A VULGAR ART

Folklore Studies in a Multicultural World

The Folklore Studies in a Multicultural World series is a collaborative venture of the University of Illinois Press, the University Press of Mississippi, the University of Wisconsin Press, and the American Folklore Society, made possible by a generous grant from the Andrew W. Mellon Foundation. The series emphasizes the interdisciplinary and international nature of current folklore scholarship, documenting connections between communities and their cultural production. Series volumes highlights aspects of folklore studies such as world folk cultures, folk art and music, foodways, dance, African American and ethnic studies, gender and queer studies, and popular culture.

FOLKLORE STUDIES
IN A MULTICULTURAL
WORLD

Squeeze This!
A Cultural History of the Accordion in American
Marion Jacobson
(University of Illinois Press)

The Jumbies' Playing Ground
Old World Influence on Afro-Creole Masquerades in the Eastern Caribbean
Robert Wyndham Nicholls
(University Press of Mississippi)

The Last Laugh
Folk Humor, Celebrity Culture, and Mass-Mediated Disasters in the Digital Age
Trevor J. Blank
(University of Wisconsin Press)

The Painted Screens of Baltimore
An Urban Folk Art Revealed
Elaine Eff
(University Press of Mississippi)

A Vulgar Art
A New Approach to Stand-Up Comedy
Ian Brodie
(University Press of Mississippi)

A VULGAR ART

A NEW APPROACH TO STAND-UP COMEDY

IAN BRODIE

UNIVERSITY PRESS OF MISSISSIPPI / JACKSON

www.upress.state.ms.us

The University Press of Mississippi is a member
of the Association of American University Presses.

Publication of this book is supported by a grant
from the Andrew W. Mellon Foundation.

First printing 2014

∞

Library of Congress Cataloging-in-Publication Data

Brodie, Ian.
A vulgar art : a new approach to stand-up comedy / Ian Brodie.
pages cm. — (Folklore studies in a multicultural world series)
Includes bibliographical references and index.
Includes discography and videography.
ISBN 978-1-62846-182-4 (cloth : alk. paper) — ISBN 978-1-62846-183-1 (ebook)
1. Stand-up comedy. 2. Comedians—United States. 3. Wit and humor—
Social aspects. I. Title.
PN1969.C65B85 2014
792.7′6—dc23   2014015283

British Library Cataloging-in-Publication Data available

For Jackson

You want to hear stupid? Major stupid? Stand-up comic. You walk onto a bare stage absolutely alone, no comfort, no help, no script or actors to support you, no lyrics and music to give you life—just yourself saying your words out of your own head, telling each person, one on one, the weirdest corners of your psyche. And everybody is judging your personality, judging whether you are worth their money, whether you make them happy. When they do not laugh, that silence is a rejection of *you* personally, only you. Not your mother. Not your piano player—if you have one. A thousand people in a room are saying, "You stink. You're nothing."

—Joan Rivers, *Enter Talking*

CONTENTS

PART 3

ACKNOWLEDGMENTS

Ron James was kind enough to allow me to follow him around on his tour of Nova Scotia in November of 2005 and provided me—unbidden—with complementary tickets to his shows. And when they did not want me driving from Truro to Sydney in the middle of a rainy November night, he and his tour manager, Mr. Terry McRae, arranged for a hotel room, going far beyond the call.

I would like to thank my colleagues and mentors at the Department of Folklore at Memorial University: Martin Lovelace, Diane Tye, Cory W. Thorne, Philip Hiscock, Diane Goldstein, Neil V. Rosenberg, Gerald Pocius, Bev Diamond, Sharon Cochrane, Cindy Turpin, Lynne S. McNeill, Stephen van Geem, Andrea Kitta, Jon D. Lee, Jillian Gould, Holly Everett, and Kelly Roubo. The high standards set by Peter Narváez and the intersection of folklore and popular culture have been influences that I hope are evident in the present work. Peter is greatly missed. At Cape Breton University, I would like to note the support of Jane Arnold, Chris Jones, Mary Keating, Dale Keefe, Peter MacIntyre, Richard MacKinnon, Stephanie MacQuarrie, Chris McDonald, Ruby Ramji, and Heather Sparling. Many thanks go to the members of the Folklore Studies Association of Canada (l'Association canadianne d'ethnologie et de folklore), particularly, Pauline Greenhill, Laurier Turgeon, Marcel Beneteau, and Jean-Pierre Pichette.

Portions of this work were presented at meetings of the American Folklore Society (Brodie 2005; 2006b); meetings of the Folklore Studies Association of Canada (Brodie 2006a; 2008a; 2009); the conference Perspectives on Contemporary Legend (Brodie 2007a); and the joint meeting of the Folklore Studies Association of Canada and the American Folklore Society (Brodie 2007b). Many thanks to all participants and panel co-presenters for their invaluable comments and suggestions. Portions have appeared in a different form as "Stand-Up Comedy as a Genre of Intimacy" (Brodie 2008b), and I thank the editors and the anonymous readers for their suggestions.

The participants of the Folklore Studies in a Multicultural World for 2012 were inordinately helpful in preparing the manuscript for final submission: I would like to thank my fellow first-time authors Joy Fraser, Peter Hoesing, Sarah Quick, Anthony Buccitelli, and Joan Saverin; mentors Jim Leary, Sharon Sherman, and (especially) Simon J. Bronner; publishers

Sheila Leary, Laurie Matheson, and (especially) Craig Gill; and coordinator Dawn Durante. This is a wonderful initiative by the American Folklore Society and the Andrew W. Mellon Foundation that should continue. As the book entered production with University of Mississippi Press, Craig Gill was joined by Anne Stascavage and Karen Johnson, who were not only efficient, expedient, and thorough but also kind and considerate.

My wife, Jodi McDavid, has always been supportive, even when she was reluctant that I follow her into the field of folklore. Her own practically innate understanding of the dynamics of folklore is something I can only hope to emulate, while her ongoing respect—in all spheres—is what I am always striving to earn.

My father, Bernard Brodie (1945–2002), played Shelley Berman's albums, let me watch Johnny Carson's *Tonight Show*, took the family to see Joan Rivers live in concert, and brought the *Carlin at Carnegie* video home from work, all before I had turned ten. Responsibility for the following therefore lies with him.

A NOTE ON TRANSCRIPTIONS

To transcribe performances, I have employed a system to indicate a variety of audience responses and to demonstrate performance rhythm.

Audience sounds [bracketed]

A	Applause
Aw	"Aw" (e.g., disappointment, sadness)
B	Boos
C	Cheers
H	Hisses
L	Laughter
O	"Ooo" (recognition of taboo topic)
S	Silence (pronounced)
W	Whoops

Qualifiers

:	Two (or more) occurring at once
→	Transition from one to other
[<___>]	Discernible words
[lowercase letters]	Limited reaction
[!___!]	Single reaction

Line breaks occur at prolonged pauses or audience interruptions or to indicate the cadence of the line. Words in *italics* are specifically emphasized, underlined words indicate that the previous audience reaction is sustained but the performer is talking over or during it, and . . . ellipses indicate false starts. The performer's gestures, "stage directions," and other nonverbal cues are {in curly brackets} and, when indicating tone or accent, qualify the words following, which are in double quotation marks [" "]. Text enclosed in | straight lines | denotes characterization. Ellipses in brackets on their own line [. . .] indicate a non-transcribed section.

A VULGAR ART

LET'S G● ●UT

Stand-Up Comedy, "Folklore" or "Not Folklore"?

I am a stand-up comedian, and I love that title. Stand-up comedy is a vulgar
art. It can be vulgar in the usual way we use that word. But vulgar really
means "of the people." It's the people's art.
—**George Carlin,** "Exclusive George Carlin Interview"

At the Perspectives on Contemporary Legend meeting in Logan, Utah, I was
presenting some of these ideas, in particular noting—what I thought inno-
cently—a similarity between what was *au courant* in legendry research and
what I had noticed about stand-up comedy (Brodie 2007a). After a brace of
encouraging questions, Linda Dégh asked the inevitable, inimitable question, "What does this have to do with folklore? This is not folklore! This is
show business!"

Good question. I wish I could have said the following.

I would like to imagine that what follows is not "not folklore" as it meets
academic standards of rigor and aims at putting its content into a larger
perspective, distinguishing it from an amateur or a popular study. Given
the appeal of writing about popular culture, in general, and comedy, in particular (demonstrated by the wealth of lay analyses of comedy available), it
is at times tempting—or easy—to stray.

I also believe that what follows is not "not folklore" because it is
entrenched in the disciplinary perspectives of folkloristics. It is not a literary analysis, a popular cultural study, anthropology, or performance and
has been little influenced by same, save that stand-up comedy has not been
studied much by folklorists but has to this point largely fallen within these
other domains.

But is it not "not folklore" in terms of its object? Stand-up comedy, by
virtue of it being a professional activity, takes that first step away from a
wholly folkloric process and bestrides the folk and popular ends of a continuum (Narváez and Laba 1986b). Despite analogies to vernacular forms
of talk, and despite the stand-up comedian's frequent use of vernacular
forms of talk, the relationship between audience and performer, in terms

of systems of exchange and in terms of spatiotemporal distance, however slight, make it "something other." Dr. Dégh's point was, in part, quite valid.

Perhaps, by way of explaining my position, I may compare stand-up comedy to country music. Country music is rooted in vernacular music and presents itself as intertwined with vernacular traditions. But it also has its own traditions, its own expectations, and its own requirements of being able to transcend locality and idiosyncrasy. This dual life—both vernacular and popular—need not be understood as disingenuous: it is simply a different beast to be considered on its own terms. Or, to be more precise and to allow for the argument for this work, given country music's intricate relationship and association with local traditions, the employment of the tools of the folklorist is a natural fit: but one must bear in mind that it is also something other.

So, too, I believe, with stand-up comedy. It is so self-evidently related to vernacular, folk, everyday talk that folklore is a natural fit and, moreover, one that illuminates elements within the tradition and technique of the stand-up comedian that get lost when it falls under the purview of other disciplines. But I am sensitive to the concerns—and at times share them myself—of those who are wary of the rush to the boundaries of folklore and thus are willing to employ the "not folklore" sobriquet. So I proceed with caution.

WELCOME TO THE SHOW

A Vulgar Art

SA: Isn't that the *worst* name for something that's . . .

EM: [:first love]

SA: . . . for something you *do*

"*Stand Up*"

Isn't it *horrible*?

EM: [high pitch, descending] "Ahhh" you know . . .

SA: Don't you feel *embarrassed* when you say it?

EM: I think because it's an *abbreviation*

for the full term of stand-up *comedy*

it's *okay*

SA: But even saying *that* is *horrible*

EM: well I don't know

would you rather be *that* or *modern rock*? [!SA:L!]

I don't know if there's a *thing* that people *do*

that's always described *great*

—Scott Aukerman and Eugene Mirman

.

Stand-up comedy is a form of talk.[1] It implies a context that allows for reaction, participation, and engagement on the part of those to whom the stand-up comedian is speaking. When it is mediated through broadcasting and recording, an audience present to the performer is included in that mediation. However heavily one-sided, it is nevertheless a dialogic form, performed not *to* but *with* an audience.

The form stand-up comedy takes, therefore, is very much the same form of intimate talk that occurs in face-to-face encounters. However, the requirements of the professionalization of this intimate talk impose a distance between the performer and the audience, whether that is the proxemic distancing of the performer being on a stage and the audience not, the indeterminate spatiotemporal distancing of stand-up recording being listened to or viewed, or the sociocultural distance between a performer from one "social category" group and an audience from another.

We are left with a bit of a paradox: how does one reconcile "intimacy" with "distance"? That is the question this book seeks to answer.

By framing the act of stand-up comedy in this manner—working toward the successful reconciliation of intimacy and distance—we are able to side-step much of the academic discourse about what role or function the stand-up comedian plays or has in society. Stand-up comedy scholarship attempts the argument of the comedian as "cultural anthropologist" (Koziski 1984) or "social mediator" (Mintz 1998), as engaged in a "minor discourse" (Schulman 1994), or on a "quest for goodness" (Fisher and Fisher 1984). But the intimate relationship of face-to-face communication momentarily suspends other extant social roles and identities.

The purpose of stand-up comedy is entertainment and its aim is laughter: it is in the form of verbal play and utilizes humor. Humor theorists tell us that the humorous is the revelation of (by the performer) or a reaction to (by audiences) a physical, intellectual, social, moral, or emotional incongruity that could just as easily elicit feelings of terror (Bergson 1900; Freud 1976; Lonergan 1957; Oring 1992). Both the context and manner in which the humorous observation is made is what differentiates the humorous from the tragic.

What critics often leave unsaid is that the identification of the incongruous implies a more or less shared worldview. The stand-up comedian and his or her audience negotiate a claim of incongruity. Simultaneously, there is a negotiation of the appropriate response to the incongruity and of the interwoven nexus of commonly held assumptions that constitutes the worldview of the group. The more the assumption is exposed as incongruous, the more the reaction elicited can be terror or grief instead of laughter. Lastly, the stand-up comedian is in a position of re-affirming his or her right to be the one to reveal this incongruity: that he or she is not making an outsider's pronouncement and judgment but knows whereof he or she speaks as a member of this particular group. To put it another way, there are opinions that one may express—or implicitly proclaim through joking and humor—among friends that one would not express in a public forum: the stand-up comedian expresses them in a public forum by turning that forum into an intimate venue. This negotiation is a continuous process with the specific audience to which he or she is performing, and thus the stand-up comedy performance is a collaborative act. If stand-up comedy is play, there is nevertheless a deepness to the play, as the collaboration with the audience can just as easily fail as succeed, and this failure is an assault on not only his or her status as a performer but as an intimate.

To immediately qualify the above statement, not all stand-up comedy is de facto profound: much of what is revealed as incongruous would be already known as such to the audience at large. The content of stand-up comedy often clusters around culturally accepted quandaries and exoteric pronouncements. Furthermore, they may not be reflections on fundamental cultural beliefs but rather on mundane particulars of everyday life. Genuinely novel revelation would be the exception rather than the rule. Audience reaction is based in part on an assessment of the abilities of the performer to express revelation in an unanticipated manner that corresponds with the aesthetic and moral sensibilities of the group. And as will be argued throughout this book, homogeneity for the group is rarely in play, and there are multiple sets of aesthetic and moral sensibilities: part of the stand-up comedian's technique is to create frisson by bringing these sets of sensibilities into conflict with each other during the course of performance, if only to reconcile them by performance's end.

Because stand-up comedy is this private communication, it is unclear whether stand-up comedy is essentially and intentionally counter-hegemonic or whether it is simply the professionalization and commodification of the forms of counter-hegemonic joking discourse present in everyday life (Limon 2001). Nor is the question irrelevant, for whatever "license" the stand-up comedian may have, it is not a totally free rein, as the issue of taste and offense has a very real consequence for his or her livelihood. The professional stand-up comedian can introduce an irreconcilable distance from a potential audience should he or she transgress some fundamental boundary. Following a tragedy, like the events of September 11, 2001, or the Aurora, Colorado, shootings, joking enters a latency period, but slowly reemerges.[2] For the professional comedian, this period of sensitivity is compounded by (a) the difference in intimacy of audience between moments of informal joke-telling and mass-mediated performances, howsoever talented they are at creating an atmosphere of intimacy in performance, and (b) the inherent professionalism and, by extension, commodification of humor, wherein the professional comedian can be perceived as profiting from the tragedy of others.

The dilemma of the professional stand-up comedian is characteristic of the inherent tension between social expectations and the occupationally required identification and exploitation of cultural incongruities. This book explores the nature of professional stand-up comedy as a field which, by its nature, is both forced to and expected to negotiate the edges of cultural sensitivity and risk, as it explores the means by which professional comedians identify and develop contextual strategies for challenging and engaging with norms of appropriateness.

The discipline of folklore, which has at its focus and object proper the communications that take place in small, intimate, informal groups, brings the appropriate perspective to the study of stand-up comedy through its examination of the mutually mediating relationship between a group's identity and the expressive forms of that group. I examine stand-up comedy using the theoretical models developed by folklorists to study traditional narrative art. Intrinsic to the role of both "storyteller" and stand-up is the notion of performance (Bauman 1975; Burns 1972; Georges 1969; Goffman 1959; Hymes 1975). Both are vernacular art forms, requiring fluency with locally situated knowledges that are particular to the culture in which they operate. However, the commodification and professionalization of stand-up comedy makes it different from traditional narrative performances: these differences include the breakdown of the intimacy of face-to-face communication that comes from larger venues and media dissemination and from the ownership of material and the emphasis on novelty that contrast against perceived notions of a shared or traditional repertoire. In part 1, I set in greater detail the case for why folklore, the discipline, is well suited for the study of stand-up comedy.

In part 2, I look at how the stand-up aims at bridging distances—both the spatial distance from the audience occasioned by a stage and the sociocultural distance of speaking to a group of which he or she is not a member. This involves using the microphone to allow for an intimate voice, manipulating visual and aural cues (the physical self, accent, costume) to be located within a particular worldview, capitalizing on the social identity of "stand-up comedian," developing a comic persona that individuates this social identity, and constructing material that addresses the concerns and understandings of the audience.

Part 3 turns to broadcasts and recordings, which introduce a further distance between the stand-up comedian and the audience, one that is not occasioned by the stage but by not being present to one another. The distances that must now be bridged require an engagement with two audiences: one immediately present to react to and thus construct the stand-up performance itself and one removed, the reactions of whom the comedian can only anticipate and who is indeterminate, whether in taste, in esoteric understanding, or even in desire to participate in the intimate stand-up event. However, broadcasts and—particularly—recordings also provide the greatest opportunity for reputation cultivation; and, thus, adapting material for their various conventions is a most important skill for the stand-up comedian to develop.

PART 1

The Opener: From Folk Talk to Stand-Up

Okay [L]

good evening ladies and gentlemen thank you for uh coming *out* tonight
to the Lakeshore Theater to see me uh *talk* [W]

that's what I'm going to be doing

this is going to be . . .

I don't know how much stand-up comedy you've seen in your *life* but
uh . . .

it's pretty *talky*

—**Paul F. Tompkins,** *Freak Wharf*

This is the opener: order your drinks, show up halfway through, skip it all
together. It's not what you came for, unless it's your friend up there and
you're just being supportive. It'll be over soon enough. But, since your
expectations are low, maybe you'll be surprised.

In this section, I begin to make the argument for why a folkloristic
approach is best suited for an analysis of stand-up comedy: as a discipline
both interdisciplinary and disciplinarily distinct, it has throughout its history synthesized a variety of approaches and applied them to the performances of vernacular culture. My aim is to demonstrate how its insights
can be applied to the cultural performances that bestride vernacular and
popular. This also looks at folklore genres and genre theory and how, while
loosely framing the materials of stand-up comedy along genre lines helps
locate the comedian as engaged in a process of interpersonal communication, stand-up comedians switch between "genres" so effortlessly that one
must look to the entire performance as an integral unit.

CHAPTER 1
Stand-Up Comedy and a Folkloristic Approach

> When I think of a storyteller, I think of an old folkie, over by a puppet the-
> atre at a folk festival. I don't think a storyteller would have been able to get
> three 90-minute specials on major Canadian networks.
> **—Ron James**

"The Sickniks" was the title of an article in the July 13, 1959, issue of *Time*.
A polemic against the rise of a new form of comedy, it identified Mort Sahl,
Jonathan Winters, and Shelley Berman as key players but reserved much of
its venom for Lenny Bruce.

> What the sickniks dispense is partly social criticism liberally laced with cya-
> nide, partly a Charles Addams kind of jolly ghoulishness, and partly a personal
> and highly disturbing hostility toward all the world. No one's flesh crawled
> when Jack Benny carried on a running gag about a bear named Carmichael that
> he kept in the cellar and that had eaten the gasman when he came to read the
> meter. The novelty and jolt of the sickniks is that their gags ("I hit one of those
> things in the street—what do you call it, a kid?") come so close to real horror
> and brutality that audiences wince even as they laugh. (*Time* 1959)

By 1960, Sahl was a major cultural force, providing material for John
Kennedy's appearance at the Al Smith dinner during the presidential campaign and earning over $300,000 a year. He even appeared on the cover of
Time that August (*Time* 1960b). Outside of his influence, most notable was
his style, so different from what had preceded him.

> Holding a rolled newspaper in his right hand, flashing baby-blue eyes and a
> wolfish grin, he states his theme and takes off like a jazz musician on a flight of
> improvisation—or seeming improvisation. He does not tell jokes one by one,
> but carefully builds deceptively miscellaneous structures of jokes that are like
> verbal mobiles. He begins with the spine of a subject, then hooks thought onto
> thought; joke onto dangling joke, many of them totally unrelated to the main
> theme, till the whole structure spins but somehow balances. All the time he is

building toward a final statement, which is too much part of the whole to be
called a punch line, but puts that particular theme away forever. (*Time* 1960b)

Partly in response, *Playboy* convened a panel of comedians for its March
1961 issue: included were Sahl, Bruce, and Winters; Bill Dana, best known
for his José Jimenez character; Mike Nichols, of the improvisational-sketch
comedy team Nichols and May; *Village Voice* cartoonist Jules Feiffer; and
Steve Allen, former host of the *Tonight Show* and an early supporter of
these comedians. Those involved in this "new," "hip," and, occasionally,
"sick" school were consistent only in identifying themselves as different
from forebears. Sahl pointed out the comedian as specialist, noting, "There
is no new school of humor. Here are just a lot of guys working now who
can't sing or dance" (qtd. in *Time* 1960b, 35). Winters saw that the "gimmick
. . . was to get away from jokes per se. . . . I pray to God we're past the pie
throwing phase" (qtd. in *Time* 1960b, 35). Allen located it in the upsurge
of youth, proved by the election of John F. Kennedy, while Dana thought
it inherently cyclic. But Nichols saw them as "all peddling a kind of *inside*
humor, which gives an audience the impression that they're the only ones
who really understand it" (qtd. in *Time* 1960b, 35). It is perhaps Nichols
who was the most prescient, as the premise of a performer and an audience
working in collusion opposite an indeterminate "outsider" or "other" has
been the dominant theme in the scholarship of the intervening fifty years.

The *Playboy* panel appears as a line in the sand, one of the first opportunities to reflect on the burgeoning "new comedy," if only within a vernacular
theory approach. *Playboy*, the *Village Voice*, and, later, *Rolling Stone*—van-
guards of "new journalism"—continued to examine it; but, despite the
commercial successes of Bill Cosby, Richard Pryor, George Carlin, and Steve
Martin, stand-up comedy, as it became known, was largely considered a
countercultural phenomenon.

As with many popular art forms, the academy was slow to recognize stand-
up comedy. Outside of a few passing references—which would posit stand-
up comedians as modern examples of the phenomenon of their immediate
interests but would rarely follow up on that point—few paid it much scholarly attention until its sudden growth in the late 1970s, coincident with
the emergence of cable television, particularly HBO. Scholars concerned
themselves with stand-up comedy as a more-or-less homogeneous entity,
a sphere of human activity that could be differentiated on the basis of
professional and amateur, original and derivative, good and bad. They all

note, implicitly or not, that a variety of performance strategies are required for the different audiences the comedian might face. But by making general statements about what stand-up comedy is, there was a tendency to conceive of it as an ideal, a pseudo-Platonic form against which all actual occurrences are contrasted. Some researchers will look at a specific adjectival group of stand-up comedians (categorized by nationality, by ethnicity, by gender, by sexuality) and contrast their work with a presumed homogenous mainstream. Others will establish a role for the comedian—moral spokesperson, jester, anthropologist—focus on one or two performers who fit their model, and then again contrast it with their unexamined "mainstream," "typical," or "regular" stand-up comedy. All implicitly present what "stand-up comedy" is and who "the stand-up comedian" is.

Within the scholarship, definitions of stand-up—and, as a consequence, the data pool from which scholars draw their observations—vary wildly. However, a set of interrelated themes emerges. The contemporary stand-up comedian does something more than tell jokes, but they must still "be funny." The something they do is observational, by the comedian grounding it in an experiential, proto-ethnographic act; reflective, by endeavoring to interpret that experience; perspectival, by taking a particular position for interpretation; critical, by privileging that position; and, above all, vernacular, by locating it in the local rather than the universal. This locality is both figurative, the assumed or anticipated shared experience of the audience and performer, and, as the performance progresses, literal: informed by the audience's reactions, the experienced comedian customizes the performance.

Whereas many do not bother articulating a definition for stand-up comedy, seeing it as self-evident, others make bold attempts.

> A strict, limiting definition of stand-up comedy would describe an encounter between a single standing performer behaving comically and/or saying funny things directly to an audience, unsupported by very much in the way of costume, props, setting, or dramatic vehicle. (Mintz 1998, 194)

> Stand-up comedy . . . is a rather strange and precarious line of work in which to succeed one must routinely win the attention, approval and laughter of a large assembly of people. (McIlvenny, Mettovaara, and Tapio 1993, 225)

> [Stand-up comedy] is a single performer standing in front of an audience talking to them with the specific intention of making them laugh. (Double 1997, 4)

In standup comedy individual performers stand on stage and say funny things directly to an audience to make them laugh. How they convey their self-identities in their routines is an integral aspect of their stage persona. (Price 1998, 256)

Stand-up comedy is verbal entertainment presented by one person to others. It is a monologue spoken to and for the audience, and its purpose is not to inform but to invoke the audience's response. It is a speech that always presupposes a reply. Applause and laughter are the audience's answers to the address of the comedian. (Lo 1998, 160)

[Stand-up] is a form of public address—one speaker speaking directly to a live audience with a variety of intents and purposes. It is both serious and not serious, because . . . stand-ups range in their talk from the most trivial details of everyday life . . . to the most potent political and social issues of the larger culture. . . . (French 1998, 57)

[Stand-up] may best be described as a humorous monologue (although the comedian usually starts his show with an attempt to engage the audience in a dialogue), presented to an audience in a seemingly spontaneous and conversational manner. (Misje 2002, 87)

Narrative [i.e., stand-up] comedians are, in a sense, like modern day jesters, publicly smashing assumptions that underlie attitudes and behaviors that exist in society. Where comedians are socially conscious, the assumptions that explode are often ideological ones. But the fact that they keep audiences laughing gives the comedians licence to provide incisive and sometimes biting social commentary. (Rahman 2004, 1)

Stand-up comedy, apparently, is difficult to circumscribe but, nevertheless, seems recognizable when encountered. Patterns of features emerge. Stand-up comedy is typically

1. a spoken, verbal performance by a sole individual;
2. in front of, to, and in collaboration with an audience;
3. with a clear demarcation between performer and audience;
4. without conspicuous staging, costuming, or props;
5. in prose and without musical accompaniment;
6. with minimal characterization;
7. seemingly extemporaneous;

8. largely autobiographical or observational;
9. presented as emerging from a particular worldview (place, perspective, values, experience, etc.);
10. claiming shared, complementary, or overlapping worldviews between performer and audience;
11. esoteric;
12. ostensibly counter-hegemonic;
13. deliberately aimed at evoking laughter from the audience to whom it is being performed;
14. taking place within an exchange economy and thus with attendant expectations of value for money; and
15. often recorded, broadcast, and disseminated as a tangible product for sale and/or for purposes of reputation cultivation.

For each feature one could easily find a comedian who would prove the exception, but most of these features would be present most of the time to virtually every performer who either identifies him- or herself or is identified by others as a "stand-up comedian." It is a skeletal description that is deliberately avoiding both functionalist approaches and necessary historical antecedents. This point is taken up again in chapter 3, where the social identity of stand-up comedian is further qualified through the lens of vernacular theory. It is a workable definition and a starting point for the work that follows.

This work is built on the argument that stand-up comedy is a complex transposition of vernacular forms of talk into a more formal, mediated context and that this more formal, mediated context introduces a distance between audience and performer that needs reconciliation. The discipline best suited for stand-up comedy's analysis is the discipline that studies vernacular expression: the discipline of folklore. Despite this, very little has been written by folklorists on stand-up comedy.[1]

In general, the assumption that underlies what few references there are to stand-up comedy by folklorists is that there is something analogous to vernacular talk going forward, whether that be in terms of the function of stand-up comedy or in the appearance of folk texts within popular performance or in the "storytelling" process. These claims to analogue are rarely tested: they remain the product of "common sense." In part, I would imagine, this is due to the concern of stand-up comedy being "not folklore," the same question I raise in the introduction. However, the claims are by no means untenable: much of the present work is concerned with demonstrating the very real connection between vernacular talk and stand-up comedy and, thus, the applicability and importance of folklore to its study.

All communicative acts presume a group of people present to the act, as performer and receiver of the message. Stand-up comedy is an explicit example of this, demonstrated by how broadcasts and recordings are—without exception—of the comedian's routine as performed in front of an audience. The comedian and the live audience constitute a group, as do, implicitly, the comedian, the live audience, and the audience at home.

Contemporary folklore is rooted in the concept of the group. At its minimum, a group has one communicator and one receiver; they are in contact with each other through the medium of communication itself, whether that be in immediate face-to-face communication, over space via some transmitting medium, or over time via some recording medium, and they have in common a shared referent required to encode and decode the communication.

For the most part folklorists study groups that are more recognizably assemblies of similar persons. There are certain broad social categories, like "American" or "children," which identify groups whose named common factors are recognized as culturally significant keywords, even to the purported members themselves, but are simultaneously contestable given the numerous interpretations of how to define that common factor. In practice, identifying a large-scale group by its common factor can be most fruitful, as the delineation of immediately consequent additional common factors by the folklorist is likely to coincide with a general consensus among the constituent members of the group under discussion. But these additional common factors do not proceed syllogistically by necessity but suggestively by implication, and the larger the group, the less the utility of these generalities as models. For these reasons, as folkloristics has developed over time, the focus has been on smaller and smaller groups that can be described less by implication than by explicit enumeration of details. Moreover, the common factors, as real and quantifiable by the folklorist as they may be, are often held with far less significance by the participants than the factors that differentiate one set of participants from the other. Identity is created, in large part, through contrast.[2]

The comedian and audience are part of a group by virtue of, if nothing else, their interaction in a face-to-face relationship. The comedian's task—especially in instances where performer and audience are in different social categories—is to deconstruct (in all senses of the word) the differences in self-identity and introduce criteria from which to create an intimate shared identity, often by virtue of contrast with a non-present "other."[3]

When I meet someone for the first time, certain cues give me an initial orienting of them within my worldview, allowing for the projection of sets of both common and opposite factors. This initial orientation is based on culturally and experientially grounded expectations for the worldview of the other associated with particular, culturally significant keywords. Such projections are prejudicial and, as such, quickly contestable. They are, however, prejudicial in terms of both commonality and difference: they have both esoteric and exoteric expectations associated with them, dependent on the particular category of keyword projected. With each new cue proffered—as I move beyond visual identify markers to their articulation of dites and narratives—my understanding of their worldview is challenged, deepened, reaffirmed, nuanced, and developed until expectations are as grounded in experience as they are in prejudices. And as they arise, I scrutinize and evaluate each cue in terms of its group referent: is this position on a topic, this articulated understanding, this articulated experience, something consistent with my understanding of the universe, something identifiably inconsistent, or something apart from but not wholly other, something new but not threatening?

Such scrutinies occur more or less spontaneously: within the context of a finite but intense contact, such as between audience member and comedian, an innumerable number of such judgments may be made. For this type of contact, one can identify the possibility of a simultaneity of having shared, complementary, and opposing worldviews, dependent on the keyword under discussion. Whereas exclusivity and dissent would be destructive in certain forms of discourse, stand-up comedy, which is play and not polemic, thrives in the milieu of difference. The sociocultural distance of performer and audience that often occurs is reconciled not though its negation but through both its recognition and the recognition of other sets of commonalities.[4]

One way of looking at the group, then, is as an association of people with shared expectations or norms: I expect members of this group—mine, yours, ours—to know this history, to share these values, to behave in these manners, to hold these attitudes, to draw meaning from these experiences. I am reassured when expectations are met; I can discover new groups, new factors from which meaning is derived, where things are unexpected but not contrary to expectations, and from which I draw a blend of fear and delight;

and I am challenged when expectations are not met, when something other happens, and I must reflect on what caused me to have those expectations in the first place.

Groups are categories for the organization of people in terms of potential future contact based on previous experiences. As models, people of the "same" group hold the "same" worldview: when seeing the world from the context of organizing principle *X*, there will be consensus as to how to interpret and engage that world. But the individual has not one but a multiplicity of organizing principles, and context dictates which one may be at the fore at any given moment: as such, he or she "switches" groups as he or she brings up and operates within a new set of expectations based on the context. Audiences are comprised of individuals, and the comedian addresses a heterogeneous group that may share many common factors (African Americans, Maritimers, trades people) but that also varies in experiences.

> But you're still the *audience*
> you all came from different *places*
> *that's* what I like
> everybody comes from a different *house*
> different apartment different *room*
> {in awe} "you left your *rooms*" [L]
> | {paranoid} "I'm leaving my *room*" |
> *must* be special
> and you come all the way here to act as a *unit*
> you ought to have a *reunion* next year y'know [l]
> get together talk about the show (Carlin 1977b*)

One of the skills of the comedian is to identify a worldview within which he or she is operating and express that to the audience more or less immediately: simultaneously, he or she must begin to indicate a position and perspective that allows for challenging the audience's expectations. Established comedians have the advantage of being known to the audience already: they can bring a more nuanced worldview to the stage. "New" comedians (new to the particular audience, at least) require a catch that orients them for the audience. In the continuum between wholly unknown to established and celebrated comedian, each is engaged in the task of establishing an intimate exchange between himself or herself and the audience, or, in other words, creating a group through talk.

Critical to any study of comedy is moving beyond text and examining the context of performance. Who is the performer? How is the performance augmented: through dress, through gesture, through posture? Who is listening? What is their reaction? Why is the performance being performed at all? In terms of the text, how is it different from other performances of this text? How is it modified by the performer to the particular performance context?

Let's make some self-evident observations. First of all, stand-up comedy is concerned with and directed toward audience reaction: the manner in which it is received is, in a manner of speaking, the whole point. Second, the texts of stand-up comedy are, or are meant to be, the performer's own creations, as an individual artist making original contributions to a realm of performance. Third, as the text is collaborative between performer and audience, the words do not make much sense—or are often not "funny," which is worse—without the audience's reaction; and the audience is responding not only to the text but to delivery, gesture, dress, and a whole range of nonverbal cues. This is evidenced, as will be discussed further, by the drastic reworking required for a performed text to work on the printed page. Fourth and finally, as stand-up comedy is a profession, where the most mercenary objective is to eventually be recorded for purposes of large-scale broadcast and attendant revenues, the text as it appears in performance *is* the urtext: once a routine is committed to a fixed medium and broadly disseminated, the emphasis on novelty requires new creations.

> Again, at Carnegie Hall [Lenny Bruce] said, "Now my humor: I dig, first,
> recall—abstraction. I can't be ponderous. People say to me, 'Hey, how come you
> don't do the bits on the records?'" The reason, he explained, was that he would
> be like the guy at a party who tells the same funny story to every neighbor who
> walks in: "And by about the fifth neighbor you really get *drugged* with him,
> man. He tells the same story and you say, 'He's *corrupt*, man, he's not funny—*I*
> could tell that story now.' . . . So that's it: if you dig hearing the same thing, go
> by your neighbor's." With the gauntlet thus thrown down, Bruce affirmed that
> he would not play the game that was demanded of him by popular comedic
> convention, the delivery of the smooth, rehearsed bits that flowed from the
> mouths of the television comedians, the false impression of spontaneity in
> entire pages of memorized chatter. (Kaufman 1997, 77–78)

Performances prior to the recorded one are, as it were, rough drafts. Whereas a traditional text may be understood as a recreation of its original performance, or as existing solely within and for the purposes of one specific context, stand-up comedy performances are teleological, in that they aim toward a final, definitive version. Stand-up comedians work through their routines, making alterations from performance to performance until they develop a honed, rehearsed version that—when performed in front of a specific audience but knowing it is to be recorded and thus the "definitive" version—will elicit the most laughter. The final version is privileged and intentionally considered the definitive version and, as it gets committed to a recording and becomes a potential source of inspiration for subsequent comedians, it is the version that enters the canon. Comedians tend to phase out or drop entirely material from their live performances that has been committed to record: it is hardly ever put on record again.

Further, with respect to the context of performance, stand-up typically takes place in specialized spaces. A complex network of venue management and staff, along with technicians and event coordinators, work with the stand-up comedian, collectively creating the impression of the solo, intimate performance. A space identified as a comedy venue—whether the permanent comedy club or a theater or festival tent temporarily labeled as such—already frames how the performance ought to be received. The specific setting provides two interpretations: firstly, an unadorned, stripped-of-artifice stage synecdochically indicates the unadorned, stripped-of-artifice performances that take place thereupon, highlighting the "authenticity" of the performance—or rather, that what is occurring on the stage is not a "performance" but one half of a direct, sincere, intimate exchange between the performer and audience—simultaneously, there is a continued definition of the situation by the performance team (comedian, emcee, club managers, and staff) to frame these performances as occurring firmly in the realm of play.

And stand-up comedy is also inherently play: it is understood as entertainment, as something enjoyed within the context of leisure time, as a commodity extrinsic to the basic economic circuits. Furthermore, the consequences of stand-up comedy do not extend into the "real world": there is a mutual understanding between audience and performer that what is said in performance does not require enactment. But the nature of that entertainment, for both performer and audience, both participants in a performative exchange, implies how the "text" presented by the stand-up comedian can so easily fail in its immediate goal of eliciting laughter. It can be found "not funny" in one of two ways: it can simply not elicit laughter as it is found trite, dull, uninspiring, or insipid; or it does not elicit laughter by it being too painful, too scandalous, too threatening, too novel. It is deep play.

The "safety" of the stand-up performance is the play-frame for a performance that (potentially) stirs up one's worldview. Roger Caillois calls this *ilinx*, or "vertiginous," play that is "based on the pursuit of vertigo and which [consists] of an attempt to momentarily destroy the stability of perception and inflict a kind of voluptuous panic upon an otherwise lucid mind" (1961, 23). The stakes—both in terms of economics and status—are equally high for the performer in either instance of "not funny," but the risk involved is substantively different: the possible consequence of rejection and anger is different from the consequence of dull stares and yawns. A successful comedian is one who consistently elicits some form of laughter, but it is the one who treads that line of disapproval, and who therefore is risking the most, that tends to be the more memorable.

I would never go so far as to suggest that all stand-up comedy is inherently profound or vertiginous or "deep" in any sense of the word, but as is apparent from surveying both the academic and the vernacular literature, the stand-up comedian is presumed to be one who articulates "dangerous" propositions. So what I am saying is that stand-up comedy has profundity as one of its ostensible goals, despite the playful garb it wears. The profound comedian is held up as one of stand-up comedy's heroes, and his or her work informs the canon.

Stand-up comedy is, on one level, an occupation. There are expectations that arise when one deigns to perform in exchange for compensation. Occupations, like any other group, have their own particular sets of techniques, technical and metaphorical jargon, and narrative histories. Biographies of stand-up comedians invariably include learning how to perform through listening and watching other performers, participating in small talk back stage and in other cultural scenes of the comedian, and absorbing a canon of both exemplary performances and performance technique. These same biographies also demonstrate the use of recordings by comedians as a source for inspiration and emulation, how they learn the craft in part from repeated listening to comedy albums.

Stand-up comedy has its own concepts of canonicity. The canon is engaged through mediated forms, specifically, audio and video recordings. When one speaks of the canon of stand-up comedy, one is mainly speaking of the routines of particular comedians that serve as exemplary executions of the comedian's art. Stand-up comedy, being a contemporary, popular genre, is a genre of novelty, so one does not learn the canon so much as learn *from* it, locating oneself within a tradition not simply to continue it but to develop and add to it.

Although there may be general consensus about canonical texts and techniques found among stand-up comedians at any given moment, canons are in a constant state of formation and evolution, and comedians may advert to and value particular performances long after the undergirding techniques have been found wanting. For such reasons as nostalgia and a sense of historical continuity, canons are fluid, dynamic, vital, adaptable, and, above all, susceptible to change.

As a folklorist, my first impulse in studying stand-up comedy, I must confess, was to immediately make strict correlations between the verbal performances of the comedian and the verbal forms and genres of "the folk." It doesn't quite work, but it's not an inherently bad place to start.

This entire book is, in many ways, an exercise in genre: in the middle of the twentieth century and centered in North America, a particular form of popular entertainment, verbal discourse comedy, emerged that, while related to previous forms, was identifiably and explicitly understood as distinct therefrom, to which the predated term "stand-up comedy" was eventually attached. As efforts began to formalize the definition of the emerging genre, both practitioners and academics suggested a variety of formal characteristics and functions, but the move toward absolutizing definitions has given way to simply sketching out some of its features—as I do above—and treating "stand-up comedy" as a keyword. In my sketch-definition, I suggest in part that stand-up comedy is largely autobiographical or observational; is presented as emerging from a particular worldview; is claiming shared, complementary, or overlapping worldviews between performer and audience; and is largely esoteric. These pertain to saying something specific about a worldview, and as such they hinge in part on what is considered "true" within that worldview.

When the stand-up comedian performs, there is a frequent switching between belief stances. At times, his or her narratives and statements are like myths, as they are not subject to debate. They are coincident with the worldview of the group and, as proof, they are met rarely with laughter but with signals of assent and agreement: whoops, applause, and vocalized assent ("Amen," "That's right."). At other times his or her words are tale-like, grasped as fictions and as unnecessary to contest as history. They are met principally with laughter at the creative distortions and imaginative and playful descriptions employed by the teller. And at other times the audience doesn't know what to think: they are opinions or accounts of events that are either contestable or are coincident with a worldview that the audience does not share or is not comfortable adverting to; or—as the audience is not a homogeneous mass—the words can divide the audience. They can be met with either laughter, which demonstrates either assent to a risky proposition or the judgment that the risky proposition is merely vertiginous play, or active booing, demonstrating dissent. One of the features of legend is that the narrative's ending, that is, the restoration of equilibrium, is suppressed in the telling, and the listener must somehow supply an appropriate ending for him- or herself (Ellis 2001, 59), which is similar to what I suggest happens both in jokes and stand-up comedy performances, where equilibrium is restored by recognizing that it is an instance of humor and affirmed by laughter.

What is held absolute, contingent, or subjective varies from group to group and, within, from individual to individual. The audience for a stand-up comedy performance varies both collectively from the performer (especially as the performer moves literally and figuratively from his or her own group) and individually among themselves: how a particular stand-up comedy item is received, how it is interpreted along that belief spectrum, and—most importantly—how well it will generate laughter will often depend largely on whether a line of sacrality has been transgressed or skirted or carefully avoided. Even though the performance setting is not sacred and is understood as play and as profane, there are limits to transgression.

But the stand-up comedian speaks more often in the first person than in the third person. The very expectations of the genre expect novelty and perspective, even among the most trite examples. First-person narratives have an explicit connection between the narrator and the protagonist: the convention is that they are one and the same. The narrator is the narrative's referent, and events refer to his or her history or worldview. That history and worldview may or may not be representative of the group: the comedian may in fact stand on the periphery of the group or, as is the case for the itinerant stand-up comedian, ostensibly, wholly outside it. The history is personal, in that it is either from the narrator's perspective or it is the narrator's own experience. So, too, is the worldview presented: it is perspectival and, as a possible consequence, iconoclastic.

Testimonials, much like myth, concern origins inasmuch as they relate events fundamental to the individual's history and worldview. They are opportunities for presenting arguments or rationalizations that orient the speaker within the worldview of the group, the former within established groups within which a momentary misalignment may have transpired and to whom one is "giving an account of oneself" and the latter for presumed but not established groups (cf. Abrahams 1975).

But the stand-up's "truth" requires the contrast of the fictive and, possibly, fanciful: something akin to tall tales. These are narratives concerning the narrator's extraordinary adventures and fantastical achievements, and what gives them purchase is how they coexist within the truth-frame of the testimonial: by doing so they become commensurate with the narrator's worldview (Bethke 1976). To dispute the history, the truth of the events, is to miss the point: they are not told as history, even when they explicitly claim to be so. Chandra Mukerji makes a similar case in her study of "bullshitting" among hitchhikers:

> To say that people feel free to lie in these situations is both an accurate description of the possibilities of "talking off the record" and a misrepresentation of the intentions behind doing so. When people bullshit or gossip, they do so not so much tell lies as create situations where events can be elaborated in non-ordinary ways. Just as a stage play is not a lie though it takes events from life and heightens their drama to make good theater, so bullshitting takes events and heightens their storytelling possibilities. (1978, 242)

Amidst testimonial and bullshitting is the personal anecdote, a narrative told as if true but subject to contestation and negotiation. The historicity of events and the worldview that informs them are open to challenge: the narrator simultaneously challenges the worldview of the audience.

A further remove from the narrative-genre-spotting exercise is the recognition that stand-ups are not always "telling stories": they are making observations and offering insights. There need not be an account of events with some sort of movement through them by a protagonist: observation is at the heart of the stand-up's vernacular ethnography approach, where they make explicit their take on implicit ideas that undergird a contemporary phenomenon, or what Alan Dundes would simply have called "folk ideas," "the unstated premises which underlie the thought and action of a given group of people" (1971, 95–96).[5]

Lastly, stand-up comedians often speak in the second person: they project events or opinions onto the audience, sometimes passively (asking, "Have you ever . . . ?" or "Has this ever happened to you?") and sometimes directly ("You're going to be driving home tonight . . ."). This direct engagement brings the audience even more fully into the performance, as their worldview is being either validated or impugned. In *Raw*, Eddie Murphy (1987*) explicitly draws the audience into his performance by speaking to women ("you") about men (both a collective "we" and the absent "him").

{emphatic gesture with each stressed word} Men must *find* and *conquer* as
　　much *pussy* as they can *get*
do not think for *two seconds* that you are the only one your man is fucking
he is a *man* and *has* to conquer women
I see a lot of you women out there going
|{emphatically} "not my man"|
yes *your man too* [L]
<u>your man too</u>
if he's not here with you *tonight*
he's *fucking* somebody [L] (Murphy 1987*)

The performer mediates between the worldview of the group and its implied self-understanding and his or her own worldview. Because they are personal they are by default interpersonal: they are not communications of the group to itself but from one to another within the group. When one is determined to be speaking for *the group*, the group allows one to continue unchallenged; when one is determined to be speaking for *oneself*, the group seeks clarification, objects, belittles, grows fearful, and challenges the speaker. Moreover, it is the group itself that determines "membership" status, and its reaction is the marker of that status. The group determines its own constituency and reinforces it through reactions (or actions): the performer may or may not be within that group at any given moment.

Jokes constitute one of the more problematic areas for the student of stand-up comedy. Comedians do not understand themselves as telling "jokes" per se: when the term is used, it is more as a coding strategy that seeks to undermine their own art form (Murphy 1987*; Rock 1994*) or simply a sardonic reminder that what they do is largely play (Hedberg 2002*; D. Martin 2006*).[6] There is also an implication that jokes are isolatable and easily repeatable narrative units, more or less independent of the teller. The artistry of stand-up comedy is the interweaving of these units into a cohesive piece whose sum is greater than its parts and which is virtually inseparable from the teller. Nevertheless, the association between stand-up comedy and the cultural keyword "joke" is such that it must be discussed.

Jokes should be understood more as instances of humor than as a particular form. Granted, they often take a form, like riddle jokes, or have recurrent motifs (rabbi, priest, and minister; Pat and Mike) and verbal patterns ("walk in to a bar") so that they are more quickly recognizable as jokes. Through whatever cultural cues are present, they may be identifiable as having a beginning, middle, and end and thus can be extracted or redacted from a longer flow of talk. But their recognition as "joke" is ultimately dependent not on form or even content but on reception.

Like legend, jokes do not provide their own resolution. The listener restores equilibrium by "getting it": recognizing the vector the narrative or sentence should have taken had it unfolded according to expectations, contrasting that against how it did unfold, and grasping the proposition one must admit to shift the former to the latter. This proposition is a folk idea, something not necessarily believed but widely known to the group in which the joke is performed: the "nature" of blondes, Aggies, Mainlanders, and such (cf. Davies 1990; Henken 2006; Thomas 1997). Getting it differs from finding it funny: the former is noetic, a consequence of understanding; the latter psychic, a consequence of affective resonance. There is a mutual mediation between the two, but one can examine each one apart from the other.

But jokes differ from legend largely with the presence of the punch line: the specifically placed endpoint that invites the audience's specific interpretation or "a device that triggers the perception of an appropriate incongruity" (Oring 1992, 83).

Stand-up comedians, for the most part (as always there are notable exceptions), do not tell jokes in the discrete unit sense typically studied by folklorists. Instead, they interweave material into a routine, which may run from five minutes to over two hours. Each unit, "chunk," or "bit" is inexorably linked with the others in the routine, the performance venue, the composition of the audience, the perceived relationship between the teller and the audience, the technological medium (beyond amplification) in which it is being transmitted, and the personality of the comedian him- or herself. Punch lines—insofar as they are opportunities for laughter—are deliberately scattered throughout any particular stream of talk, narrative or observational. The stand-up comedian may switch between narration and didactic commentary throughout a given performance text (wherein didacticism must be as loosely construed as are "anthropologist," "cultural mediator," and all quasi-functionalist qualifiers of the stand-up comedian). Especially given how stand-up comedy routines are first-person narratives, there is an investment in the ultimate situation of the characters, and the text ends with resolution: it is typically funny, but its function is to bring the narrative to a conclusion, not to be the endpoint of a long buildup of appropriate incongruity. If the laughter is loudest (or if it actually generates applause), it is not expressly for the concluding line per se but for the recognition of the cumulative and now concluded routine.

As an illustration, the following is an example from Lorne Elliott's routine "Shopping." It is self-contained, with a beginning premise (including an overture encompassing an even more self-contained quasi-narrative), a middle, and an end.

I'm a married man I should tell you about that

and I've figured out some things

you've got to figure out in your marriage ah

what you like *doing* with your wife and what you don't

I know for a fact I don't like going *shopping*

with my wife

Christmas shopping that's the worst

show me a shopping mall around Christmas

five minutes I want to take hostages [L→A]

you too eh?

I've got my Christmas shopping down to an art now anyhow

I just flip everybody a *loonie*

say it's a *gift certificate* for a *dollar store* [L:a]

I know for a fact I do not like going *grocery* shopping with my wife

she always uses me as a *stand-in* on the *check-out* line [L]

{hesitation noises, sounding like "I mean, she's got"} well you got the shopping
     cart there

she takes an empty *shopping cart*

puts a loaf of *bread* in 'er [I]

goes over to the *cashier's* line

says | *stay here* | [L]

then she's off foraging [L]

so I'm staying there

Humming along with the Muzak [I]

reading the cover of the National Enquirer two or three times [I]

lady arrives with a bunch of *groceries*

I see no sign of my wife

so I *let her in*

then my wife arrives | {high pitched} "what are you doing" [I]

{very fast and precisely articulated} "your job is to keep the place in line if you
     can not perform this simple function I will divorce you and marry someone
     who *can*" | [L]

she drops off the groceries that she has foraged

and she's back to *foraging* [I]

so I'm moving up the line

{sinisterly} "and I'm not letting anybody in" [L]

but I'm getting near the *cash*

and there's no sign of my *wife*

and the ladies who have formed in this line behind me *by this time*

they're starting to *smell blood* [I]

I get the *feeling* if I *leave* for a *second*

just to *see* where my wife *is*

the second they're out of my *sight*

they're going to scatter my groceries and throw my shopping cart out the *door*
    [I]

and that explains that lone broken shopping cart you see in the parking lot of
    every grocery store [I]

they're from guys who have *left their post* [L]

so now I'm up to the *cash*

{dramatic pause} and no sign of my wife

I'm feeding stuff through as *slowly* [I]

as I can *do it* [I]

and the women behind me are all *casting daggers* at me

still no sign of my wife

I've got *nothing more* to feed *through*

so I'm buying stuff off the shelves [L]

{exasperated and drawn out} "and they put the most useless garbage in the
    world [L] for just such an eventuality as this" [L]

label-maker repair kits [I]

I had to buy *three* of those [I]

I don't even have a *label-maker* for god's sakes [I]

{quickly, excitedly} "I've *cleaned out* the shelves by the time my wife arrives

big armload of groceries

pushes her way to the front" |

| {high pitched} "I'm with him! I'm with him!" |

and *I'm* saved but at the back of the line

there's this guy

empty shopping cart

one loaf of bread

and I'm thinking oh-oh he's got it worse than me [I]

I've cleaned out the shelves next to the cash [L] (Elliott 2000*, track 7)

The laughter that is occasioned by the last line is in part from the line itself but no less from the recognition that the story has reached its natural and logical resolution. The bigger laughs occur after the comments on taking hostages, on the loonie (the standard nickname for the Canadian dollar coin) as gift certificate, on being a stand-in at the checkout line, on the threat of divorce, and on the origins of the lone broken shopping cart. And it is perhaps only the loonie as dollar-store gift certificate that could be easily reworked into a stand-alone joke. The question arises about what else is being performed if not jokes?

One could suggest that a joke is precisely that form of humorous narrative that can be—and is—abstracted from its original performance context. What makes a joke a joke, in other words, is that the listener (and the collector) can make it wholly independent from a specific performer and treat it as an isolatable or discrete unit. It is based not in personal but in collective worldview. Were one to incorporate wholesale someone else's joke into one's own repertoire, one would still need common ground with the original teller in order to effect a similar interpretation and reaction. The greater the manipulation required for the listener to abstract it or the more inextricably the specific performer weaves it into their repertoire, the less one can successfully transfer it across repertoires. These bits sit nestled in the midst of a larger performance and are extracted only with difficulty.

Eddie Murphy makes this point explicitly in his stand-up comedy concert *Delirious* from 1983. He is speaking to a young child in the audience, who Murphy imagines to have expected performances of his characters from *Saturday Night Live*. The following section does double-duty, as he notes how inextricable his material is from the flow of his entire performance, while what he says also serves as an illustration of an extract from a performance that is not—by most definitions of the word—a joke. It is also worth noting that the bit takes place within five minutes of the end of the performance, which allows for references to elements previously performed:

> Here's a little joke for y'all
> {Turning to crowd at large} y'all can listen to it too [L]
> 'cause I know *lots* of times people see my show and then go to work and try to
>   tell my *act* and fuck my jokes *up* on the job and shit [L]
> they're like | {in Caucasian voice} "and then he said *'goonie-googoo'* [L]
> and he had a GI *Joe* up his ass! | [L]

> *'hey-hey-hey* I'm Mr. *T*
> I'll rip your *cock* off with my *ass'''* | [L]
> and a dude will be standing going
> | {dry and sarcastic} "yeah that's very funny shit" | (Murphy 1983a*)[7]

That said, there is a significant stand-up comedy strategy of including within the final minutes of an act material that is more easily retold the next day at the proverbial water cooler as a means of promotion (Stebbins 1990, 15); and, again, Murphy's routine is about five minutes shy of the end of the concert.

A similar but far graver observation was made by Lenny Bruce almost twenty years prior. Bruce had spent much of the last few years of his life defending himself on obscenity charges, and the trials became fodder for his onstage performances. He repeatedly returns to the theme of context over the course of the performance recorded as *The Lenny Bruce Performance Film* (1992*), in a routine about police giving evidence about his performances.

> *I* do my act at perhaps uh eleven o'clock at night
> little do I know that 11:00 a.m. the next morning
> before the grand jury somewhere
> there's another guy doing my act who's introduced as Lenny Bruce {sotto voce}
>   "in substance" [I]
> | Here he is: Lenny Bruce {sotto voce} "in substance" |
> a *peace* officer
> who is trained for
> to recognize clear and present dangers not make believe
> does the act
> the grand jury watches him work and they go *that stinks* [L]
> *but I get busted* [L] (Bruce 1992*)

One should further distinguish between the manipulation required to abstract a joke from one context and the subsequent artistic or aesthetic manipulation the individual performer may choose to employ in order to render a unique performance. *The Aristocrats* (Provenza 2005*), a documentary about a joke type known to most stand-up comedians, but one which is performed backstage as an exercise in comedic artistry as opposed to onstage as part of professional repertoire, demonstrates how a text with a fixed and formulaic opening and closing but with unlimited liberty in the middle section can be made distinct with each performance. The formulaic pattern allows for its infinite variation: like most jokes when reduced to their structures, it is context-independent until it is performed.

In the end, "joke" is only ever an emic category. Something that is identified as a joke within a culture can certainly be studied and labeled as such by the folklorist, but the connotation remains of a cultural phenomenon that can be abstracted from its context. This work treats the term "joke" only within this context, as a keyword implying a culturally recognized instance of humor, not as a generic form. But if stand-up comedians don't tell jokes, what do they do?

The form of talk that is most coincident with stand-up comedy is "small talk," talk that is understood by the participants as primarily concerned with the establishment or reestablishment of interpersonal relationships and less with instrumental communication for the facilitation of a specific, concrete goal. It is ostensibly a form of play only insofar as it is not a form of work. It may prelude more "serious talk"; and in part it is a recognition that, although particular lines of authority may be required in order to promulgate particular tasks, and these lines of authority are manifested in serious talk, the formal hierarchical structures do not by necessity extend into all aspects of the relationships between participants: hierarchical divisions are contingents and not absolutes, and relationships are not merely instrumental but can be built on fellow-feeling. Small talk is not so much concerned with building consensus as it is with building community in which diversity can be fostered. It builds intimacy. It is not inconsequential, as it is not trivial: rather, it is non-consequential, in that it does not require enactment.

Small talk is thus a frame of talking in which the talkers are allowed a license for a certain ambiguity in regard to the connection between what they are saying—whether in narrative or in belief statement—and what they "actually" hold to be true. The elusiveness of meaning and the allowed license of talk have their limits, as the relationship between talkers will only allow so much encroachment by one talker into another's central core of what they hold to be true. The parameters of what is allowable in small talk—including whether small talk is even permissible to any extent—are contextually set, defined by a negotiated understanding between talkers, and continuously renegotiated through the act of small talk itself. The truly playful aspect of small talk stems from the testing of those parameters, where assumptions are deliberately challenged, held up to scrutiny, mocked, or rejected, whether through an explicit discourse on these assumptions or implicitly through their enactment in narrative, all the while retaining a frame of non-consequentiality.

In brief, they're talking shit.

"Talking shit" is the non-consequential talk of casual, intimate, quotidian encounters: it is an exchange of ideas and opinions, often venturing away from units of worldview to disquisitions on a particular idea, supporting that argument with narrative examples and so forth. It can erupt into other genres but always returns to its flow (Bell 1983). Barbro Klein describes a similar form of talk using her father's term "skitprat" (shit talk); within the context of informal conversations among family and friends, her father

> took advantage of nuances in conversations and other kinds of interaction in order to stage stories and other forms of verbal art in which he utilized a number of stylistic devices and verbal techniques to make the past come alive: rich metaphors, play with dialects and other paralinguistic resources, traditional migratory motifs and turns of phrase, cultural historical explanations and elaborations. (2006, 79)

All writers on stand-up comedy, without exception, specifically emphasize that a stand-up comedian is on a stage talking with an audience. Stand-up comedy is neither a series of narratives nor a series of jokes: it is a form of small talk that can make use of a variety of genres and breakthroughs to performance, all at the service, however, of the social, interpersonal, and collaborative nature of its shared creation between performer and audience. Insofar as the success of the stand-up comedy performance, the impetus for it to continue, and its ostensible goal are all the audience's reaction in the form of laughter, the audience cannot help but be part of the performance.

Coincident with a discussion of such emic gentrification as "small talk" and "talking shit" is—much like in the above discussion of jokes—the process of trivialization as a coding strategy (Radner and Lanser 1993). These genres of marginality (evidenced by the minimalizing words used in their names) are explicitly perpetuated as not only non-consequential but also inconsequential by the participants themselves: in part, so that, should the transgression of boundaries go beyond the acceptable confines of play, the participants can restore the play frame through reference to genre and, in part, so that, should those outside the participating members express concern about the content, assurances of the non-consequences can be quickly made.

Strategies of coding allow for discourse to take place in the presence of, but outside the notice of, power: groups emerge as subcultures whose aesthetic forms are in part defined by their coded relationship to their dominant culture's forms. Trivialization encourages the dismissal of what is said by marking it off from the serious, and an entire discourse framed as small talk and joking can allow for the avoidance of consequence. It impels one to frame the performance as play until such time that we cannot reconcile it as such. Eddie Murphy dramatizes this point in *Raw*, in the conclusion to the routine discussed above.

> I know there are a lot of guys sitting out there right now going like this too
> | {angrily} "yo Ed shut the fuck up man" [L]
> {alternating between obsequious smile to person at side with "quit it" gesture of
>   hand drawing across throat}
> {more angrily} "I didn't spend all my money for this motherfucker" | [L]
> 'cause you're going to be driving home tonight with your wife in the car like this
> | {suspiciously inquisitive} "you don't really be fooling around like Eddie Murphy
>   says do you" |
> | {steering and smiling broadly} [L] ha ha
> no baby that's just *jokes* | [L] (Murphy 1987*)

In everyday small talk, people exchange information, share interests, express opinions, and mutually reaffirm their commonality while not obviating differences. There may be some elements of functionality to it (and some elements of mere convention), but it is not an instrumental form of talk. The inertia of the exchange is interpersonal, as the roles of performer and audience move between the constituent participants. Other relationships beyond that of audience and performer—male/female, elder/youth, employer/employee, oppressor/oppressed—have an influence on how balanced that back-and-forth movement may be in practice, but a surfeit of egalitarianism and collaboration is maintained. On occasion, focus may be drawn (or may be given) to one of the participants as he or she elaborates on a particular point. This focus is typically granted through implicit consensus by those present on the anticipation of meeting expectations of a culturally and contextually appropriate performance and, should those expectations not be met, the granting of focus may be withdrawn. When focus is granted, however, the performer is never dislocated from the audience, which must continually reaffirm the performance's continuation. It is forever dialogic. If a performed text is of a type where, irrespective of the presence or absence of an audience, it would both produce an intelligible text and vary little from version to version, one is encountering something other than small talk.

Stand-up comedians do not tell jokes: they do not tell stories, spout proverbs, or spread legends. They talk on a stage with an intent to be found funny. Like in small talk, they engage in a flow of discourse with "an" other; and then, often, and *within this primary talking frame*, they tell jokes and stories, spout proverbs, and spread legends. In other words, again just like everyday conversation, my immediate point is that stand-up comedy is a dialogic form. No matter how one-sided the conversation between the performer and the audience might be, there is a required reciprocity between performer and audience.

We can see this negatively through the questionable success of transliterating live performances into the recording studio or onto the page (as is discussed later): without the audience's reaction, however coerced or manipulated by the skilled performer that reaction might be and however little it "interferes" with the narrative flow of the performance, the text is incomplete. The stand-up comedian needs an audience, not like an author needs a reader or an artist needs a muse, but like a skier needs snow. Stand-up comedy is the only mass-mediated cultural performance activity whose normative consumable product is a recording of a live event.

Much like folklore, popular culture is recognizable when encountered, and yet it is difficult to identify those features common to all instances thereof. To study popular culture first requires its distinction from other spheres of culture, typically, from "high" or "elite" culture. Such distinctions are not absolute and are, in fact, identifiably perspectival, as the judgment of what is or is not mere fashion is the prerogative of power elites. Certain popular culture products are elevated to elite cultural status when their value, in terms of retroactively having met some criteria, is recognized by elites: the films of John Ford, the illustrations of Robert Crumb, the writings of Charles Dickens, the music of Robert Johnson, the stand-up comedy of Lenny Bruce. Such an elevation—their admission to "the" canon—often entails their preservation through their institutionalization, wherein they are kept safe from the very whims of fashion that either gave rise to them in the first place or allowed for their commercial viability.

Popular culture is similarly distinguished from folk culture: we tend to place the products present within small-group, immediate, intimate cultures in one frame (i.e., folk culture) and the products present within large-group, mediated, and widespread cultures in another (i.e., popular culture). North America (at least non-folklorists therein) tends to see folk cultures as occasionally engaging in and being influenced by the products of popular culture but, in the main, being isolated from it.

Some have suggested that popular culture is more or less the culture that emerges from the people in their manifest differences and has attained or found a broad popular appeal: popular culture is discerned as that which is pleasing to most, in that it overcomes difference, and thus it is determined by consensus (Fiske 1989, 20). It is, in a way, either a confluence of the products of folk cultures or the product of a single folk culture that has found large-scale purchase. This works well, although it fails to take into consideration that broad dissemination implies access to conduits of dissemination through direct or indirect control of media and that popular culture rarely conflicts with the interests of those who do wield control. A perspective based on power is almost in direct opposition to any optimistic reading.

John Fiske (1989), among others, has therefore argued for a third, mediating position: that one should talk of "mass culture" as the product of Theodor Adorno's "culture industry" and "popular culture" as what is made therefrom (1991, 24). Though fruitful, this approach introduces a certain rigidity to the differentiation between the producers and consumers of popular culture. While this model is highly effective, it has its limits. By emphasizing the unidirectional aspect of mass mediation, this model tends to gloss over the culture industry's propensity for not reacting to popular consumptive trends unless those trends are pervasive and apparent and their reaction serves the hegemonic need. A further limitation is the supposed homogeneity of the culture industry, related to its reactive element. Producers of popular culture are understood to make available products for which there is a demand—which the producers themselves may create—and which allow for the perpetuation of the hegemony. Esoterically, people believe that the culture industries see them as a mass, occasionally broken up into demographics but otherwise virtually interchangeable.[8] Exoterically, they believe the culture industry to be a juggernaut that, although ostensibly divided into different corporations in competition with each other, is in fact cooperating in the production of content meant to appeal to the broadest consumer base, independent of aesthetic value. When genuine aesthetic value is chanced upon, the industry is quick to imitate until it becomes conventionalized and, ultimately, a further commodity.

Stand-up comedy introduces a distinct complexity to this argument that, surprisingly, allows us to sidestep it, if only momentarily. Because the performance is always in part to an audience immediately present to the performer and whose response is part of the overall created text, the rigid distinction of a producer/consumer model breaks down. We immediately return to the issue of power and cultural taste when it is asked how a particular comedian gets to be in front of that audience through the apparatuses of club bookers and agents judging the comedian's adherence to the local aesthetics of performance, and this is compounded when we question the comedian's access to mainstream outlets like television and radio. But at its core we have a performance comprising collaboration between a performer and his or her audience.

Stand-up comedy introduces another complication. The two "products" of stand-up comedy are performances, whether that be an intangible live performance for which tickets are sold (or covers are charged, drinks are more expensive, etc.) and for which the performer is paid or a tangible recording of same, able to be redistributed through media or through stores. An audience's immediate and active engagement with the producer/performer's product is manifest in all instances. With broadcasts, there may be a passivity to its reception, although it can quickly shift to an active engagement, from the simple aesthetic response of laughter to the pursuit of further work by the comedian, to repeated viewing or listening, and—ultimately—to the incorporation of routines into the individual's own repertoire (as Robert Stebbins suggested [1990, 15]). At its core, however, is audience engagement: laughter is both the ends (the validation by the live audience of the comedian being found funny) and the means (data for the subsequent listener to consider in judging whether the comedian could be found funny).

> Sometimes people laugh and nothing comes out of their face
> this is what upsets me the most
> I *look* at them and I can *tell* they're laughing and enjoying themselves
> but they're silent laughers
> I don't *need* them here
> get out [L]
> they're just {mimes enthusiastic silent laughter} [L]
> you only hear them when they need *breath*
> to fuel their *shit non-laugh* (McIntyre 2007*)

This differentiates it from popular music, which is experienced both through live performance and recordings but for which the live recording is the exception rather than the rule. Stand-up comedy, however mediated it becomes and however great the spatiotemporal distance between performer and a specific audience member, is always formed by, and thus retains, the intimacy of face-to-face communication.

For stand-up comedy, we find ourselves in an indeterminate place between mediated and intimate cultures. Stand-up comedy is inherently folkloric, as it is performed in front of an immediate audience. The economics of stand-up comedy, however, are directed toward turning a live performances into an object—something that is not subject to further variation and can be sold as a commodity and broadly disseminated through distributive or redistributive networks.[9] But unlike the immediate analogue of musical recordings, which for the most part are recorded in studios and can be reworked into something approaching the ideal version from the perspective of the artist and producer, stand-up comedy recordings are based on live performances. They may be selected from a number of versions to create the best one,[10] but they contain within themselves the manner in which they have already been received: there is laughter, applause, heckles, and all other manifestations of audience reaction. They both record and suggest response.

Stand-up comedy products, when viewed through the lenses of popular culture studies, have already been subjected to some form of active reception: as such, they are more difficult to classify as hegemonic or counter-hegemonic. On one level, comedy brings with it an aura of counter-hegemony, as humor is one means to the revelation of inconsistency within a system. At another level, as comedy builds on exoteric assumptions, it can strengthen cohesion within a group by "othering" those outside it and, as such, can just as easily serve hegemonic interests. They are small-group focused and, as it were, filtered, but they aim at broader dissemination. There are narrowcast aspects to its distribution but, from the individual comedian's perspective, not necessarily to its original intention.

So we have a further breakdown in the absolute distinctions between folk and popular culture and are presented instead with a continuum (Narváez and Laba 1986b, 1). This model places, at one end, artistic expressions within a small and intimate group with slight or nonexistent spatial and social distances between performer and audience and, at the other end, artistic expressions transmitted through technological means to or in mass societal contexts, with significant spatial and social distancing between performer and audience. This model therefore focuses on differences of neither content nor socioeconomic class but on group size and medium of transmission. Although we can make judgments on individual performances or even performance genres as being "more one than the other," everything commonly referred to either as popular culture or folk culture exists somewhere in between these two ideal types, where performances are transmitted via various configurations of sensory and technological media (1).

By suggesting the continuum model, one navigates through some of the apparent contradictions and inconsistencies of the various approaches to popular culture. First of all, if one positions "folk group" as one's basic element of the model, one begins with a model that has as its focus notions of similarity but not homogeneity: there are factors shared, and one can rightly talk about the group as a whole without disallowing the possibility of further complexities to one's analysis. Second, as groups are defined by their common factors, one can use the cultural product as the common factor: it is not directly the product per se that makes for a common factor, but the experience of the cultural product; it is not blue jeans, but the experience of blue jeans; it is not the films of Adam Sandler, but the experience of the films of Adam Sandler—these make for the common factors of groups in terms of popular culture. Furthermore, small groups are no less operating within the context of small-scale hegemonic pressure—the weight of "tradition," the local "institution," however defined—than are large-scale, mass groups: the same patterns of resistance and the self-awareness of interstitiality that appear within folk contexts repeat themselves in macrocontexts. Lastly, as any study of culture beyond the statistical or theoretical eventually must return to the actual reception of the cultural product within a real context, popular culture studies can only ever ultimately be framed within small-group contexts.

Such an approach also seeks to address the issue of what defines "the people." As folklorists have struggled to define "the folk," they ultimately dispensed with pedantic nominalism and defined "folklore" as any artistic or intimate communication in small groups. A group that can be identified as such has an integrity all its own. When attention is turned back to the large-scale group, integrity becomes a nebulous issue: the lack of intimacy and spatial contiguity between performer and audience, particularly in mass-mediated performances, and the attendant indeterminateness of the intended audience tend to break down the group integrity ideal. One of the performer's (or performance team's) responsibilities is to create intimacy through the performance, overcoming the obstacle of unidirectionality and distance.

Despite the large formal structures responsible for its broad dissemination—culture industries, as it were—stand-up comedy is the product of individual creators and performers: along the folklore–popular culture continuum, it begins firmly at the folklore end, as it is performed within an intimate small-group context and, unlike other popular culture products, commodified by cultural industries, and it explicitly retains that small-group frame by including a record of its reception. To lose sight of the initial performance context—including the audience, which indicates the primary group for whom the performance is intended—is anathema to stand-up comedy research.

One of the further distinctions to be made when discussing the applicability of folklore study to stand-up comedy is the commercial aspect of the latter. There are distinctions to be made between the amateur and the professional, but this distinction is not made merely on the basis of performance competency. Rather, there are separate expectations for each, of which performance competency is but one. Just as important is the active cultivation of cumulative reputation and goodwill by the performer, in a manner similar to that described by Neil Rosenberg (1986) in relation to country musicians. Rosenberg proposes a model through which one can understand the complex relationship between purely avocational performers and those for whom performance is an occupation (153–57). The distinction of amateur and professional has an emic connotation of the latter lacking in musicianship: should that lack be shown to be demonstrably false, the emic distinction is maintained by identifying the professional not in terms of musicianship but in terms of being an "entertainer," one whose skills transcend that of mere musical ability. Ron James distinguishes "having the goods" of being funny from "having the balls" of working at professionalism:

I wanted them to *know* that it just wasn't
| *Oh* fuck that's the guy who was funny in *high school* and *university*
look where he is *now* |
and *everybody*
thinks that
and
it just wasn't . . .
it just wasn't that *way*

I had the goods but a *lot* of people had the goods
but a lot of people didn't have the *balls* (2005a)

These transcending skills—the balls—concern the cultivation of reputation. Being funny is honed through a growing competency and fluency with
the group's ideals of performance and its repertoire. Eventually, a comic
voice begins to take shape: a style and a repertoire that are recognizable
as genetically related to established modes but are simultaneously distinct.
The comedian's mastery of and potential contribution to the artistic realm
are recognized and actively sought out. In time, the personal accomplish-
ments and abilities of the performer become so well known to the audience
that individual repertoire and perhaps even skill become less important: it is
the person and the personality more than that person's abilities that people
come to see. The voice has emerged into a well-crafted, idiosyncratic persona
and the performer's reputation—and even repertoire—proceeds him or her.

This ascension is not so simple, however, if the comedian moves away
from his or her starting point. It is one thing to master the aesthetic expectations of one's home constituency—of one's folk group—but reputation
and cultural fluency might not extend past the borders of that group. The
professional comedian, like the professional musician, has the impetus
to perform in larger and larger markets, moving past local to regional,
national, and maybe even international. Locally, your reputation may pre-
cede you, but when you move to play to a different crowd, you are not only
not assured the audience's goodwill but may not be familiar with this new
place's aesthetic expectations. Using Rosenberg's terms, a local "craftsman"
may be only a "journeyman" on the regional scene, and barely considered
more than an "apprentice" on the national stage.

A baseline of worldview that is less defined by locality than by the inertia and precedence of the popular tradition itself needs to be understood
before one can be idiosyncratic and unique, as one needs to comprehend
what, precisely, one is idiosyncratic *to*. When a larger market is understood
as an amalgam of constituent smaller markets, each with widely varying
tastes, and with a commensurately greater reliance on the "delivery" of performance through broadcasting and recordings, the professional must be
willing to alter style and repertoire in the direction of maximum generality. Furthermore, one of the distinctions between both an amateur and a
professional and the various tiers of professionalism is the skilful use of the
media to aid in reputation cultivation.

There are two further qualifications for this model's immediate applicability to stand-up comedy: firstly, whereas the musician may require an

apprenticing stage in which technique is honed and group expectations of performance and group repertoire are learned, for the comedian, with stand-up's emphasis on novelty and "originality," the requirement to develop new texts necessitates writing one's own material from the very beginning. Secondly, whereas for the musician the penetration of larger markets—reputation establishment—comes primarily through broadcasting and sales of studio-recorded music, and only secondarily and infrequently through face-to-face interaction (i.e., distance precludes a constant interaction between audience and performer in all markets), the comedian's main form of market penetration stems from the broadcasting and sales of live recordings that were recorded in a specific locale. These performances have a "double-market" context: they must in some manner operate within the immediate, specific expectations of the specific audience present at the venue while simultaneously operating within the mediated general expectations of an intended but unknown audience.

By virtue of its interdisciplinarity, folkloristics has historically borrowed concepts and approaches from a wide array of disciplines to shed light on its object proper, informal interaction in small-group contexts. I have laid out several of the more general approaches that this book will use to explore stand-up comedy.

Most stand-up comedy implies a level of performed autobiography. At first one gives some of that biography through an explicit introduction, but over a comedian's career some form of persona is established, mostly concerning the life lived offstage or off the road. It is one of the factors which further makes material unique to the performer and harder to transfer across repertoires. Furthermore, returning audience members bring a foreknowledge of this persona to subsequent performances, and a framework for how to interpret a specific performance is already established. The intimacy of the performance style makes intimates of the performer and audience: even for the unknown comedian just starting out, the ultimate goal is this establishment of intimacy.

I have been arguing the analogies between stand-up comedy and vernacular forms of talk: now is the time to turn to the differences. Once there is a distancing between teller and listener and once the performance becomes less ephemeral, the media of that distancing—from something as simple as a stage to something like digital distribution of performances—changes the talk.

PART 2
The Middle: Creating Intimacy over Distance

We go out naked.
—Johnny Carson

This is the middle: a solid performer who maybe just needs more exposure before making the move to headlining. A few months from now he or she might be on television and you will sit up, listening for material you heard live and smiling at the recognition.

I have been maintaining that stand-up comedy is a form of talk that on the surface is more or less indistinguishable in potency from everyday forms of vernacular discourse. Much of stand-up comedy's appeal is precisely its contiguity with small group talk, as opposed to oratorical or theatrical modes. Stand-up comedy is certainly a performance, but much more in keeping with "styling and profiling" than with the performances of the conservatory and proscenium. The expressive or artistic patterning of everyday talk falls under the purview of folkloristics. Nevertheless, the study of stand-up comedy as a form cannot consist of a wholesale application of the tools and genres available to the folklorist without taking into account that which distinguishes it from everyday talk.

Much of the rest of this work operates within the folklore and popular culture continuum described in the last chapter. This model suggests that spatiotemporal distance between performer and audience is the principal distinguishing marker between folk and popular performance and that the various media of transmission are connectors between audience and performer.

This section concerns the separation of performer and audience through the use of a stage and how the microphone subsequently bridges that distance and returns the talk to the intimacy of face-to-face encounter. Then we cover how the comedian bridges the sociocultural distance that is typically there, the consequence of the professional comedian's itinerant life.

It ends with a denouement on how the stand-up comedian, both of professional necessity and by virtue of being "trapped" in this social identity, can never fully bridge that distance, as there is always the expectation of being an outsider.

CHAPTER 2

Where Is the Stand-Up Comedian?: Stand-Up on Stage

Some people think I'm *high* on stage
I would never get high before a show
because when I'm *high*
I don't wanna stand in front of a bunch of people *I don't know* [L]
that does not sound *comfortable* [L]
like when you're high and a joke doesn't work it's *extra scary*
it's like | whoa what the hell happened there [L]
I am retreating within *myself* [L]
why have all these people *gathered* [L]
and why am I *elevated* [L]
why am I not facing the same way as everyone else [L]
and what is this *electric stick* in my hand | [L]
I like the *way*
this is *situated* here
it seems like you guys were *chasing* me
closing in
and then said | fuck it let's sit *down* |
—Mitch Hedberg

We experience through our senses—taste, touch, smell, sound, sight—and to be present to a thing allows for the potential of experiencing that thing with all senses. When that thing is a person, we are approaching intersubjectivity and intimacy. Spatial and temporal proximity—being there—is our assurance of authenticity, much like courts privilege eyewitness accounts and dismiss hearsay (Auslander 1998). For performances, being there allows us to avail ourselves of all our senses for the interpretive act of understanding and judging and not having some experiences cut off from us by an intermediary. And in stand-up comedy, which is dialogic in form, there is a requirement for the immediate presence of someone at the comedian's performance to react and thus move the performance along. Let's look at the various mediations of stand-up comedy performance that still imply the spatiotemporal co-location of performer and audience and the experience of the live event.

We can take as our baseline, one theoretical end of our continuum model, the unmediated performance. "Unmediated" is a misnomer, of course, a conceit for our model: language is a medium, as are tone and gesture and costume and stance. But we allow, in our ideal type, for the possibility of an immediate and spontaneous coding and decoding of linguistic, paralinguistic, and kinesic symbols between performer and audience.

This event is, first of all, communicative. There is at least one "encoder" (performer) and at least one "decoder" (audience member) between whom there is direct, person-to-person communication, and communication happens through a coded message—using linguistic, paralinguistic, and kinesic codes—transmitted through audio and visual channels, which generate continuous perceptual responses interpreted by performer and audience as feedback (Georges 1969, 317). It is also a social experience when the social identities of performer and audience member imply a known set of rights and responsibilities: the performer needs to meet the expectations for performance shared by the two, while the audience needs to interpret the performance as such (and not as some other form of talk). Ron James put it thus:

> He also realizes people have certain expectations about his shows and he tries to give them what they came for. He has seen some of his own comic heroes perform and he doesn't appreciate it when people don't give their audience the best they've got. [James said,] "I don't want to sleepwalk through a set. I never want to do that. . . . I've seen some bad shows and paid a dear price for the tickets. That kind of experience stays with you. I want people to walk out of my shows feeling great. And it can be really exciting out there when everything's working, when you get the wind in your sails. There's a double relationship when I'm out there. It's my responsibility as a comedian to deliver and the audience's responsibility to enjoy the journey." (qtd. in Gallant 2003)

They may, and most likely do, have other social relationships, but this pairing is most prominent at the time of performance, conditioned as it may be by other relationships. The event has social uses, which can be articulated by participants, and social functions, which can be inferred through analysis.

If the social use or social function warrants it, the assumed identities of performer and audience member can be switched. One can easily imagine a session of "swapping stories," wherein the identities are continually reversed. But we also recognize the status accorded particular members of groups who have a certain mastery over both the group's repertoire and its preferred mode of aesthetic patterning and whose presumptive identity as "performer" may be an a priori in any group interaction. Furthermore, certain other reciprocal social identity pairings—parent and child; two lovers; employer and employee—may determine the assumption of the performer identity. Nevertheless, in our ideational model, there is nothing that inherently limits the assumption of particular identities to particular participants, as the distinction between performer and audience member is one that lasts only for the duration of the performance event itself.

As it is a professional activity, the plasticity of this model does not immediately apply to stand-up comedy. There is no sense of anticipation that the performer and the audience member will actually switch roles, nor that the distinction between performer and audience member is mere happenstance. However, as the talk that is performed on stage aims at replicating this intimacy and informality, it can be retained not only as a model for one end of our folk and popular culture continuum, but also as an aspirational model for subsequent performances.

"Stage" could be understood in one of two ways. Ostensibly, any place where any type of performance is taking place could be called a stage. The performances of everyday life determine by context what specific areas are considered front stage, backstage, offstage, and so on. Specialized stages (for example, commercial establishments such as restaurants) may develop over time that help to facilitate the "impression management" and control of the situation that are required for such interactions (see Goffman 1959). Similarly, as one shifts from interacting behaviors to performances that are expressly and intentionally artistic, ludic, affective behaviors, participants, both performer(s) and audience, may position themselves in a manner that, through kinesic and proxemic codes, indicates the audience's collective focus on the performer. In his study of English monologue traditions, Kenneth Goldstein notes how the monologist

> invariably stands up to perform, thus rising above the seated audience, or, if the members of the group are all standing, then the performer draws back. Both actions serve to establish the social and dramatic distance required for

the performance and to explicitly indicate the separate and distinct roles of the parties to the interaction. (1976, 10)

In these instances, stages are ad hoc, temporary spatial distinctions between performer and audience and disappear at the end of the performance event.

But the stage as meant for our purposes is a concrete and physical entity. It is a pragmatic concession to the size of the group present or potentially present for the performance: it would be unwieldy for a crowd to rearrange itself spontaneously to give focus to one individual. Sight lines and the projection of sound—increasingly problematic issues as the crowd gets larger—are further issues.

A dedicated space solves these problems but alters the nature of the performance. Most immediately, the stage makes formal the distinction between performer and audience.[1] George Carlin, in "Goofy Shit" from *Toledo Window Box*, speaks to the minimized participation of the audience that the stage engenders:

> Yes you *are* in this you can say *anything*
> you like you don't have a lot of *lines* granted right on
> you have to think of them but . . .
> it's often hard for me to *understand* them
> because oddly enough these places were built for the voices to go | *that way* | [L]
> and what *I* hear is | {distorted sounds like a record played backwards} | [L→A]
> I have to turn around and hear | {angry} "get off there you asshole" | [L] (1974*)

By making such a distinction, there is effected a movement from performance to what Milton Singer has called "cultural performance" (1972), or, in Richard Bauman's formulation, a conception of performance

> as a specially marked mode of action, one that sets up or represents a special interpretive frame within which the act of communication is to be understood. In this sense of performance, the act of communication is put on display, objectified, lifted out to a degree from its contextual surroundings, and opened up to scrutiny by an audience. Performance thus calls forth special attention to and heightened awareness of the act of communication and gives license to the audience to regard it and the performer with special intensity. Performance makes one communicatively accountable; it assigns to an audience the responsibility of evaluating the relative skill and effectiveness of the performer's accomplishment. (Bauman 1992a, 44)

As a stage facilitates the signaling of such a performance—one which is of a different order from face-to-face, unmediated performances—the kinesic and proxemic codes of being on or off the stage also serve to change the expectations of the performance event from both the performer's and audience's perspective. As Johnny Carson put it, "You were *different* from other people. You were up on the stage and they were sitting down here, and there's a certain, I don't know if you want to call it . . . power, but it makes you different" (1979). Their interlocking nexus of rights and responsibilities is supplemented with a tacit testing of the performer's assumption of the storytelling identity.

For example, the rap artist Ice T, interviewed for the Comedy Central series *Heroes of Black Comedy*, expressed it this way: "Every black man got a little comedy streak in him: all of us think we can shoot the dozens and say something funny. So, it's almost like, when you hit the stage at the Apollo [Theatre in Harlem] or something, the audience is like [crossing arms defiantly], '*Make me laugh*'" (Ice T 2002*). In an unmediated performance, should the performer fail to live up to his or her responsibilities, the performance would simply dissolve, with focus shifted elsewhere. With the introduction of the stage, the intensity of the focus on the performer is such that, should that same failure occur, the performance cannot simply dissolve: the stage accentuates the failure.

Nevertheless, within stand-up comedy the intent is to retain both the connection with the audience and the notion of the stage as a concession to performance and not a divisive structure. In an interview that appears as a special feature on the DVD of *The Original Kings of Comedy* (Lee 2000*), Cedric the Entertainer describes his style:

> When I go on stage I try to take the energy of
> this is all my *living room*
> all these people *my friends*
> and I'm just up here *entertaining* them
> for a few minutes (Lee 2000*, "Bonus Scenes")

Staging for the stand-up comedy performance is minimal. Typically, there is a stool, a microphone stand, and a neutral backdrop.

The backdrop is either a blank wall (frequently brick) or a curtain. At times, there are more elaborate backdrops, but they tend to be abstract or impressionistic. In the case of specific comedians, there may be some attempt to indicate something of the particular comedian's worldview,[2] but the economics of touring often prohibit anything so elaborate. Furthermore, comedy performance spaces, either permanent ones like comedy clubs or temporary ones like theaters, are more often than not going to be shared by more than one comedian over the course of an evening: anything too idiosyncratic would be ultimately counter-productive to one or more of them.

Most historians of North American stand-up comedy trace its origins to vaudeville, burlesque, and variety theater (Franklin 1979; Mintz 1977, 1998; Stebbins 1990). The names that are often invoked as antecedents of stand-up comedy include the Marx Brothers, W. C. Fields, Jimmy Durante, George Burns and Gracie Allen, and so forth. While their influence is present, particularly in reference to the anarchic, surreal, or absurdist nature of some stand-up comedy performances, stylistic antecedents would be found more in the masters of ceremonies for variety shows. As an intermediary between audience and act, and as "filler" between acts, they had the onus of responding to audience reaction, smoothing over any adverse reactions, and contextualizing the following act, all done with a drawn curtain behind them.[3]

Within the coffeehouse circuit of the 1950s and 1960s, the aesthetic was based in part on the reclamation of found space: basements, in particular, in Greenwich Village were popular due to their being inexpensive. In Eric Lax's biography of Woody Allen, Art D'Lugoff, owner and founder of the Village Gate, is quoted as saying:

> Where I settled was a rather reasonable place because no one else wanted to go there and I got a decent price for a big space. There was a tradition of coffee shops from the old country that continued. Midtown had nothing like it. The area was ripe for something to happen culturally and the business could support itself. Folk music was self-contained; there was not a big expensive group to pay. (in Lax 1992, 144–45)

Max Gordon, founder of the Village Vanguard, recounts a similar economic rationale for the basement locales of his own club (1980, 19–25).

The original look, albeit born from an economic need, was perpetuated by the interrelatedness of class consciousness and "authenticity" in the folk revivalist movement. Robert Cantwell, in "When We Were Good: Class and Culture in the Folk Revival," provides a history of this interrelatedness and frames it in part in terms of "style" (1993, 39).[4] Eric Lax writes, "The bare-brick-wall backdrop for the acts that is so common in clubs today was first used at the Bitter End" (1992, 145). Contemporary stand-up comedy clubs, including chains like Yuk-Yuks, intentionally install brick facades as part of the décor. The brick wall for the comedy stage has reached the point where it is now iconographic for stand-up comedy; and one notes its metonymic use in *The Simpsons* and in packaging for books (Carter 1989; Sankey 1998), albums (Regan 1997*; Rock 1997*, 1999b*), and videos (*Best of the Improv* 2001*; *Laughing Out Loud* 2003*).[5]

In both instances, the curtain and the brick wall, the impression created is that of performance abstracted from any artifice. If it is theater, it is theater removed from any of its trappings, with nothing intruding on the intimacy between audience and performer. "It is often stripped bare of any competing symbology . . . , so that the talk itself is highlighted as the dominant symbol" (French 1998, 90–91). Similarly, in Rachel Lee's study of Margaret Cho the "focus [is] on the literal site of performance (the bare stage) as a space of assemblages, as a platform for revealing the body's infirm boundaries and borders as well as its embeddedness in histories of migration" (2004, 109). Ron James, lamenting how comedy on television is presented, told me in an interview, "You know what you should be concentrating on? What's being said" (2005a).

The stool, although it can on occasion be used as a prop, more or less serves its utilitarian function. It can double as a table but is principally used as a seat, even though sitting is just as often a piece of stagecraft as it is a concession to tiredness.

> I see we ah
> we have a *stool* here
> that's good
> comedians work for
> *what*
> half an hour a *day*
> but we might want to take a *break* at any time [L]
> I guess the message here is *don't* underestimate our laziness (Barker 2008*)

The last object, once one considers the stage and the stool, is the microphone. All three are part of the "found landscape" of a comedy performance: their presence as utilitarian objects is not only not a contradiction of the abstraction and minimalism of the stage but also an *a priori* for and a convention of the genre.

The microphone serves a basic function: amplification. Through it one is able to transcend the acoustic limitations of physical space and have one's voice projected without recourse to shouting. It makes one loud without forcing one to be loud. As such, it changes the nature of what one says and how one says it. The medium of the microphone, therefore, not only alters the stand-up comedy performance but also allows for new expressive forms to take place on the stage.

Parallels can be drawn to other forms of expressive behavior. In his 1965 article "An Introduction to Bluegrass," L. Mayne Smith writes of the requirements for bluegrass musicians to orient themselves in relation to a microphone, not only for the general purpose of being heard in a large venue but also so that naturally quieter instruments can be heard and not overpowered by the louder instruments playing alongside. Bluegrass is a musical style where the impression given is of simplicity of style (albeit with proficiency of musicianship) but with a highly developed understanding of the use of microphone as instrument. It is a style that emerged with the advent of the technology and cannot exist without it.

Singing is the area that has been most closely scrutinized with respect to the effect of the microphone. Paula Lockheart writes, in her article on the history of early microphone singing, that with the introduction of the microphone in both broadcasting and live performance,

> [the] volume, pitch range, and vocal production of both the men and the women became closer to that of their conversational speech, and the presentation of text became more like that of conversational American English in pronunciation and phrasing. (2003, 380)

Simon Frith, in *Performing Rites*, indicates how

> [the] microphone made it possible for singers to make musical sounds—soft sounds, close sounds—that had not really been heard before in terms of public performance. . . . The microphone allowed us to hear people in ways that normally implied intimacy—the whisper, the caress, the murmur. (1996, 187)

Robert O'Meally notes that Billie Holiday, "whether in clubs or on recording dates, . . . continued to deliver her lyrics as if only for one or two listeners whom she addressed face to face" (1991, 32). Roy Shuker summarizes the affect of microphones by describing how they "revolutionised the practice of popular singing, as vocalists could now address listeners with unprecedented intimacy" (2001, 52).

The connection between microphone singing techniques and the intimacy of speech has also been made. John Szwed draws comparisons
between Miles Davis's use of the microphone, Frank Sinatra's use of it for
voice, and the naturalism in acting for the camera extolled by Konstantin
Stanislavsky:

> In the same era when audiences were becoming accustomed to closer and more
> intimate looks at actors on film, the mike removed the need for musicians and
> singers to struggle to close the physical distance between themselves and the
> audience. (2002, 188)

Kate Augestad likewise notes the crossover between naturalistic speech and
singing:

> The microphone invited a different way of pronouncing the words, a more clear
> diction and a new singing style that came to reflect the *vernacular of everyday-
> like speech*. Microphonic singing enabled *a speech-like voice* production to be
> used. . . . Singing that comes close to speaking seems to signal something popu-
> lar, something trustworthy, something everyday-like. One often sees that the
> most popular singers are those who manage to combine a speech-like way of
> singing with a kind of natural, but subdued virtuosity, in an easy recognisable
> form of competence that still comes forward as something extraordinary in its
> ordinariness. (2004, 46–48, emphasis in original)

Through projecting the human voice at its natural register, either
through space in the case of live broadcasting or through time and space
through recordings or the broadcasting thereof, an illusion of intimacy can
be created despite those space or time distances.[6] A performer can be heard
within a room without recourse to shouting: he or she can talk in a manner
commensurate with one-on-one communication.

I dwell so much on this history because the importance of the microphone on the history of stand-up comedy is both self-evident and profound. Just as "red hot mama" vocal stylings gave way to crooning, the use
of amplification allowed for comic performances in a voice that did not have
to struggle to be heard above a crowd. Short one-liners could give way to
longer pieces. Whispers, mutterings, and going off on tangents become
possible again. As Allison McCracken wrote about crooners, "Not only did
[they] not project their voices in traditional ways, but they also chatted

with their listeners; they created an identifiable personality" (1999, 392). So too could the comedian: a patter could be built up that was not simply a stream of jokes but an interplay of genres. The reaction garnered from the crowd did not need to be exclusively laughter: a proposition could be put forth, which could elicit a reaction from the crowd, which could then in turn be developed and defended. The comedy performance thus became a creation of both performer and the audience.

It is my contention that stand-up comedy only exists as a form with the advent of the microphone. Although this newly available intimacy between performer and audience does not have the exclusive unidirectionality of a broadcast or a recording, where the audience may be an active or passive listener but cannot alter the performance (as is discussed below), neither is there the potential for the switching of assumed identities of performer and audience member. In the relationship between performer and audience, power resides with the performer. The amplified performer's voice literally overpowers that of any one member of the audience. The more the audience operates as a collective, the less it can articulate its position with any precision or nuance. The microphone, in conjunction with the stage, allows for the performer to control the situation by continually drawing focus to him- or herself.

> I once said
> I love doing stand-up
> but I also think I just like to hear my voice amplified (Glass 2010*)

Insofar as the microphone is an instrument, vocal performers not only work around but also exploit the limitations of the technology. As was mentioned above, part of the way the microphone changed the nature of the performance was the newfound ability to speak at a natural register and nevertheless be heard. The inverse to this is the occasional need for the performer to speak outside of a natural register, whether in a whisper or scream, and maintain a more or less consistent volume level. This is typically achieved through the simple act of drawing toward or away from the microphone. At times, the distancing is taken to an extreme. In *Raw*, Eddie Murphy (1987*) leaves the microphone on the stand during a retelling of a heated argument at a nightclub; as he simultaneously distances himself and projects his voice away from the microphone, only snippets of talk are picked up and amplified, and the performance takes on the character of a dumb play.

Conversely, getting too close to the microphone introduces distortion, over-amplification, and additional reverberation. This is often used to great effect as a means of switching voice and employing characterization when the stand-up comedian is interjecting an authoritarian or contrarian characteristic to part of his or her text, an oral—and aural—parallel to the use of italics. In "Teenage Masturbation," from *An Evening with Wally Londo Featuring Bill Slaszo* (1975*), George Carlin drops his pitch and introduces distortion on the word "fantasized" when he says, "We didn't know that we *fantasized*; we thought we thought about people." In "Travel Tips," from his *Live at McCabe's* album (1992b*), Henry Rollins recounts being molested while on a childhood trip to Greece: when his assailant first approaches him with the offer of a pack of gum, he asks the crowd, "What's the big rule, everybody? *Don't take candy from strangers.* You've got that one embedded in your head." In either instance—moving away from or toward the microphone—the process of amplification and its "unnatural" presence are alluded to. Even when the comedian is quoting him- or herself in the context of a personal experience narrative, the use of this form of distortion is to indicate that a voice other than the performer-narrator is present to the audience.

Others have used the properties of microphone distortion to create sound effects. Michael Winslow has built a career around an uncanny ability to imitate various mechanical effects—notably, gunfire and machine noise—using only the microphone. Bill Hicks had a routine wherein he would imitate Jimi Hendrix's distorted electric guitar. In *Delirious*, Eddie Murphy (1983a*) imitates the sound of his aunt falling down the steps, interjected with her imprecations to Jesus to help. Andrew "Dice" Clay, in one routine from his *Dice Live at Madison Square Garden* concert (1994*), holds the microphone to his Adam's apple to imitate the sound of someone talking with an electronic voice box. I asked Ron James, in my interview, why he had not made the move to hands-free microphones:

IB In Halifax you had a microphone on a *stand*
    with a wire
    and each night you come out
    you take the mike off the stand
    you move it behind the stool
RJ yeah
IB and you don't really use the microphone as a *prop*
    you don't sort of . . . really use its *amplification*

RJ no
IB its capabilities for *distortion*
    you don't use it as a makeshift *phallus* or anything
    um . . .
    have you ever thought of using *hand's free* mikes
RJ yeah
IB have you *done* so
RJ yeah I did it in my first special *Shakey Town*
    'cause it was a one man *show*
    beginning middle and an *end*
    it was more of a *theatrical* presentation
    and I think that I would ah . . .
    I just don't do that *now*
    because I've got to make the sound of the *fart*
    of the *Huns'*
    coming over the *altar*
IB the *whoosh* sound
RJ yeah
    so that's a *technical* response to that (James 2005a)

On *Class Clown*'s "Sharing a Swallow" (1972b*), George Carlin makes admirable use of the prima facie function of the microphone by using it to amplify the sound of swallowing: holding the mike directly to his throat, he emphasizes the two parts of the swallow, pausing between them for optimal effect.

Much as a performer without benefit of electronic amplification might change his or her voice through timbre, pitch, or volume or supplement it with gesture and sound effects, the sonic qualities and limitations of the microphone provide the performer with further opportunities for vocal modification and supplementation. It is used sparingly, however, as it draws attention to the presence of artificial amplification and thus tends to be an interruption into the conversational and "natural" flow of the comedian's intimate talk.

It would be tempting to ascribe some totemic meaning to the microphone—a modern "talking stick," as it were—but there is nevertheless ample evidence that the microphone is symbolic of the act of stand-up comedy itself. Just as the brick wall is metonym, so too is the microphone; and its use on book jackets (Borns 1987; Nachman 2003; Schwensen 2005), albums (Foxx 1997*; Rock 1997*; 1999b*; Seinfeld 1998b*) and videos (Rock

1999a*; Seinfeld 1998a*, 2002*) to represent comedy is equally ubiquitous. The expression "on [or at] the mike" as a shorthand for the stand-up comedian's life and work is a commonplace (Stebbins 1990, 40; see also Bernie Mac's use of the phrase in "The Kings of Comedy" episode of *Heroes of Black Comedy* [in Billing and Upshal 2002*]).

Chris Rock provides an interesting example of the use of microphone as metonym: in addition to its conspicuous use on his album covers, part of his trademark is to drop the microphone to the ground at the end of a performance: when it is dropped, the performance is done, with the implication that it is never to be repeated. This derives from an early successful performance when he was starting out: Eddie Murphy was in the audience and asked to see Rock, who was the only African American comedian present. At the end of Rock's set he half-dropped, half-threw the microphone to the floor (in Quinn 2002*).

But perhaps the most explicit example of the microphone as representative of the act of stand-up comedy is from Damon Wayans (1990*) in his HBO special, *The Last Stand?*, filmed at the Apollo Theatre in Harlem. On the final show of what was then to be his last stand-up comedy tour, he begins by telling the audience how it is to be his last performance, as he is doing comedy for money. In due course, he ends the performance and smashes the microphone against the stage. The camera lingers on the electronic detritus.

If one wanted to take the totemic nature of the microphone seriously, one could also suggest that microphones are inherently phallic. Microphones as phalli are nothing new: John Hellmann, writing about the appropriation of blues terminology by the Rolling Stones, notes that, "in 'The Spider and the Fly,' [Mick] Jagger uses a common metaphor in the blues argot to spin a personal story of an after-show seduction, identifying himself as a leering spider seducing a willing fly who likes the way in which he holds his 'microphone'" (1973, 371). Lesbian comic Marjorie Gross observed that the physical act of standing on stage holding a microphone is "like holding a penis" (qtd. in Parker 2002, 19). But the stand-up comedian occasionally takes the implicit and makes it explicit. The minimalism of the staging means that the comedian has few props at his or her disposal: the diegetic microphone can easily "become" a penis for illustrative purposes.

In *Raw* (1987*), Eddie Murphy describes an episode where "your woman" has gone down to the Bahamas in an effort to clear her head: as she walks along the beach, "all of a sudden a dude named Dexter walks up, Dexter St. Jacques, who'll walk up swinging his dick." He then grabs the cord about two feet from the microphone and makes slow circles in front of him like he was swinging a watch on the end of a chain. The action is repeated—a callback—when it is revealed that the boyfriend is back in New York. And on a third occasion, when they are going back to his place to "just talk," the same length of cord and microphone is slung over his shoulder. In Chris Rock's *Bigger and Blacker* (1999a*), the microphone is tentatively and perfunctorily fellated as he describes "women that give you just enough head to shut you up." Margaret Cho, in *I'm the One That I Want* (2000*), repeatedly grabs at a limply held microphone to illustrate the perils and consequences of the sexual relationship between two alcoholics.

Microphones can be used as representations of non-phalluses, of course.[8] David Cross uses his to emulate a bong in his performance on *HBO Comedy Half Hour* (1996*), while in Eddie Murphy's *Delirious* concert (1983a*) it represents an ice cream cone. But the association with the microphone as phallus is strong. In the *Lenny Bruce Performance Film*, a documentary recording of one of Bruce's last shows in 1965, he opens the show by grabbing the microphone and using it as an aspergillum (the rod used for sprinkling holy water). He then tells the audience that he likes to use that gesture, as it is an example of "eye of the beholder," and that only Catholics interpret it correctly. As he recounted on stage, when he went to trial,

> I said
> |make sure to tell them it's a gesture of benediction not masturbation|
> I would never make gestures of masturbation 'cause I like ladies
> I'm concerned with my image and I know it offends chicks (Bruce 1992*)

The microphone cord and the stand can also both be used as props. In addition to the Eddie Murphy *Raw* use already noted, George Carlin, during his *On Location: George Carlin at USC* concert (1977a*), takes his lead from the whipping effect of a random tug on the cord and develops it into a sustained cord movement, with the ad lib, "'Within the first few moments he had the snakes going.'" Henry Rollins, in his *Talking from the Box* performance (1992a*), begins by binding the microphone to his hand with the cord, a technique developed, no doubt, when he was the lead singer of the seminal Los Angeles punk band Black Flag. In the former instance the cord is a reality whose presence is adverted to by Carlin so that it can be subsequently forgotten. In the latter the cord is a part of a routinized prelude to a performance, although it may be a consequence of affectation or habit.

In his *Wired and Wonderful* concert (2002*), Lee Evans begins his act *in medias res*, miming speech and then beginning halfway through a sentence, as if there had been a microphone malfunction. He then takes the stand, which in this instance is a gooseneck, and, while making appropriate sound effects, sprays the audience with machine-gun fire, before moving the stand to the side. Louie Anderson, a comedian whose short act in the early days was based more or less entirely on his being overweight, removed the mike from the stand and put it to one side, telling the audience that he was doing so "so you can see me" (qtd. in Carter 2001, 140). In such instances, the stand is an obstacle, the removal of which is incorporated into the comedian's routine, either spontaneously or, in the case of Anderson, deliberately.

If one wishes to maintain the impression of pure performance, one must be careful to use discretion when utilizing the found landscape. Steve Harvey, during his *One Man* special (1997*), only uses diegetic props once: when imitating the actions of a black man getting fired from a job, he overturns the stool and pushes the stand over. Margaret Cho's phallic use of the microphone, noted above, is the only instance of its use as prop in an hour and a half of performance: for her *HBO Comedy Half Hour* show (1994*), she never removes the microphone from the stand and touches it only to rest her hands during extended applause or laughter.

However, a problem with the physical reality of the microphone is how it interferes with the smooth performance of gesture. For performers who wish to incorporate more complex gestures, the microphone must on occasion return to the stand. In his routine about women and checks, which begins with the microphone in his hand, Jerry Seinfeld (1990*) seamlessly brings the stand forward and returns the microphone to it in order to effect the "quick-draw gunslinger" pose for the checkbook and identification and then removes the microphone again and continues with less elaborate gestures. Removing the microphone from the stand typically implies the desire for additional movement around the stage: leaving it on the stand means staying in one spot. With the former, gesture is limited (while talking) to one hand; with the latter, two hands are possible. In combination, the comedian is allowed an ample freedom of movement.

The stand is also used for leaning on and other non-gestural kinesic movements. Dennis Miller rarely if ever removes the microphone from the stand: he will occasionally hold onto the stand and sometimes will lean forward when emphasizing a point, bringing the stand with him. Comedians will also sometimes simply fidget with the stand, adjusting the height or angle, when neither gesture nor stillness seems either appropriate or possible. With cordless microphones, which intend a greater freedom of mobility for the performer, the need for a stand has diminished (sometimes the microphone is lying on the stool for the performer), but it is still in use, precisely to allow for complex gesture.

As technology develops, the use of hands-free microphones has become a possibility: several physical or prop comedians—Carrot Top, Gallagher— have been using them for years. Prop comedy is somewhat outside of the purview of this discussion; however, for the non-prop comedian, the hands-free microphone allows for a freedom of gesture that is not dependent on returning to the same spot and replacing the microphone on the stand. In her biography of Billy Connolly, Pamela Stephenson phrases it thus:

> Billy's live performing has been liberated by the radio microphone. He resisted it at first, clinging to his old stand and hand-held mike, but now he can move more freely over the whole stage, and use both hands. He strides back and forth, crossing the audience from side to side, almost forcibly yanking people into the world he's exploring and drawing them together as he explores the depth and width of the space as well. (2002, 364)

Robin Williams and Eddie Izzard are two further examples of contemporary comedians who refrain from hand-held microphones when they have the option. Notable is their use of gestures: the former quite natural and the latter quite theatrical. There is something less formal about the absence of a microphone: gestures can be more natural and uninterrupted, and the distinction between performer and audience in terms of physical referents is now back to the onstage/offstage dynamic. Charles Goodsell has written about how different kinds of political discourse arise in legislatures with hidden or exposed media of amplification (1988, 298). With hands-free microphones, amplification is still a presence, but it is not given physical form.

Nevertheless, the decision to go with or without a microphone is occasionally outside the comedian's domain. As will be discussed later, in the section on television performances, variety shows dating back to Ed Sullivan and continuing to late-night talk shows of today typically use the boom mike. Conversely, just as shared spaces have backdrops suitable for the widest assortment of worldview, so too do they have the amplification equipment suitable for the widest assortment of comedians. The comedian needs to be able to adapt his or her use of gesture to the circumstances of performance. Given the reliance on the microphone for performance,

Robert Stebbins locates it as one of the "things that go wrong onstage," the coping with which further serves to distinguish amateur from professional (1990, 92). Larry Horowitz developed a rating sheet for his stand-up comedy classes taught through Yuk-Yuk's in Toronto; it is used to evaluate amateur acts: the question "Do they use the mike well?" is listed under "skills" (in Stebbins 1990, 80).

An appreciation of the microphone is central for an understanding of stand-up comedy performances. Amplification changes the nature of the relationship with the audience: it is an enhancement of the unidirectionality of mediated performances that is a natural extension of the stage: at the same time, it reintroduces a level of intimacy by enabling the voice to be used in its natural register, allowing for natural speech patterns that more closely resemble face-to-face communication and dialogue. Furthermore, it is part of the diegetic landscape of the stage: it becomes not only something that must be dealt with as a potential obstacle but something that can be employed as a device that goes beyond and enhances verbal communication. Finally, it represents the act of stand-up comedy itself: as occupation, as social role, and as calling.

When Andrew "Dice" Clay sold out Madison Square Garden in 1990 (1991*, 1994*), it marked the first time that a North American comedian had filled a sports arena. Thus comedy hit the scale that popular music hit twenty-five years earlier when the Beatles played Shea Stadium. The distance from performer to his audience had surpassed its natural limit: without the aid of video projection—which is to the seeing what amplification is to hearing—one can speak of the performer and audience being present to each other in only the most notional sense.

As many sporting and musical audiences now anticipate a supplement for their immediate experience with video projection (in part from the routinized experience of watching these sorts of events on television), the venues are already set up with the technology, and the comedians who play these venues can avail themselves of it. Lee Evans's *Wired and Wonderful* concert DVD (2002*) provides an excellent referent, as there are moments where a wide, establishing shot includes the video screen, and it is clear that the crowd at Wembley is being shown something different from what the audience at home is seeing. What is being shown to the crowd, how the performance is affected by the directorial choices of the team running the video display, is ultimately not much different from what would be shown in a video-recorded or filmed performance, as will be discussed below: the audience member, however, has the benefit of switching between the immediate, albeit spatially distant, and the mediated, albeit spatially close, performances. Philip Auslander, in his appraisal of the impact of what he calls "mediatized" culture on live performance, briefly notes the emergence of video projection:

> The spectator sitting in the back rows of a Rolling Stones or Bruce Springsteen concert or even a Bill Cosby stand-up comedy performance is present at a live performance, but hardly participates in it as such since his/her main experience of the performance is to read it off a video monitor. (1999, 24)

Auslander's stance is reasonably evident in such expressions as "hardly participates in it as such," and (although I oversimplify his argument somewhat) he appears to suggest that mediatization is something that happens to extant art forms and performance genres, not something that creates new ones. Nevertheless, his general argument—that although being physically present at a performance event is commonly understood as somehow more authentic than experiencing it through a mediated form like broadcasting or recording, the performance itself is already going through some process of mediation (amplification, video display)—remains problematic for a performance genre like stand-up comedy that is predicated on (a surfeit of) interactivity. It is perhaps because of this distance between himself and the audience, complemented by the interrelated phenomenon of the Madison Square Garden concert being less a comedy performance and more a popular culture event, that in the weeks between the concert selling out and the concert itself Andrew "Dice" Clay performed two unadvertised and largely improvised and interactional shows at Dangerfield's in Brooklyn; they were recorded and released as *The Day the Laughter Died* (1990*).

With the media of the stage, microphone, and video, we have made a more or less full transition from vernacular talk to cultural performance. There is a clear demarcation between performer and audience: kinesic, proxemic, and aural cues are now directed fully toward the performer, who is granted control over the situation, albeit with the audience's expectations of providing a "good" performance. It is what is referred to as the "live performance," which appears to indicate explicitly no disjuncture in time and space. However practically distant the audience might be from the performer in the foregoing, the two are present to each other: however large, diffuse, and heterogeneous the audience might be, the performer is performing to it and for it and, collectively, it is reacting and responding back, propelling the text forward. As the audience is constituted by individuals, each audience member has the potential to contribute to and affect the performance through a reaction and response (including the absence of a reaction or response). That potential is very real for those who are immediately within the field of intimacy of the performer, and perhaps approaching only notional for those in the furthest reaches.

There may indeed be a practical limit to the extent that the performer does not have recourse to their own amplification or video projection and can only see or hear particular audience members through the unaided senses. Thus the first few rows become a "proxy" audience for the entire venue, although the comedian is careful to include the furthest members through alternating eye contact between the closest and furthest members and references to "the people in the back" and by surveying the audience, where answers are gauged through applause or cheers. The performer, who uses the mediation of stage, microphone, and (on occasion) video projection, and the audience, which is fluent enough with mediation to ignore it partially, are in the same place at the same time. Irrespective of mediation, the performance is, for all intents and purposes, immediate to the audience, experienced with all five senses, and in real time.

If the microphone and video projection bridge spatiotemporal distances between audience and performer, they do not bridge cultural distances. It is one thing to engage in face-to-face talk with someone, but that alone does not make someone your intimate. How does this stranger engage with an audience, reconciling the distance not of the stage to the floor but of differing worldviews rooted in their different, respective social identities outside of the performance context?

CHAPTER 3
Who Is a Stand-Up Comedian?: The Social Identity

[Joseph Campbell] says that the role of the *artist*
is to stand *outside* the village
but he's also got to *understand* them
Jerry Seinfeld in one of his uh . . .
unusually *profound* moments I found
when he's not talking about what to do with the *soap* when it gets thin
he said that we're contemporary *shamans*
I mean we're invited in to the village to tell them what's *going on*
and then we go back *out* again
and Dennis Miller said we're essentially *assassins*
we come into a place make a hit and *leave*
we come in at *night* make a *hit*
we *kill 'em*
and we *leave*
—**Ron James,** interview

I have been arguing that the stage introduces a distance between the audience and the performer, while the microphone and, recently, video projection bridge that distance. Indeed, without amplification, speaking at a natural register in front of a crowd of any size is almost impossible, so stand-up comedy as a form cannot exist without the technology: furthermore, that technology in turn becomes symbolic of the act of stand-up comedy itself. Such is the apparatus of stand-up: the material culture and media that constitute the found comedy landscape. But it takes far more than being heard to be recognized as an intimate. Breaking across physical distance is one thing, but breaking through cultural distance is another.

Earlier, I was examining some conceptions about what stand-up comedy is and what the stand-up comedian does. These questions can be rephrased as efforts at determining *who* the stand-up is. Apart from academic conceptions, however, there also exist vernacular conceptions of the person of the stand-up comedian. To identify oneself as "stand-up comedian" is to assume a social identity with a number of connotations and expectations.

Non-theorists go to performances by stand-up comedians—or are members of a broadcast audience or are participants in listening to audio recordings or watching video recordings—with this set of expectations already in place, knowing it to be a performance of a particular kind. Even if they do not know the particular comedian, they come to the performance informed by a "type."

There are no better sources for determining this set of expectations than fans of stand-up comedy and the comedians themselves. Stand-up comedians understand themselves as figures in the culture: they have an informed understanding all their own on the role of the stand-up comedian in modern society. They also have, as professional necessity, a need to establish not only their identity as a stand-up comedian, as an artist, but also their worldview.

Let's begin by examining how fans and comedians understand the role of the comedian and comedy through the lens of vernacular theory. Then we turn to a study of the narratives that comedians tell about themselves, offstage and on, that complement their onstage performances of non-autobiographic material. These narratives frame the performed material for the audience, providing the lens through which it is meant to be interpreted.

Starting with this chapter, I begin to refer to the comedian Ron James as my primary example; but, rather than introduce him at this point, he will be introduced in a manner that emulates an audience "coming to know" a comedian.

One of the dissatisfactions of reading academic literature about stand-up comedy is the sense that, for all the earnest theorizing, each attempt at explanation tends to ignore what fans or, more frustratingly, stand-up comedians think about it. For one example, Robert Stebbins notes how "common thought holds that the early career of all stand-up comics is affected by two contingencies: a tension-filled childhood and adolescence during which they were either the class clown or the life of the party or both, both being manifestations of psychological problems" (1990, 60). He does not attribute this common thought, and he goes on to qualify this by saying, "Our sample does not always conform to this image" (60). But for our purposes it is this common thought that is of interest, as it speaks to a perception of the social identity of the stand-up comedian, or what I call vernacular stand-up comedy theory.[1]

In interviews and elsewhere, stand-up comedians have a lot to say about the figure of the stand-up comedian in society, his or her function, and the nature of stand-up comedy. I would contend that not only is this process of self-reflection a natural consequence of the specialist, but also, inasmuch as their presentation of self offstage contributes to their interpretation onstage, it is a professional strategy.

Andres Lombana interviewed Dana Jay Bein, a stand-up comedian who also teaches stand-up at the Boston Center for Adult Education:

> "Comedy is like no other," [Bein] continued, "it started as tragedy but now you are putting it out there as humor." From his point of view, failure and pain were in the origin of comedy. "Everybody has that instinct to laugh of other [people's] failures, or even your own failures. You see somebody gets splashed by a car driven into a big puddle in a rainy day, and one of your instincts is to laugh," he said. . . .
>
> "The only way to really defeat other people making fun of you is to get on the board and start to make fun of yourself, kind of show them that it doesn't bother you," he added. "Then, self-deprecation comes to the next level when you find your own voice in that self-deprecation." Nowadays, Bein takes "self-deprecation" as the most effective way to connect with his audience. "I make fun of myself and not only does it make the audience comfortable of who I am as a performer but it also gives me the green light to make fun of other things as well," he said. (qtd. in Lombana 2007, paras. 4, 6)[2]

"Tragedy," whether the explicit failures and horrific events of a life or the mere failure to meet the socially constructed expectations of one's culture, is the touchstone of stand-up comedy for Bein, who can transform it, through honest address, into something emancipatory: what is more, that he has been made marginal through these failures allows him to expose the failings in others.

Similarly, for an entry in his *New York Times* blog, Dick Cavett wrote about the impulse that drives comedians:

> Coming up through the ranks of any calling can be rough, but that battered soul who survives the early years of courting the comic muse comes close to knowing what only the soldier knows: What combat is like.
>
> What puts that vulnerable soul standing up there in the most brightly lit part of a room, clutching a microphone, to be judged by skeptical and often hostile strangers?
>
> Desire to be loved is surely part of it, cliché though it be.
>
> What better substitute for real love than a sea of eager faces, beaming, laughing, applauding and celebrating your existence? (2008, paras. 5–8)

Cavett, who started his career as a writer for Johnny Carson before turning to stand-up in the 1960s, is tapping into a common theme in the comedian's story: audience approval—love—as a substitute for approval and love from some other, less ostensibly contingent source. The immediacy of the audience's reaction, whether approval or humiliation, may make stand-up comedy the most extreme example, but this need for love is more related—in this vernacular psychology way—to the general urge to become an artist or, more accurately, performer. Johnny Carson made a similar point in response to a question about when he knew he wanted to be a performer:

> I think it's when you find out, at least for me, that you can get in front of an audience and be in control. I think that probably happened in grade school, fifth or sixth grade, where I could get attention by being different, by getting up in front of an audience or even a group of kids and calling the attention to myself by what I did or said or how I acted. And I said, "Hey, I like that feeling."
>
> When I was a kid, I was shy. And I think I did that because it was a device to get attention. And to get that reaction is a strange feeling, it is a high that I don't think you can get from drugs. I don't think you could get it from anything else. The mind starts to do things that you didn't even realize it could do. It's hard to explain. (1979)

Cavett is reticent to explore too fully any further underlying motivations for comedians, specifically, but the mantle was picked up in a variety of comments to his post, many making reference to Lenny Bruce in response to an aside Cavett made about him ("whose alleged genius largely escaped me"). Without negating Cavett's observation about the need for approval, the themes that emerge strongest are a sense of distance, marginalization from the dominant culture, and the related desire to make informed observations about that culture.

"Mirror" and "reflection" and "seeing differently" are metaphors commonly employed: "They simply see or interact with the world which is antithetical to most peoples' prosaic perceptions" (David Chowes, in Cavett 2008, comment 11). "[We] get to hold up a mirror and say, 'hey, this is life!'" (Kehau Jackson, in Cavett 2008, comment 108). "Bruce . . . reflected America's puritan image back on itself" (Martello, in Cavett 2008, comment 18). "Lenny's mortification was more of an individual comedic mirror-image of the society at large from which he sprang" (John Blake Arnold, in Cavett 2008, comment 61).

This reflection, however skewed through comic artistry, is coupled with a sense that it is true, and truth and honesty become guiding principles: "So, others laugh at seemingly strange comments which were never conceived (by them)—because there is a degree of or complete validity" (David Chowes, in Cavett 2008, comment 11). "Comedy is essentially an expression of truth. That's why when people laugh the loudest, they often say, 'That's so true!'" (Kehau Jackson, in Cavett 2008, comment 108). "Richard Pryor . . . wished he could be more honest on stage" (Leo Flowers, in Cavett 2008, comment 118).

And this mirror is held either outside of or trapped within the larger culture it is reflecting: "I think comedians . . . always suffer from strong feelings of inferiority coupled with an aggressive, competitive nature" (Rob L., in Cavett 2008, comment 9). "Lenny's humor is the humor (but not the language) of people in exile waiting for G-d to redeem them. It is the humor of man caught in a system run amok. It is a moral humor" (Yehuda Jordan Kaplan, in Cavett 2008, comment 106). In a different context, Richard Pryor puts is thus:

> These guys on stage now, being all cool, saying they were influenced by me, show me when I was cool. I never said "Dig me. Look how cool I am and how messed up everybody else is." Hell, I got all the material I *need* just on how messed *up* I am. I mean, how screwed up a brother I gotta be to stand up in front of a million strangers and say "Listen to *me*"? Yes, stop what you're doing and listen to me so I can make you laugh—so the sound of your laughing drowns out the voices in my head. (Pryor 2004, ix)

But Cavett's comparison to combat resonated as well: "I have to wonder why anyone would willingly step in front of an emotional firing squad" (Elizabeth Fuller, in Cavett 2008, comment 23). Ron James made that comparison in my interview with him, but with a sense of exhilaration, not trauma.

> Oh *jeez* I had a corporate gig
> I don't play the clubs anymore
> but I had a corporate gig a while ago where they were all *hammered* in the *daytime*
> and I was playing a *pub* in Halifax
> and it was *great*
> I had a small *stage*
> and it was like I had that
> *second show Sudbury knife in my boot* set
> y'know where you just had to *survive*
> and your wits are *singin'*

but you know
it was just . . . it just
it felt so *alive*
y'know it's *combat* man
it's *combat* (James 2005a)

Elsewhere James mixes the combat metaphor with the idea of it being a calling:

I think *stand-up*
Is the Promethean *fire*
it *burns* you [IB: It's a different order]
it's *dangerous*
there's no safety
you walk away from this *cut*
you walk away with *wounds*
you step up to the *plate* in this thing
with a *legitimate* calling
it's life or death
it's *true* (James 2005a)

This seeming contradiction, that metaphors both of violence and of a redemptive love can be equally extended to the stand-up comedy performance, is tied into the idea of "good" comedians purposely exposing themselves to risk, and that the greater the risk the greater the reward. It is tied into the painful honesty that looking at the mirror requires. It is tied into the tension of someone existing simultaneously outside and inside the group.

These themes are frequent in the stand-up comedian's story. At times they are merely implied, where coded hints of marginalization are peppered throughout a routine. At other times they are made explicit, either on the stage or off. The comedian works to establish the social identity of stand-up comedian by identifying his or her story as containing these elements, thus providing the frame through which his or her performance is meant to be interpreted. The process of establishing the social identity relationship of comedian and audience is in large part itself conditioned by the multiple social identities of the social personas of the participants.

The stand-up comedian is engaged in an exchange with an audience: he or she is an outsider who becomes accepted as an intimate by the audience, who are in turn expecting humorous insight. Laughter becomes a sign not only of approval but of acceptance. When an audience comes to a stand-up comedy show, whether they know the particular comedian or not, they are expecting this sort of interaction.

Before stand-up comedians even open their mouths, they are seen. As such, their appearance already sends a set of stimuli to the audience that frames how the subsequent performance is to be interpreted. Whether control over the elements of their "personal front" (Goffman 1959, 24) can be exercised (costume) or not (physical characteristics), they are often either used by stand-up comedians or addressed and then moved beyond. They serve to locate them in a particular worldview, if only to be immediately flouted.

As an embodied being, the stand-up comedian's physical appearance can immediately locate him or her within a particular interpretive framework for the audience. The comedian can either use this to advantage or introduce a qualification. Once, on the *Tonight Show*, Bill Cosby recounted his first appearance on the show, twenty years previous:

> I came out—the guy put Lena Horne's makeup on me—I walked out and I was going to do my karate routine. And I hadn't really thought that it would be funny. But I guess the people were so conditioned to see a black person come out—they said okay, he's gonna talk about the back of the bus and the front of the restaurant and the side of the tree—and I walked out and I said I wanna talk about karate. And they went wooo hah hah—and I almost backed up and said, "Well, what's so funny?" Then I went into the routine. (qtd. in R. Smith 1997, 54)

Physical characteristics have denotations—sex, genetic ancestry—but also connotations, socially constructed and historical categories such as gender and ethnicity. These connotations extend to what topics are going to be considered, and these expectations can in turn quickly be either affirmed or flouted. What these expectations are is determined by the local audience, and the issue of relevance may be obscure to a mediated one: in her appearance on the "Prairie Crop" episode of *Winnipeg Comedy Festival*, comedian Erica Sigurdson began her set with "You guys can probably tell by my *ears*. I'm with the *Icelandic* contingent," which, in a part of the country with a substantial Icelandic community, occasioned her first laugh of the set (Sigurdson 2004*) but which I personally could not understand. W. Kamau Bell put it even more succinctly:

The *moment* I step on stage I'm a black comic
the *moment* I step on stage
and then it's up to *me* to sort of decide
how do I want to *play into* that or *subvert* that (2013*)

Body type further influences how the comedian is perceived, although it is mostly those types that diverge from cultural standards of "normal": conspicuous tallness or shortness; conspicuous thinness or fatness; for men, conspicuous muscularity or frailty; for women, conspicuous shapeliness or underdevelopment. "Attractive" and "unattractive," even more contingent markers of identity, further cue the audience toward how to interpret the comedian. Darby Li Po Price, in his discussion of American First Nations stand-up comedy, expresses it thus:

> Standups are expected to address how their distinguishing physical features such as ethnicity, race, gender, or body type inform their experiences and comic world-views. Indian identities may serve as central, secondary, or even minor aspects of routines, and may be conveyed in numerous humorous ways. (Price 1998, 256)

Although one might hesitate to phrase it in this manner, Ron James is "ethnically Maritime-looking." His is a physiognomy and body type similar to many people in the Atlantic Canadian provinces: fair-skinned, medium height and build, vestiges of red hair. In the course of his act he makes reference to this "Celtic" physique, particularly as a child, but to suggest that it does not somehow frame an audience's expectations would be naïve. He uses a routine in performance that is also used in his official biography and in interviews:

> Ron was a non-stop stuttering, freckle faced red headed kid, who weighed only forty-five pounds until he was fifteen years old and thirty-seven of that was his head! With a pedigree like that, was comedy even an option? . . . [W]hen the circus came to town his mother had to hide him. He was educated in a public school system during a day when teachers would dwarf toss you for singing a wrong verse to God Save the Queen. He "took air" often. (*ronjames.ca* 2004)

> "I happen to have a colourful palette to use, the real friends who graced my mother's kitchen. I was just a little kid sitting on the counter. I weighed about 45 pounds until I was 15, and 37 pounds of that was head. It was a great perch to have if you're gonna end up doing what I do.
> "With a pedigree like that was comedy even an option?" (qtd. in Ward 2005)

His appearance and his interpretation thereof allow him further license to make claim both to a Maritime persona and—especially with the "was comedy even an option?" tag—to the social identity of stand-up comedian.

Not having control over physical aspects of their appearance, comedians either use this to their advantage or, when desirable, deliberately flout those expectations. With time, as their individuated narratives are performed and cultivated and they become known, their physicality doesn't so much recede as ceases to be the only data the audience has for interpretation: the "what he or she is" gives way to the "who he or she is."

But there are aspects of stand-up comedians' appearance over which they can exercise immense control. Clothing, grooming, and comportment contribute to a front, a presentation of self that indicates and informs the desirable interpretation. Stand-up comedians make deliberate decisions on how to present themselves on stage.

When Mort Sahl first began performing in the 1950s, one of the first things to distinguish him was his dress, "the signature cardigan sweater, slacks, loafers, rumpled hair, open collar, rolled-up shirtsleeves" (Nachman 2003, 50). It was distinct insofar as it was so very much not a discernible costume, a deliberate effort to look indifferent to appearances.

> "It occurred to me that you mustn't look like any member of the society you're criticizing. What could I be? I went out and got myself a pair of blue denims and a blue sweater and a white button-down shirt open at the neck: graduate student. And I went out there and I did it and it worked. It let the audience relax." When he wanted to discard the sweater later, it was already part of his image and he was stuck with it. (Nachman 2003, 58)

When George Carlin tried to make the switch from his character comedian style of the 1960s to the countercultural comedian style of the 1970s, the first thing he changed was his appearance.

> George is back on TV and has another album out, but he sure looks different. The ties, jackets, and tuxedos have been replaced by T-shirts and jeans, he has a long pony tail where his hair used to stop, a gold earring is sticking out of one of his ears, and his eyes seem suspiciously blurry. Actually, his eyes always looked like that only nobody noticed. Anyway, this woman wanted to know how come, at age 35, he's suddenly turned into a hippie. So, for the thousandth time, George explained this phenomenon.

"Well, the reason that I only showed what I used to show was because I thought that would help me get what I wanted, which at the time was a half-hour TV series. And, oh yeah, I wanted to be an actor. I wanted to get all the movie roles that Jack Lemmon turned down. But then I decided that I'd really rather be myself. Which is what you see now." (Werbin 1972)

Carlin was at pains to indicate how the self he was then presenting on stage was his authentic self, in large part because it was a change from how he had looked in the past. Carlin spoke about it on stage as well:

> One of the
> things that occurred when I began to uh
> just y'know feel some *changes* happening to me
> uh naturally I was kind of still entertaining uh
> in *gin joints* y'know
> I mean I realize they sell gin here
> but it's really not the same as
> as middle-class *nightclubs* where I spent like a *lot* of years
> and it was *weird* to start having *hair* and start having a *beard* (1972a*, "The Hair
>   Piece")

To suggest that there is deliberateness to the "anti-costume" aesthetic is not to suggest disingenuousness, although the deliberateness of the costume is derided by the anti-costume crowd, especially when it is part of the performance. In the documentary *The Comedians of Comedy*, there is an exchange on this topic between the stand-up comedians Brian Posehn, Patton Oswalt, and Maria Bamford that turns into an improvised routine:

> Posehn: There was that one . . . remember that guy in San Francisco that had to
>   wear a Hawaiian shirt every time he went on stage 'cause
>   his j—his opening joke was always about the Hawaiian shirt
>   it was like uh
> Oswalt: I don't remember that guy
> Posehn: was uh | I know what you're thinking
>   did he blow Don Ho for that shirt |
>   and uh
> | no I blew Don Ho 'cause he's a *great entertainer* |
>   and that was his opening joke *every night*

Bamford: Oh but come on that's not . . .

Posehn: yeah but he had to wear the *Hawaiian shirt* every night to get to *that bit*

[. . .]

I love the idea of like that you're mad . . .

it's like somebody else dressed you

Oswalt: Yeah

{looking down at his clothes, angry} | "what the fuck is . . ." |

{grabs his shirt and points to it, still angry} | "look at this *shit*" |

Posehn: | What happened to me |

Oswalt: | *Look at this* |

Posehn: | Look at what happened to me on the way here . . . |

Oswalt: | fucking *ridiculous* |

Posehn: | . . . and this shirt I jumped into . . . |

Oswalt: | oh, these guys . . . |

Posehn: | . . . this shirt I put on and buttoned up |

Oswalt: | . . . these guys *jumped* me and put this *shirt on me*

and they sewed it to my skin and I'll

I'll never be able to take it off |

Posehn: | I *have* to talk about it

that's the first thing on my . . .

'cause I know *you're* thinking if I *didn't* mention it . . . |

Oswalt: | it would be *crazy*

Posehn: | my shirt is *so insane*

that you couldn't even *concentrate* if I didn't bring it up

because you'd be watching

| *when is he going to talk about his crazy fucking shirt* |

Oswalt: | god if a shirt like that got put on me *I* wouldn't have a joke |

but I *know* that you're thinking that I will

and I do

because I'm a *comedian*

I'm a *comedian*

professional comedian | (Blieden 2005*)

Costume-as-prop considerations aside, the aesthetic of dress for these comedians is that what they wear onstage is essentially no different from what they wear offstage. A distinction between audience and performer is reified when dress indicates "costume" and the impression of a stylized performance. Stand-up comedy works within the illusion of extemporaneity. If the impression is that the stand-up comedian has in essence emerged out of the audience and moved on to the stage, removing themselves spatially only for the purposes of being seen for the duration of their enactment of the stand-up comedian social identity and then returning to the audience upon that enactment's completion, then anything that smacks of premeditation introduces an interruption into that sense of the extemporaneous and intimate.[3]

There is a second connotation to the "non-costume" that is an extension of that emergence from the audience theme: that what they wear onstage is essentially no different from what the audience is wearing. This point is potentially moot, because there are moments when that is expressly not the case: Sahl and the transforming Carlin were expressly differently attired from their mainstream audiences. However, their dress was consistent with the group from whose worldview they aimed to speak. Like all forms of costume, it can mark solidarity with one group while it marks distinction from another. It becomes, in essence, a statement of what *they* would wear were they members of the audience.

The white suit that Steve Martin wore as part of his stage persona (which was predicated in large part on the vacuity of performance) likely marked the moment when the "slick" suit disappeared from the stand-up comedy stage. But suits remain a staple of the stand-up comedy wardrobe. They tend to be unobtrusive, formal items of apparel. One exception to this is among African American comedians, who often wear exquisitely tailored and colorful suits, something very much a part of twentieth-century African American tradition.[4]

> On Sundays and in their other leisure hours away from work, however, urban blacks regained control of their bodies and of their souls. Shucking off their work clothes—the overalls and maids' uniforms that more often than not were a mark of the degradation frequently associated with their employment—ordinary African Americans dressed up like "fashion plates" and congregated in convivial black spaces. (White and White 1998, 245)

In other words, if we can fairly say that a stand-up comedy performance, particularly of African American comedians, is a "convivial black space," then the clothes worn by comedians onstage are no different from the clothes they would wear were they to be in the audience. Filmed performances and ethnography both bear this out; the clothing of the audience tends to complement the clothing of the performer when they are members of the same social identity grouping, irrespective of which social identity: African American, southern white, urban bohemian, Atlantic Canadian.

Until 2005, whenever Ron James appeared on stage he invariably wore a flannel shirt. It is the dress he employed for the publicity posters for the concerts, the pictures he supplied to the local theaters for their in-house bulletins and websites, and how he appeared on his own website. In a 2002 *Globe and Mail* article on the flannel shirt as "the uniform of the Canadian Everyman," James was specifically interviewed on the topic.

> James, the veteran standup comic (who always sports a plaid shirt on stage) and the star of the quirky TV series *Blackfly*, says he remembers years ago when someone told him to, "'Get your look and stay with it.' That phrase always stuck with me.
>
> "The plaid in my shirts represents, and I don't want to sound too lofty, the regional diversity of the country," James says, very seriously. "It doesn't reek of urban pretension. I don't think the content of my shows reflects a sophisticated urbanity. And the shirt puts me on the same page as those 700 folks who just came to hear me at a hall in Cranbrook, B.C., or the crowd that might assemble at the neon-lit Mirvish theatre in Toronto," James adds.
>
> "It is an equalizer. If my content is a tapestry of Canadiana, then that's what my shirt reflects." (G. MacDonald 2002)

By the time I followed him on tour in November of 2005 for a leg of his Atlantic Canadian tour, the flannel was still part of his wardrobe but not the only shirt in circulation. He would alternate between a red cotton shirt with khakis and a variety of flannel shirts with black casual pants. In *Quest for the West* (2005*) (filmed before but aired after this Maritimes tour), James wears the red shirt and black pants, and in the following year's *West Coast Wild* (2006*) the shirt is burnt orange. Having firmly established his "Canadianness" and trusting that this interpretation of him will be brought to the performance by the audience, he no longer needs to demonstrate it through material objects like a costume as explicit as the flannel shirt. Again, like body type, its prominence gives way as the "what he is" is replaced by the "who he is."

Although not atypical for Canadian comedians, and not a dress sense particular to the Maritimes, James's overall costume nevertheless reflected the dress choices of much of the audiences in the three cities on this leg of the tour and, being neither too casual nor too formal, it appeared at the very least in keeping with a Maritime sensibility of appropriate attire.[5] In my fieldnotes I was struck by what the audience members themselves were wearing. For the most part they too wore presentable casual attire:

the men wore Dockers pants, solid-colored button-up dress shirts with no ties, nice but comfortable shoes. At the first Halifax show I wrote, "People aren't really 'dressed up' per se: more like going-to-a-bar attire." This was in the context of noting how they were "really middle aged—white exclusively, predominantly Anglo." In Pictou I wrote, "In general, an older crowd, dressed clean, casual, but not too flashy." In all the venues, the majority of the men in the audience were wearing clothing similar to James: to put it another way, on stage Ron James wears what a Maritimer like Ron James would wear to an event like a Ron James performance.

In part because the whims of fashion vacillate to greater extremes and are thus in retrospect less forgiving for women than for men,[6] the dress of women comedians has sometimes been caricatured as androgynous, the donning of mannish sports jackets with shoulder pads, trousers, and the occasional waistcoat.[7] The literary critic John Limon in his study of abjection and stand-up comedy made the observation that the more successful comic persona for a woman stand-up comedian was nonsexual (2000, 120). Framing it this way, however, suggests that it is a successful strategy in a world where women's experience is not interesting, let alone fodder for comedy.

The debate about how women present themselves on stage is inextricable from the ever-present and unnecessary question of whether women are funny, something that is still a going concern in vernacular theory arguments about the nature of stand-up comedy. A *Vanity Fair* article tackled the issue, which of late has been compounded with another observation: "It used to be that women were not funny. Then they couldn't be funny if they were pretty. Now a female comedian has to be pretty—even sexy—to get a laugh" (Stanley 2008, 185).

Whether Limon had a point is debatable: he may have been right but for all the wrong reasons. It may have been an accident of history that, just as African American and Hispanic comedians needed to present themselves in a particular way to get time and notice on a predominantly white comedy circuit, so too did women have to present themselves in a particular way to get time and notice on a predominantly male comedy circuit. Furthermore, women didn't have the same narrowcasting opportunities as emerged within the African American comedy market in the late 1980s and early 1990s, with shows like BET's *ComicView* and HBO's *Def Comedy Jam*, to develop viable and highly lucrative careers wholly separate from the mainstream clubs. Since that time a number of women comedians— Margaret Cho, Ellen DeGeneres, Janeane Garofalo, Sarah Silverman, Rosie O'Donnell, Roseanne Barr, Maria Bamford, Brett Butler—have attained enough of a place of prominence that women comedians in general are no longer seen as the aberration they once were. And thus, since the 1980s, the forms of dress are also less caricatural than they once—ostensibly—were: women stand-up comedians wear on stage what they would wear were they going to see themselves perform.

Accent is another indicator of social identity. Not only can it confirm or flout ethnic identity, it can connote national, regional, socioeconomic, sexual, or gender identity. It is something that can be an affectation, granted, but that affectation is more likely to be an exaggeration rather than a deliberate falsehood.

Henry Cho is a Korean American comedian raised in Knoxville, Tennessee. The epigrammatic quote on his website is "I'm an Asian with a Southern accent. To a lot of people, that right there is funny" (Cho 2006). In his early television appearances he would assure the audience that there was nothing wrong with their television sets. For a profile on Asian American personalities, it is "his jaw-dropping accent [that] was the springboard for a roaring comedy career" (Nahm n.d.).

In his early career, Jeff Foxworthy would make a similar advertence to his Georgian accent. During a performance filmed at Rascal's Comedy Club in Montclair, New Jersey, Foxworthy began with a bit on regional differences based on the southern accent.

> This *is* my real voice
> this is how I *talk*
> it is a *y'all* so
> go ahead and *laugh* at that now
> I *love* to work up here
> because y'all think we're so
> so much *goobers* down in the South [L]
> [. . .]
> you *can't be cool* with a southern accent
> you can take us somewhere *nice*
> somewhere like a *nude beach* on the *French Riviera*
> we'd be out there going
> | *damn* [L]
> this is a good place to *fish* here [L]
> {hollered} "hey Ed bring the *cooler*" |
> we'd be going up to naked women

| hey you don't know where we can pick up some *red wigglers* do ya | (in Rascals
2003*)

Ron James's accent evidences a biographically validated blend of New-foundland, Cape Breton, and downtown Halifax. It is decidedly Eastern Canadian, although not identifiably of one place. His is not the strong, affected accent of character comedians like Jimmy Flynn, Andrew "Dice" Clay, or Roy "Chubby" Brown, but neither is it the same as his normal speaking voice. There is an aspect of Dell Hymes's (1975) breakthrough to performance where performance competency and audience expectations require an elevated or heightened presentation of the self. As James put it:

You know
maybe my accent's a little exaggerated a bit
I get called on that from time to time
they say | you don't sound like that in real life |
but I say
I don't know
when I'm channeling something out there. . . (James 2005a)

James's accent is also mentioned frequently by reviewers and inter-viewers.

His speech is full of interesting metaphors and stream-of-consciousness jokes and he uses words like visceral and catharsis more naturally than a university professor. But the sentences roll so quickly off that Cape Breton tongue and his accent is so engaging, the nuances of his story are easily missed. (Hepfner 1999)

The rapid-fire pace of James' marathon routines—delivered in that distinct Maritime accent, hey?—covers so much territory, it's enough to send Olympic gold-medal triathlete Simon Whitfield into premature retirement. Among a gazillion others, there was his macarena-on-speed talk 'n' dance regarding the joys of camping, the conspiracy behind the Disney Channel, and the differences between the earthy, hard-faced Tim Hortons' staff and the phony, "Up With People" smiles of the Starbucks folk. (Nathanson 2001)

"They gave me a bun on Air Canada that was as hard as the hobs of hell," he says in an East Coast accent. "Stale? This thing came off the table at the Last friggin'

Supper. And in the middle was a slice of ham so thin the pig never even felt it comin' off his arse." (Dunn 2003)

Just like his physical appearance and his stage costume, his accent aids in locating him in a particularly Maritime or Atlantic Canadian identity, although he allows a certain ambiguity as to precisely where in Atlantic Canada we should place him.

Irrespective of the particular content of their talk, stand-up comedians have their embodied selves at their disposal to create an image and present a front for their intended interpretative frame by an audience. It not only appears on the stage: it is in promotional materials like flyers, posters, and websites, and, in the case of accent, it is the voice they use in interviews. These expectations are in part conditioned by history, but that conditioning can be the very content of the talk itself.

In his book *Acting*, John Harrop makes the following observation:

> At the simplest level, the muscleman, the Miss Universe contestant, and the stand-up comedian are projecting themselves. They may be making adaptations to the conventions of the performance, but they are not playing a character . . . [and] only the actor is both present on stage and yet at the same time absent, replaced by the illusion he or she creates. (1992, 5)

Contra Harrop, I would suggest that the comedian *is* replaced by the illusion he or she creates and that the created illusion is that what is projected *is* him- or herself. One could suggest a taxonomy of comedians along a spectrum, with one end being a wholly natural performance, with no distinction between performer and performance, and the other end being a pure contrivance, with no pretence of direct correlation between performer and performance. The performative aspect is made most clear with "character comedians" like Pee Wee Herman, Andrew "Dice" Clay, or Judy Tenuta, for whom the worldview presented through their onstage personae is not meant to be understood as coincident with their offstage life. The adoption of a different persona through costume, props, and voice modulation is an explicit expression that the worldview they inhabit onstage—however artfully rendered, and, in the case of Clay especially, however difficult it is for the audience to disassociate from their own worldview and enter—is a fiction. This fiction is nevertheless grounded (or "groundable") in the expectations and experiences of the audience as a satire of, or foil to, consensus reality.

But such is the case for all comedians, even for those whose onstage persona is presented as indistinguishable from their offstage persona. There is an argument to be made here about Baudrillardian processions of simulacra (Baudrillard 1994): what is the difference between the perfectly rendered map and the territory to which the map refers? Another, less post-modern but equally fruitful, framework is Erving Goffman's (1959) notion of "front," the manner in which we portray ourselves to the world in everyday life.

On- and offstage does not imply that the persona or front is wholly dropped once the spotlight is off. One of Neil Rosenberg's (1986) insights into the distinction between the amateur and the professional is how the latter is skilled at rapport and reputation cultivation and uses a variety of methods—mainly the media and interview—to project a memorable persona that frames the eventual onstage performance and the audience's expectations thereof.

Unlike the musicians Rosenberg was studying, the stand-up comedian is not solely displaying technical proficiency at an instrument or demonstrating mastery at performing and subsequently contributing to a culturally acceptable repertoire. The comedian is performing the self. The worldview expressed onstage is expressed offstage, outside the framework of "performance" but within the professional necessity for building rapport and reputation. The audience brings what they know about the comedian to the performance, derived from both prior performances and the media, so the comedian is well-served to take as much effort to frame the offstage talk as he or she does onstage talk. And there is a mutually mediating relationship between the extant expectations of who the comedian-as-figure is—marginal/marginalized and lonely, which grounds and informs the perspective they bring—and the individual comedian's particular story. Stand-up comedian is a social identity to which the individual comedian actively and continually lays claim.

In *Sounds So Good to Me*, Barry Lee Pearson made a contribution to the understanding of the bluesmen's art by paying attention to their stories: "I wanted them to tell me the story they usually tell when they present themselves to the public" (1984, xiii–xiv). Pearson's insight is in part predicated on how the bluesman—his focus is on the generation of bluesmen "rediscovered" with the blues revival of the 1960s—understands the interview as a part of the "blues business" (35), and that "because a tradition of the interview has led over the years to the same questions and to a certain degree the same answers, they develop a predictive awareness of what to expect" (37). The bluesman is "creating an artistic version of his past" (39), one that "authenticates his background and justifies his claim to the blues-man's role" (30).

> For better or for worse, they learned the advantages as well as the disadvan-tages of their ambivalent role. While musicians may chafe at being typecast, they often share their public's beliefs concerning who they are and what they do. . . . But earning the right to play the blues and be recognized as a bluesman demands an ideological commitment and the creation of a public persona. (Pearson 1984, 122)

Stand-up comedians are doing something similar. Through the opportu-nities at their disposal, they present themselves as persons who conform to the audience's beliefs about who they are and what they do, thus earn-ing the right to be recognized as "stand-up comedians." When they are unknown, in the "apprentice" phase of Rosenberg's paradigm, they only have the resources of their onstage performance and, hopefully, an accom-modating emcee to authenticate this claim to the name stand-up comedian. As journeymen, these resources are complemented by the beginnings of a cumulative reputation: they have been seen before, they have been given performance time by recognized authorities, their performances may have been mediated in some way (predominantly by broadcasts), and there may be the beginnings of interest in their offstage life. The audience members are exposed to more opportunities for discerning whether, why, and how they should interpret this person as stand-up comedian. As craftsmen, they are fully adept at using the media to tell their stories or present their worldview, they have been more heavily mediated through broadcasts and quite possibly through recordings, they have been given performance time by even greater recognized authorities, and their performances are actively sought by audiences. If they reach the celebrity level, they are known as much for whom they are as for what they do on the stage.

The autobiography, the stand-up comedian's story, is not reflective: it is anticipatory. It is not "How I got here" so much as it is "How I got here to be with you tonight." It is aimed at the "next" performance to a specific group of people. When the comedian speaks to local media—radio, newspapers, local television—and to a local audience, he or she takes pains to emphasize some connection with the local. Ron James has proven quite adept at this, emphasizing these connections, whether vicarious or real. For his 2002 tour, his first to bring him to Newfoundland, he was interviewed for the Corner Brook *Western Star*.

"People say 'what about Los Angeles, especially for comedy?' No one produces comedy like Americans, but for every person that wins down there, there are a thousand people that do not," James responded. "Six hundred people laughing in Corner Brook sounds exactly the same as 600 people laughing in Los Angeles."

. . .

James is eager to visit Newfoundland for a couple of reasons. His father's family is from Burgeo, and James is looking forward to rediscovering these roots. Secondly, the adventure of visiting a new place is something that appeals to the comedian.

"I can't wait for Newfoundland," James said. "To be able to see these places and experience new places, that is a real plus to me. I talk a lot about new places and my experiences travelling it. I always come away from a new place with 20 minutes of new material." (in Callahan 2002, 20)

James begins by emphasizing the importance of laughter as universal and stresses that a successful performance is always irrespective of place. He locates the province in his own biography and makes mention of how the new experience will contribute to his repertoire. And he echoes a similar sentiment wherever he goes: "'Six hundred people laughing in Medicine Hat on a Tuesday night sounds exactly the same as 600 people laughing in Las Vegas,' he says" (Lewis 2002); "'At the end of the day, 1,000 people laughing in Nepean with a blizzard outside sounds exactly the same as 1,000 laughing in Las Vegas when it's warm'" (Ward 2005); "James says an audience of 2,000 in Calgary sounds the same as an audience of 2,000 in L.A." (Mitges 2006).

When that media or audience is national—for example, in mediated performances—the emphasis on locality is lessened and the stand-up comedian emphasizes some connection to regional, national, or (in rare instances) international identity. But in all instances, there is some emphasis, even if only implicit, on the social identity of the comedian as culturally understood and on themselves as meeting the audience's expectations for fulfilling that identity.

Typically for stand-up comedy performances, the right to assume the stand-up comedian social identity is a given, as the audience members, through the necessary act of transporting themselves to the performance venue or, in the case of mediated performances, selecting the performance to play, have already tacitly and provisionally accepted the assumption of the stand-up comedy audience social identity even if the particular stand-up comedian is an unknown entity. Commercial apparatuses are in

place—critics, bookers, programmers, compères or emcees, and so forth—
that vet the comedian by proxy, providing assurance that the comedian will
perform "in accordance with socially prescribed rules with which he [or she]
and the other participants in the storytelling event are familiar" (Georges
1969, 318).[8] Again, making the comparison to musicians,

> the higher up the market scale the performer rises, the more impersonal and
> uncertain performer-audience relationships become. Decisions about reper-
> toire, style, performance context and other aspects of career are determined
> less by direct feedback from the audience. Mass culture mechanisms—trade
> charts, sales figures, the opinions of others inside the music business—become
> increasingly important and usually add to the pressure for change [away from a
> local, idiosyncratic repertoire]. (Rosenberg 1986, 159)

When referring to established acts, the performance context typically
presumes a pre-existing relationship between audience and performer. For
less-established acts, the performance context is often a series of comedians presented over a stretch of time in order of increasing notoriety, pre-
sided over by an established comedian (who may be the same comedian
as the final comedian of the night). The presiding comedian—the emcee—
contributes his or her own reputation and audience goodwill to the show,
performs at the beginning of the show and between acts, and, most importantly for our immediate purposes, introduces the lesser-known comedians
to the audience.

As one example, in the HBO special *Cedric the Entertainer's Starting Line
Up* (Small 2002*), the comedian Cedric the Entertainer (Cedric Kyles) hosts
an evening of new comedians. For the concert, filmed in the boxing ring of
the Biloxi Grand Casino in Biloxi, Mississippi, Cedric, having performed for
fifteen minutes, makes introductions in the style of a ring announcer:

> This first comedian coming to the stage
> has been
> *ripping shit up* [L] all around the country
> performing on the Bud Light Comedy Tour with Cedric the Entertainer
> he hails from *Jacksonville Florida*
> weighing in at an *even*
> one hundred and thirty-five pounds soaking wet with work boots on [L]
> this brother is *naturally* funny
> *please* welcome to the stage

a member of the *starting line up*
Roland Powell
let him hear it (15:53ff)

This next comedian
that I'm about to bring to the stage
hails from *Houston Texas* [C]
he has a comedy record of *numerous* shows
and *numerous* standing ovations
he is pound for pound one of the funniest *Latinos* in comedy
ladies and gentlemen please welcome to the *stage*
Juan
Villereal (27:10ff)

I want to bring this next comedian to the stage ladies and gentlemen
this next comedian is coming to you direct from *Memphis Tennessee* [C]
he's a *smooth* brother with a very quick wit
he's *known* as the brother of a *thousand* voices
and *just* as many personalities
please put your hands together
for *Tony*
Luewellyn! (44:17ff)

Alright
this next comedian I'm bringing to the stage
he is a Mississippi *homeboy* [C]
representin' the *seuth'*
this brother is *joke-for-joke*
one of the *funniest* young comedians in the country
he is a *fool* by nature
he said that he did not want to have a career of shellin' *peas* [L]
all the way from *Jackson Mississippi* [C]
y'all show some *love*
for *J.J.* (56:07ff)

In this manner, the "craftsman" emcee asks that the extant personal goodwill between him- or herself and the audience be extended to these more or less unknown comedians. In effect, if we take Rosenberg's (1986) model of markets and status seriously, these comedians may be accurately categorized as "craftsmen" in their local markets and "journeymen" in their regional ones, but as their market shifts to national, their status drops to "apprentice." Through the sketchiest of biographies, incorporating a presentation of generalized professional credentials, a statement of geo-social provenance, an attestation to his or her comedic skills, and, if necessary, an advertence to particular possible counter-expectations (i.e., Powell's small stature; Villereal's "Latino" designation in a predominantly African American panel of performers and a predominantly African American audience; Luewellyn's use of mimicry), the emcee contextualizes the performer and the performance to come.

Jason Rutter (2000) has made a similar argument for British stand-up comedy venues and the tradition of the "compère" (the functional equivalent of the North American emcee).

> The compère is a constant figure in British stand-up venues. It is compères who manage proceedings and organise the performance and who act as an anchor for the evening's events in the venue. It is they who have a responsibility to ensure that the evening's entertainment coheres as a "social occasion." . . . Compères are more than just announcers who bring on the act. They provide continuity between acts who often have varying reputations, divergent styles and or different performance skills; perform routines between acts using their own material; pass comment on performance skills; share details of the evening's itinerary. Further, they encourage the audience's participation in the proceedings on stage. (Rutter 2000, 464)

Rutter identifies six "turns" evident in the compère's talk: contextualization (giving background details), framing of response (directing the audience to greet the comedian with a certain attitude), evaluation of comedian (commenting on performance skills), request for action (typically applause), introduction (naming), and audience applause (466).

Mitch Hedberg makes light of the standard introduction in his appearance on Comedy Central's *Premium Blend*.

> Anyone see me on the uh
> *David Letterman* show [S:!A!]
> *no* {laughs}
> *no* man
> *four million* people watch that show
> and I don't know where they *are* [L]

but I believe it's a good *introduction*

for a comedian | you might have seen this next comedian on the David Letter-
man show |

but I believe more people have seen me at the *store* [L]

and that might be a better *introduction*

| you might have seen this next comedian at the *store* | [L]

<u>and people would say</u> | *hell yes* I have | (Hedberg 1998*)

One of Ron James's first televised stand-up comedy performances was in 1996, on an episode of *Comedy at Club 54*, a show recorded at the epony-mous club in Burlington, Ontario, for Hamilton's CHCH (an independent station since subsumed into the CanWest Global network). Although a sea-soned professional entertainer, he was relatively new to stand-up comedy: he was, in effect, in an apprenticeship stage. The producer and host, Ben Guyatt, read his introduction off of an index card.

Moving right along your next act this evening

get a load of this

this guy was on the *main stage* at Second City for a number of years

he's got over *thirty*

television appearances

he *co-starred* in the movie Ernest Rides Again

please welcome

the very *high energy* and *fast paced* storytelling

of Mr. *Ron James* [A:C]

<u>give him a hand</u> (qtd. in James 1996*)

As James walks to the stage through the crowd, in this episode of *Comedy at Club 54*, he assumes a hyperkinetic crouching hop, which he maintains throughout the performance, confirming Guyatt's "high energy" state-ment. As he speaks his Maritime accent comes across strongly, frequently punctuated with an interrogative "huh." He wears a flannel shirt. After a quick remark about adjusting the mike stand ("Let's get this microphone down to circus performer level huh"), he begins with "I live in Toronto by the crystal blue waters of Lake *Ontario* [L] / a lot of good that does you can't *swim in it* eh [L] / *mind you* it's great for developing your film," at which point he mimes the act of dipping photographic paper (1996*).[9]

A "performance team," which extends past the emcee and the perform-ers to include the stage crew, the promoters, the designers of the space, and the audience itself, is engaged in the creation and maintenance of a small-talk frame. Such is the case for large-scale tours premised on introducing proven local or regional acts to a larger market, but even for open-mike nights at local comedy venues: before the performer has started to speak, a frame has been created that anticipates that what follows will be "funny." Whether or not it is funny will largely be a consequence of the comedian's ability to (a) establish relevancy by demonstrating active participation in the worldview of the group through adverting to points of commonality; (b) establish interest by demonstrating active nonparticipation in the world-view of the group through the provision of a different perspective on topics of the group's concern; (c) conform to the audience's aesthetic expectations of what constitutes a "good" story; and (d) reaffirm that what is said is simply talking shit, talk among intimates. However, it is the host or emcee and the comedian, when he or she is an unknown quantity, who through their performances establish some sort of biographical sketch, however limited, to further authenticate the legitimacy of the performer's claim to the social identity of stand-up comedian.

Reputation is cumulative. Most stand-up comedy implies a level of performed autobiography. At first one gives some of that biography through an explicit introduction, as in the Cedric the Entertainer examples above, but over a comedian's career some form of persona is established, mostly concerning the life lived offstage or off the road. It is one of the factors that further makes material unique to the performer and harder to transfer across repertoires. Furthermore, returning audience members bring a foreknowledge of this persona to subsequent performances, and a framework for how to interpret a specific performance is already established. The intimacy of the performance style makes intimates of the performer and audience.

Stand-up comedians are characters in their own narrative, of their own making. They profess to have had certain experiences and express certain opinions not merely in front of but to an audience. Those experiences and opinions are, going back to William Bascom's (1965) definition for legend, intended to be "regarded as true," and the audience makes a determination of the truth behind them. But legend-like testimonial statements and personal experience narratives blend with tall tales. The audience is expected to try to determine what is true and what is play. The comedian provides cues and clues and will quickly try to establish how best to guide a particular audience toward the preferred interpretation. His or her aim is not to assist them in the discernment of an actual truth but to deliver whatever will pay off with laughter, at the time or over the course of the performance. These are offered within the context of ostensibly non-performative off-stage narratives that, outside of the play world of the stage, are not subject to the same negotiation of truth as the onstage variants

CHAPTER 4
Who Is This Stand-Up Comedian?: The Performance of Self

Sometimes when I work I try to say something of *importance* you know
I think about *racism* and how sick
how big of a *sickness* it is for our country
I think that racism is the biggest problem we've *got* in this country
Some people think it's *drugs* and *crime* [A]
<u>but I think it's *racism*</u>
I think that racism is so *stupid*
I cannot see *disliking* a person because of the color of their skin
I only wish that people did not dislike me because of the color of *mine*
but this is *America*
that's how it goes
—**Steve Harvey,** *One Man*

I have been demonstrating how the stand-up comedian makes the claim to the culturally significant social identity of "stand-up comedian." This social identity, demonstrated by vernacular theory about the stand-up comedian as a type, is largely focused on someone having a perspective and speaking from margins. The right to claim this social identity is done through a collaborative apparatus of venue, emcee, and onstage autobiographical snippets, until such point as the stand-up comedian has access to an offstage performance of biography. It is also cumulative, and as he or she becomes known for being a stand-up comedian he or she no longer has to demonstrate and legitimate a claim to that identity.[1]

Now I examine how the stand-up comedian makes claims to further complementary social identities that serve to locate him or her in relation to the audience beyond that single pairing of "stand-up comedian" and "stand-up comedy audience." If the social identity of stand-up comedian is a sketch of marginality, the performer needs to fill in that sketch with detail. Comedians locate themselves and their narratives in a specific time and place, their sense of marginalization is made more explicit, and they establish a relationship with the audience in terms of shared, overlapping, complementary, or—at times—contradictory or oppositional social identities that exist independent of the performance relationship. Again, I will be using Ron James as my primary example, although I will be framing the arguments with examples drawn from differing contexts.

While on stage, stand-up comedians project their personal charisma and tell their stories just like other professional performers do.[2] But stand-up comedy is a different kind of performance. Musicians, for example, perform music, and the non-musical moments are easily distinguishable from the musical moments. Stand-up comedians, on the other hand, talk, and to distinguish absolutely the "charisma-projecting" talk from whatever else is going on in their routine is difficult at best and, perhaps, ultimately quixotic. Moreover, in music, where narrative songs are often performed in the first person, the protagonist within the songs sung is meant to be understood as rooted in the worldview projected by the singer through his or her non-musical narrative, but the singer and the protagonist are not necessarily contiguous. Such is not the case with stand-up comedy, where the narrator is understood as "the same" as the protagonist of his or her first-person narratives.

Stand-up comedians are never not performing the self while on stage, as the incongruities they present in their efforts at humor are determined to be "appropriate" and therefore "funny" (Oring 1992, 1ff) in part by the audience reconciling its flouted expectations with its comprehension of their personas. However, one can certainly make the observation that there are moments on stage that are more explicitly autobiographical than others. In the brief time available to the apprentice comedians, they, in collaboration with the emcee, hint at a way to make their biography understood and lay claim, somehow, to the social identity of the stand-up comedian.

In *Cedric the Entertainer's Starting Line Up*, Juan Villereal, who is Mexican American, needs to emphasize some commonality with the African American crowd and begins by reestablishing his personal connection, and debt, to his host:

> *Keep* it going one more time for Cedric please man [A:C]
> I know you all clapped for him but *please*
> *keep* it going for Cedric man
> trying to make a Mexican some *money*
> and I *want* money man 'cause I've been *poor* for like a long *time*
> I *know* you fuckers 've seen me on *BET* and I've done some shit but
> don't let that shit *fool* you people

I've still got *co-signers* and shit [L]
my caller ID says *out of area* I don't answer that shit *either* bro [L]
{gesturing keeping the phone on the cradle} | uh uh uh
that shit says *unavailable*
I'm unavailable *too* then don't answer that shit | [L] (in Small 2002*)

Without having explicitly tried to forge a connection with the audience by claiming a shared identity, his discussion of poverty at least decenters him from a position of power. J. J., on the other hand, implies that for him comedy is a career of last resort:

I appreciate these few *giggles* you're all giving a brother because
I'm *tired* of switchin' jobs every six months
this is *it* [L]
I tried a *lot* of shit before I started doing comedy
I tried working at *UPS*
and I thought I was going to *move up* and drive the *truck* [L]
they wanted my little skinny ass to start at the *bottom*
unloadin' all of them heavy-ass boxes
I'm in there *cryin'* and every god damned thing man [L]
I go tell my little *supervisor*
he tells me | go get one of them belts that go around your waist |
I'm like | *man* that shit's not working
my back *still* hurts | [L]
I ain't return from break one day like | *no* we don't want this shit | [L]
I told them I was going to get some water
I went *straight* to the *car* [L]
[. . .]
I *appreciate* these few giggles 'cause
when I look back on my life a brother like me could not depend on school for *no* job
I was a *dumb* fucker (in Small 2002*)

Access to broadcasting, whether live or prerecorded, and to distributed mediations like LPs and DVDs allows for stand-up comedians to have their performed persona known to a particular audience in advance of a performance. They cannot be assured that the audience will have necessarily seen them before, but there is a good chance that they have had some exposure, either by chance through broadcasting or directly through purchased mediations.[3]

By the end of his performance on *Comedy at Club 54*, his first televised stand-up appearance, Ron James had made explicit reference to having relatives in Newfoundland and mentioned that he was from Nova Scotia, that he lived in Los Angeles, and that his Maritime accent would stand out on occasion. This was woven into a routine about the misunderstanding Canadians had about the intensity of the hot weather in Los Angeles, coupled with the misunderstanding Americans have about Canada in general. Although very little of the material is autobiographical per se, enough hints are given, with particular reference to his Maritimes persona, to provide something of a framework for interpretation.

James made the transition from improvisational theater and comedy acting to a one-man show and finally to stand-up comedy. He is perhaps an unusual case insofar as the content of his one-man show (James 1997*) was explicitly autobiographical, detailing his time in Los Angeles and his struggles to find work there. *Up and Down in Shakey Town: One Canadian's Journey through the California Dream* had been developed and performed in theater venues rather than stand-up comedy venues:[4] there was in that time a run in April and May of 1994 at the Factory Theatre Studio Café in Toronto (Kirchhoff 1994); a taping the following year for broadcast on CBC Radio (Mietkiewicz 1995); a recorded performance filmed on March 21, 1997, but unaired until June 6, 1999, on The Comedy Network (*Halifax Daily News* 1999); an appearance at the Edinburgh Fringe Festival in August 1997 (Corrigan 2001); and a two-week run at Halifax's Neptune Theatre in June of 1999. The one-man show structure, with a beginning, middle, and end—and the use of light cues and music—was broadcast and framed as a stand-up comedy performance and became his first mediated stand-up comedy project (James 1997*). It still occasionally appears on The Comedy Network, and the entire performance is available on its website. On the strength of this show, James was awarded Best Stand-Up at the first Canadian Comedy Awards in 2000.

There was significant overlap of his more theatrical work with his stand-up comedy work: *Shakey Town* was a going concern between 1994 and 1999, and his stand-up comedy dates from 1996. James's (1996*) *Comedy at Club 54* performance draws heavily on *Shakey Town*, particularly and explicitly the episode set in Los Angeles, where the material is a direct transplant. By the time James made the switch to stand-up comedy full time, he had the benefit of a fully fleshed-out persona to build upon.

Shakey Town begins with the title song from the Roy Rogers and Dale Evans film *San Fernando Valley* (English 1944*): the opening credits of the *Comedy Now* version are superimposed over a clip from the film. He takes the stage, wearing his flannel shirt, and begins:

Well that *music* you were just *listening* to there
is being sung by *Roy Rogers* and *Dale Evans*
from a film called the *San Fernando Valley*
and I saw that film for the first time as an *eleven-year-old* kid at the *Capitol* The-
          atre in *Halifax Nova Scotia*
it was *nineteen-sixty-eight*
of course their film was made in nineteen-forty-one [L]
it took a while for movies to make it back home in *those days* [L]
but *so what* if it was in black and white
it was a Saturday afternoon matinee and it was a *western*
and while grisly sleet from the Atlantic pounded on the doors *outside*
inside
safely cocooned in that warm of hum of movie screen
I watched Roy and Trigger ride across those forever hills a chaparral and sunny
          southern California
and that night when my head hit the *pillow*
I faded into *dreamtime*
whispering incantations to that place *far away*
and I *believed*
a few years ago with family in tow I took my *own* journey there
hopped a 747 Conestoga *wagon* [L]
to follow well-worn trails on the jet stream *west*
like so many other *beaming pilgrims* before me [L] (James 1997*)

All that is needed to understand the performance is included within this
opening section, as it frames the Maritimer as outsider to the larger, more
wondrous world of California, as mediated through fantastic images. The
entire show concerns James's efforts at regrouping following the cancel-
lation of the situation comedy that brought him to California and leads
through to the eventual development of the one-man show itself.

When stand-up comedians reach a certain status, they have access to
opportunities to become known outside of their purely performative
moments: they are sought out by media or are successful in their efforts to
garner media attention. Again, like bluesmen and country musicians, they
become practiced in being interviewed. The interview becomes central to
their efforts to frame performances and claim the social identity of stand-
up comedian. Outside of the "duty" to be funny, the stand-up comedian has
the opportunity to present his or her story, and it is in this non-comedic
performance where many of the tropes of the vernacular theory of stand-
up comedy are enacted.

In an interview for the book *Revolutionary Laughter: The World of Women's Comics* (Warren 1995), Joy Behar (prior to her mass exposure as one of the co-hosts of *The View*) uses her own biography to express a point about stand-up comedy in general:

> It empowers you not to be victimized. One of the reasons people become comedians is so they can say these things about themselves first. For instance, growing up I had really, really kinky hair. Everybody used to tease me about it; they called me Brillo head. My fifth grade teacher used to call me Brillo head. I was hurt by this, so finally I started to make jokes about my hair. I'd say, "I've got a Brillo head" first, before anyone could say it to me. This defuses it; it takes away their power to hurt me. (Warren 1995, 15)

In that same volume, Brett Butler is interviewed. For the preamble, Roz Warren notes, "[Butler] married at age twenty and endured an abusive relationship for three years before getting out," and "Her fans love Butler because she's a survivor. Because she's funny as hell. And because she doesn't take shit from anyone" (Warren 1995, 38). Over the course of the interview, Butler twice mentions—albeit only in passing—this marriage: "When I did get on stage again, after a grim first marriage, I felt that I had things to say" (39) and, later, "On the subject of bombing, like the marriage I left in which I was battered for three years, I honestly feel that I had to go through that to become who I am now" (42).

Ron James was born in Glace Bay, Cape Breton, Nova Scotia, the child of a Cape Breton mother and a Newfoundland father. When he was nine, the family moved to Halifax, Nova Scotia's capital city and the largest in Atlantic Canada. After finishing a BA in history at Acadia University in Wolfville, Nova Scotia, he moved to Toronto to become a comedic actor: he joined the Second City Theatre Company, appeared in several films, including *Strange Brew* and *The Boogeyman*, and was an earnest do-it-yourselfer in a Home Hardware national advertising campaign. He was nominated for a Genie Award, the Canadian film industry award, for his supporting role in *Something About Love*. A short-lived sitcom, *My Talk Show*, brought him to Los Angeles in 1990 where, when it was canceled, he found himself working for a landscaper, pulling a tree out of Robert Urich's yard. His need for work led him to try monologues at local comedy clubs, and, when he returned to Canada two years later, he parlayed his experience as an Atlantic Canadian in America into *Up and Down in Shakey Town*.

It was more this experience in California than James's childhood that becomes his master narrative, over and above what gets performed on the stage: being a Maritimer in Los Angeles frames the outsider perspective; being out of work frames his drive and ambition; his ambivalence about the promises of American success frames his desire to succeed in Canadian show business; and the entire experience forms the background of his early solo work.

> The Down East comic and Second City alumnus returned to Canada in 1993 after mixed experiences from his stand-up years in Los Angeles.
> "We were in *Newsweek* on Tuesday, cancelled on Thursday and on Monday I was pulling a tree out of Robert Urich's front yard with my buddy's pool-digging company." (McKay 2000)

> He stayed three years in L.A., working standup. "I'd put my name in a hat with 30 other people and the detritus of the American dream would filter down from Topanga Canyon, the 'illegitimate' sons of Charles Manson, with songs of pain and angst." And what material was James doing? Canadian. Stories about deer hunting in the Maritimes or comparing the stormy Atlantic coast to the idyllic Pacific coast. (Posner 2001)

> After 10 months, the show was cancelled and Mr. James became yet another actor struggling in Tinseltown. He had some luck with commercials, doing voice-overs for Fruit Loops and other products, but eventually it was costing him more to live and work in Los Angeles than he was getting paid.
> That's when he moved back to Toronto and started over. Mr. James looks back on his Hollywood experience as bittersweet. (Bouw 2001)

> The start of his Canadian dream began when his wife, June, urged him to take his stories to the small cafés in Los Angeles, to test his ability as a standup comedian and the worth of his material. He found that his tales of deer-hunting, among other stories, were funny to all sorts of people. So they moved back to Toronto, where he worked on his craft at The Laugh Resort. He wrote a standup routine called Up and Down in Shakey Town: One Man's Journey Through the California Dream.[5] (James 2005b)

In my interview with him, he brought many of these themes together, including a brief admission that he keeps stock phrases at hand to explain his time.

> My model for doing this was hitting the wall in Los Angeles as an actor in 1991 and knowing full well that I was the only person responsible for *my life*

period
no *middle ground* in America
no *safety net*
no *small town* to run back to
no *nothing*
no *idyllic halcyon* day to try to embrace during the two months of summer in *Cape Breton* in Ingonish
no *Queensland* Beach outside of Halifax anymore
it was just *me* man
and I *knew* . . .
you know a person can go *everywhere*
in the world
and uh
not be *happy*
and I knew that a *declaration* of self
would make me *happy*
and I'd always *done that*
through being *funny*
and when I hit the wall in *Los Angeles* in '91
was out of work for eleven months
and I started going up to these *amateur nights* on Ventura Boulevard
this was after ten years of pretty *serious*
employment in Canada
and there's no *middle ground* down there
and my wife said at the time she said ah
| just go up and read those *stories* that you're reading to me all the time |
and I wasn't even a *stand-up* I'd go up and *read them*
and I used to . . . and I *told* people
I don't know if I did this
observation before
but I just do it for my own *volition* rather than an *audience*
I do it to let them *know* that it didn't happen overnight
I do this phrase to let them *know*
that it's been a *long road* since I was funny in university or high school
or my *kitchen*
| I've shared the stage with the illegitimate spawn of the Charles Manson clan who came down from the Topanga Canyon warrens with their poetry and prose
lookin' for the love that Charlie never *gave* |
I wanted them to *know* that it just wasn't
| *oh* fuck

that's the guy who was funny in *high school* and *university*
look where he is *now* |
and *everybody*
thinks that
and
it just wasn't . . .
it just wasn't that *way*
I had the goods but a *lot* of people had the goods
but a lot of people didn't have the *balls*
and a lot of people didn't have a
a *healthy recognition*
that your *time* is only so limited on this planet
to *achieve* the thing you want to
a recognition of death is a celebration of life
full circle
when I came back to Toronto from Los Angeles
I knew this was the place I had to make it work
and to quote the *wizard*
I had to follow my *bliss*
and my *bliss* was always *this*
that's all I have to say (James 2005a)

James's Los Angeles experience may have a certain flexibility to it depending on the audience and performance context: on stage it is the stuff of comedy; in his brief interviews with the press it is an explanatory background narrative that serves to inform what the audience can expect; and in the long interview it takes on the aura of personal myth and testimony. Had the events that the narrative relates not happened, he would be a fundamentally different person. It is an existential story that concerns origins, it informs his career and his personal life, and it forms the basis for a belief system.[6]

In an interview one is subject to the interviewer's questions: they can be anticipated, as interviewers may have a particular agenda or angle they are more interested in pursuing, but they are not guaranteed. When the recorder was turned off after our interview, Ron James said that I had some good questions, some of which seemed to genuinely surprise him: he was able to answer all of them, but not with the same practiced air of many of the other, more routine questions.

When comedians have reached an even greater status, they frequently become the subjects of unauthorized or authorized biographies or write their own autobiographies. Often, stand-up comedians who have become the subject of biographies, or who initiate or are approached to write their autobiographies, have typically attained a level of fame in a sphere outside of stand-up comedy alone. Dick Gregory's *Nigger: An Autobiography* (1964) was written more from and about his involvement in the civil rights movement. Albert Goldman's *Ladies and Gentlemen—Lenny Bruce!* (1974) was written almost ten years after Bruce's death, when he had already become an icon for the counterculture. Some have attained that fame through television work, like Tim Allen's *Don't Stand Too Close to a Naked Man* (1994), Brett Butler's *Knee Deep in Paradise* (1996), Jerry Oppenheimer's unauthorized biography of Jerry Seinfeld (2002), Bernie Mac's *Maybe You Never Cry Again* (2003), and George Lopez's *Why You Crying?* (2004), or through film, like the biographies of Woody Allen (Lax 1992), Bill Cosby (R. Smith 1997), or Jim Carrey (Knelman 1999). A certain number of autobiographies are written by older or retiring comedians as a form of life review, like Rodney Dangerfield's *It's Not Easy Bein' Me* (2004), Bob Newhart's *I Shouldn't Even Be Doing This!* (2006), Don Rickles's *Rickles' Book* (2006), or Steve Martin's *Born Standing Up* (2007); all of these comedians have achieved success in other spheres as well.

Unauthorized biographies tend to be either intentionally glowing and effusive or intentionally disparaging and critical. In either instance, their primary materials are previously published sources like press interviews, original interviews with people outside of the comedian's active circle, and archival material dating from before the comedian was able to (or thought to) exercise control over his or her press. However, both are useful sources for information about the comedian's life, and the glowing biography also emphasizes how the life story fits into the extant social identity of the stand-up comedian. Authorized biographies are rare, especially as the comedian is often presumed to be a writer, thus questioning the need for someone else to write for him or her: the exceptions to these are the posthumous biography, sanctioned by the comedian's estate, and the extended journalistic profile.

The biography provides the opportunity to uninterruptedly reframe the stand-up comedian's story. Sometimes it is to salvage a damaged reputation or a potentially damaging moment: Joan Rivers's *Enter Talking* (1986) was published at the launch of her own talk show on the then new Fox Network, a consequence of which was a very public falling out with Johnny Carson, for whom she had been the permanent replacement host for the *Tonight Show*. Although it is not the focus of the book, Rosie O'Donnell's *Find Me* (2002) was her first public statement about her homosexuality. British comedian Russell Brand's *My Booky Wook* (2007) is as much a memoir of his infamous drug problems as it is of his professional rise.

Even when the biography is more in keeping with the transference of routines to the page (as discussed in chapter 7) and less a biography per se, the comedian who has been able to reach a status that makes book publishing viable will use it to his or her advantage. In all instances, publishing becomes yet another venue for the cultivation of a comedian's reputation.

As has already been suggested, it is practically a trope of stand-up comedian culture that comedy derives in part from a marginalized voice: it is a recognition of inconsistencies—seemingly incompatible positions—within a dominant structure that are accepted by that structure and help to sustain it, only to be exposed by one who is by virtue of circumstance neither privy to the inner workings of said structure nor a beneficiary thereof. Marginality—"outside" enough to be distanced from the power structures and "inside" enough to understand the implications of the power structures—is a first step.

The point that has been stressed throughout this work is that stand-up comedy is a speech event that requires an audience. It is a dialogic form: there are both performer and audience and, while the former is the principal actor in the exchange, the performance is cooperative, moving forward via the audience's reaction to the performer's text, often in the form of a nonverbal or terse verbal utterance or ejaculation, which variously expresses assent, recognition, disagreement, outrage, bewilderment with request for further explanation, or delight at bewilderment sated. Laughter and, to a lesser extent, applause further propel the text forward. The audience makes a judgment of the performer's right to engage with them and validates that right throughout the successful performance, indicating that the stand-up comedian's responsibility to provide a comic performance is being met. Despite the power of the performance ultimately residing with the performer, stand-up comedy is a genre predicated on having someone beyond the performer interpret, develop, and shape it as it progresses, which makes it distinct among professional solo performance genres.

The audience is historically situated. The comedian adapts a potential performance (a type) to meet the expectations of that historically situated audience (creating a version). However, as will be discussed in chapter 7, the most readily available and accessible versions are commercial record-ings that are intended to serve a larger market: the performer is deliber-ately aiming to meet the expectations not only of the immediate audience but also of an indeterminate, physically and temporally distant audience. In such recordings comedians heed the local audience in order to establish and maintain rapport, and thus elicit the greatest possible response—sup-portive dialogic utterances, alongside peals of laughter—which by proxy will hopefully translate through psychic contagion to an analogous reaction by the "home" audience. However, for the most part the idiosyncrasies of a purely localized performance are passed over in favor of a broader appeal. What is the nature of this "appeal"? Or, more precisely, what is being appealed to?

Given the nature of the professionalization of stand-up comedy, the stand-up comedy audience is not a single person but always a group of Rob-ert Georges's story listeners (1969). The audience members quantitatively have in common the primary characteristic of co-presence at the particular performance event, and by extension they are likely to share consequent social identities that their presence at the event implies, above all, an initial willingness to participate in a stand-up comedy event as a "story listener." The venue's location—country, region, municipality, neighborhood—implies national, regional, or local sympathies: its cultivated reputation (say for alternative or family-friendly comedy) or its cumulative reputa-tion for its other performance uses (music venue, casino, theater) further contextualizes the constitution of the audience; and the price of admission may alternately indicate either the disposable income of the audience or the willingness to spend to participate in the event. The performer's expecta-tion of the constitution of an audience is based on a series of implications extrapolated from the context of the performance. With rare exceptions—those being either comedians who have reached such a level of notoriety and fame that they could be described as celebrities in Neil Rosenberg's (1986) sense or comedians whose performance material is principally a series of one-liners (such as Emo Philips and Steven Wright)—performers adapt their material to their audience.[7] But what form does that adaptation take? And so I return to the same question as before: What is the nature of this appeal?

But stand-up comedians are also performers: they do not simply pas-sively operate within a "Western" worldview. Rather, they actively create or invoke the worldview in which their talk is meant to be interpreted. Like Georges's example of father and son as a social identity pairing, there is a social identity pair that precedes the storyteller and story listener identity: unlike Georges's father and son, however, the social identity pairing for the comedy performance is in large part a creation of the performer, who simultaneously addresses and moves beyond statistical or quantifiable associations and establishes a bond of common cause with the audience, permitting the story-teller identity. This common cause is often in relation to an other. One way of building intimacy is suggesting that you and I are equally distinguishable from someone else: that alone may be sufficient to initiate an engagement.

If the social identity "stand-up comedian" is equivalent to a type, then the specific and distinct persona he or she cultivates is equivalent to a version. In the last chapter I demonstrated how, even in the sketchy biographies that the emcee provides for the apprentice comedian, there is some effort to locate the comedian within a particular worldview so as to better orient the audience to how the act is meant to be interpreted. This persona is enacted on stage, developed over time, and, as it becomes better known to its potential audiences, can mature: less effort need be expended on proving the type, as the version has an established history and the flow of talk can, more or less, pick up where it left off. The audience brings foreknowledge not only of what *a* stand-up comedian is, but of who *this* stand-up comedian is. The comic persona is the stand-up comedian's projection of a character who is, simultaneously, meant to be identical to his or her "real" self.

A complexity stems from the economic necessity for the professional comedian to frequently operate outside of his or her specific small group. Within the small group each member, performer and nonperformer alike, shares in an accumulated and cumulative nexus of interlocking terms and relations that forms the baseline of a common worldview. Some may have only a tentative grasp of this worldview, some may have a mastery over certain areas, and some may have a broad and rich understanding of most areas. Should a performer emerge within this group, his or her success or failure as a talker will be judged in part on the basis of a mastery of the group's canons, its repertoire of modes of talk, motifs, and topics. And, as Neil Rosenberg reminds us, with any folklore form it is necessary to distinguish between individual competence and ideals of performance (1986, 165).

When one moves outside of one's immediate indigenous group (using "indigenous" not to denote any meaning other than that group in whose context and worldview one primarily arose), there may be a great amount of overlap between the worldviews of the new group and that of one's own. The criterion for success or failure as a talker within this new context remains the same: an audience's judgment of demonstrable mastery of this new group's canon. For a performer whose worldview is largely but not wholly contiguous with that of the audience, he or she has two options: either obfuscate the points of difference and thus enforce the impression of a contiguous worldview or advert to the points of difference and thus frame one's presence in part through the esoteric and exoteric understandings the two groups have about the other.

The comedian may, and typically does, do both, vacillating between an insider and outsider identity. Indeed, peripherality and interstitiality appear to be base requirements for the comedian. When one speaks of a group, of course, one is typically referring to an ideal type, in which each member is interchangeable. We know this to be a mere convention that allows us to continue using "group" as a term with meaning, despite our recognition that within groups (a) there are distinctions of complementarity and (b) constituent members may also belong to other groups. Active participation in a group is the conscious advertence to points of commonality and deliberate inhibition of points of difference.

By whichever humor theorist one chooses, one is told that comedy stems from the artful revelation of some underlying double meaning, discrepancy or contradiction. A humorous performance is one in which the performer, for however brief a moment, communicates having figuratively stepped aside and seen the discrepancy. There is a deliberate advertence to a second possible interpretation, one that is in contrast to the straightforward "commonsensical" interpretation of "the group." Occurring as it does within a non-consequential play frame, the recognized discrepancy need not be resolved nor its consequences dwelled on. Were it to have occurred in a frame of consequentiality, we might then be talking about the tragic, for which resolution is sought. If active participation in a group is the conscious advertence to points of commonality and deliberate inhibition of points of difference, then what is occurring in humorous performance is a simultaneously active non-participation in a group, meaning the conscious advertence to points of difference.

Whereas the quotidian humorous performance need only be a consequence of a temporary "stepping outside," the professional comedian, who is persistently needing to be funny, must be persistently "stepping out." The comedian, then, is one who has a solid grasp of the worldview of the group but who has also moved outside (or beyond, or the spatial metaphor of your choice) of that worldview and has gained a separate perspective that highlights inconsistency and discrepancy. Whereas all group members are both of the group and outside it, the vocational stand-up comedian, much like the artist, cultivates interstitiality while maintaining a non-consequential frame.

If the vernacular theory of comedy sees the stand-up comedian-as-type as marginalized, as rooted in loneliness and the need for approval, and as seeing the world from a different perspective, the comic persona developed and portrayed by the stand-up comedian-as-version needs to establish *how and from whom* is he or she marginalized, *how* is he or she lonely and *from whom* is he or she needing approval, and *from what* does he or she see the world.

In a North American context, one can quickly identify comedians who are representative of a marginalized group. There are comedians who are women, black, Asian, Hispanic, Jewish, homosexual, visually impaired, obese, southern. Their comedy is not wholly defined by their identification with marginalized groups, but an *a priori* marginalization provides an entry into the comedic universe, and there is an established comedy vein into which they can tap.

Wholly defining the comedian's voice as *a priori* marginalized, however, leads to a difficult dilemma: how does one account for the comedy of comedians positioning themselves as representative of groups that are—by any objective, measurable, sociological, or historical standard—not marginalized? One can avoid the question, which is simply laziness, or one can argue that they are somehow not performing comedy, which is a conceit.

Instead, the marginalization is a subjective framework created by the performer in collusion with the audience. This is the technique by which comedians representative of groups so clearly not forced into the margins—the proverbial middle-class white male—are able to maintain an outsider stance: Dennis Miller evokes a political universe in which the literate and intelligent, like himself, are cast aside in favor of a lowest common denominator; Larry Miller evokes a civilized demeanor above the fray of current lapses in judgment and sense. This claim of marginalization need never be "proven," simply argued and accepted by the audience, and, as it occurs within a realm of play, the consequences of understanding the world in such a manner are nil, as it is a framework that can be dropped at the end of performance.

Brad Stine, the American conservative and born-again Christian stand-up comic is a particularly strong example of an explicit self-marginalization.

> In his set, Stine hit some familiar notes, "I'm a conservative, I'm a Christian, and I think the United States is the greatest country that has ever existed on the face of the earth!" he shouted, provoking one of four standing ovations.

"And, because of those three belief systems, when I die, by law, I have to be stuffed and mounted and placed in the Smithsonian under the 'Why He Didn't Get a Sitcom' display." (Green 2004, 52)

The same issue can be approached by asking "marginal to whom?" For as much as a comedian may or may not be identifiable with a marginalized group, it is more important to establish a common ground with an audience and, as such, identify an other in contrast to whom both performer and audience can find common cause. Differences, if any, can be quickly addressed or ignored in light of a greater similarity, in contrast to an other which appears to have some semblance of power, domination, or influence over or threat to those present. The object is to build upon the established exoteric assumptions of the audience and identify oneself as *primum inter pares* at articulating those assumptions. The challenge is to do so without losing one's soul, especially when the group one is contrasting oneself and the audience against is in reality a historically marginalized one.

The shared connection between audience and performer is a fragile one, which must be maintained and reaffirmed throughout the performance. The parameters can also shift and, as the audience itself is not homogeneous, the performer can claim common cause with the multiple social identities of the constituent members, framing him- or herself in opposition to another identity component over the course of the performance (taking sides with men over women in one routing, then African Americans over whites in another, etc.). One continually, sequentially, appeals to a common cause that is shared by the plurality if not the majority of the audience: the antagonism that may arise from those left outside simply fuels the catharsis from their eventual and inevitable reintegration.

For a Canadian audience, the easiest way for a performer to build a legitimacy to his or her voice is to shift focus to the United States and distance him- or herself from it. It is a strategy that works equally well for American performers as it does for Canadians, even if the plurality of what is to come is immersed in American references. Canadian comedians can make more of this by providing the second half of a compare-and-contrast approach through the use of Canadian-specific references. In a market as fluent with American culture as Canada's—through both direct media penetration of American networks and cable channels and indirectly through Canadian broadcasters' purchasing of syndicated American products—a voice framed within a Canadian perspective is one distinct enough to catch the attention of an audience and make it stand out.

Such was the theme of "Sleeping with the Elephant" (see James 2004*), a specially commissioned show at the Winnipeg Comedy Festival in 2003, named for a remark of Pierre Trudeau's about the Canada-US relationship and hosted by transplanted American comedian Jebb Fink.[8]

> Near the end, along comes Ron James who is, as usual, a bundle of fierce energy. His rapid-fire rants are always well written and scathing. But even he gets into the territory of cliché. On the topic of American television, he says this: "Survivor? Surviving in the tropics, nonetheless! Jeez, we're a winter nation. I'd like to see those Darwinian foot soldiers of the American dream tucked into a minus-40 lean-to up there in Lake of the Woods country!" At this point, there is raucous cheering in the Winnipeg theatre. (Doyle 2004)

James was the only Canadian stand-up comedian asked to perform on *Late Night with Conan O'Brien* when it did a week of shows from Toronto in 2004. And, in one of his more recent routines, he continues his American material: "Talking about obese American tourists on [a] trip to Mexico he says, 'Jeez, it's not 9/11 that's killing that country, it's 7-Eleven!'" (Doyle 2005).

But Canada is also a country of regions. Some are identifiably so simply by means of geography, while provinces like those in the west, whose borders were largely conventions based on lines of latitude, developed regional identities as their respective political autonomies and settlement patterns emerged over the last century. Running alongside geographic distinctions is the historic development of settlement, with the early settlement of the Maritimes by Acadians, Irish, United Empire Loyalists, and Scots, the settling of Quebec by the French and Ontario by the English, Loyalists, Scots, French, and Germans, the establishment of a Pacific Ocean presence in British Columbia, and the "filling in" of the Prairies with the acceleration of immigration in the latter half of the nineteenth and the first half of the twentieth centuries, especially from Eastern and Northern Europe. The consolidation of economic and political power in central Canada gives rise to Ontario as bourgeoisie, the "urban" in an urban/rural dichotomy that is echoed both in the micro scale throughout Canada's regions and on the macro in its relation to the United States.

Thus, being twice-removed or twice-marginalized, first from the dominant culture of the United States and second from the dominant culture of Central Canada, Maritimers in general and James specifically are allowed a certain license in what they can get away with saying. Their *de facto* marginalization becomes representative of all instances of the marginalized. An analogy may be to Nebraskan Johnny Carson or Indiana's David Letterman: a Midwest sensibility (no matter how long removed from that context their lives may have taken them) can be invoked that instantly allows for rapport through the establishment of a distinction between themselves and a dominant East or West Coast culture.

Parallel to Atlantic Canada's sense of displacement is the recent phenomenon—recent in that it now has economic and political consequences—of western isolation. The economic boom of Alberta and the Oil Sands, reserves that are said to dwarf those of the Arabian Peninsula, albeit in a form which only recently has been feasible to develop, means that the West is the source of much of Canada's overall economic health, which engenders a reappraisal of its place in the Confederation.

As discussed in the last chapter, prior to any interpretation of his spoken "texts," Ron James uses a variety of devices to frame his performance within a particular set of audience expectations, that of the, in his words, "happy-go-lucky" Maritimer. In both local Maritime performances and transnational performances, James is able to play on an audience's *a priori* expectation for a Maritime identity, which helps to delimit, but not exhaustively so, the interpretation of what is to come.

Although he has not lived in Atlantic Canada since 1979, Ron James's Maritime identity is very much part of his performance persona. Primarily through accent and speech play, but also through costume and musical accompaniment, he establishes and cultivates a heightened persona of Atlantic Canadianness.[9] Reasons for this may not be immediately apparent to the non-Canadian. But, as television critic John Doyle put it,

> Television comedy in this country is dominated by East Coast wit and it flourishes because the regional attitude and sass is used to mask a much more savage, anti-establishment comedy that wouldn't be tolerated if anyone else tried it. The best of Canadian TV comedy of the last two decades [. . . is] anchored in a colourful language that's just outside the mainstream. The style is rooted in regionalism, a literal and figurative distance from the mainstream and the centre of power. The accent is a scalpel used to eviscerate the pomposity and smug assumptions of the rest of Canada. (2003)

His Atlantic Canada persona—more or less localized depending on the press audience—is often explicitly identified in the press, whether through his own words or those of the reporter.

James grew up in what he calls "a real colourful neighbourhood and a very active kitchen.

"There was a swinging door in my mother's kitchen and this great pantheon of personalities that came through who were all really lacking in any kind of formality.

"I was so fortunate to be sitting on the counter when all those shenanigans were going on and somebody was making rum toddies and somebody was making a face and somebody was playing accordion and somebody was falling down and it was fractious, passionate, humorous and contentious." (James, qtd. in Hepfner 1999)

"The essence of that piece [*Shakey Town*] was comparing where I was born and raised in the Maritimes—by that water—to the Pacific, and the juxtaposition of myth meeting reality; the California that I saw in movies, in books and on TV with the one I was living in and investing in." (James, qtd. in Spevack 2000)

"Maritime audiences are quick to respond—which is one of the things about being at home I like," he says. "There's a Maritime voice behind my work, and the Maritime way of looking at things fuels the comedy." (James, qtd. in Pedersen 2001a)

"I think there's a certain Maritime point of view to my work," notes the longtime Toronto resident, attempting to pull back the curtain without giving anything away.

"There's a tradition where I was born of standing on the porch watching the rest of the country have a party through a big picture window. You get a greater predisposition for humour." (James, qtd. in Rubinoff 2001)

James moved to Halifax from Cape Breton when he was nine and believes his comedic sense—honed on the stage of Second City in Toronto—is innate to Nova Scotia's kitchen culture.

"When you're sitting on the kitchen counter and the door is swinging off its hinges with the characters coming through, you learn something from those guys with their rum-toddy grins, their sun-burnt arms. I feel fortunate I had that." (James, qtd. in Smulders 2003)

Of course, Ron James is also a known entity: already, by buying tickets, the audience has a certain set of expectations based on reputation and previous experience. James is by all accounts a craftsman at the national level: his reputation is such that his theater tours typically sell out in all regions of the country, and his television specials and his television series are not only feasible but profitable for the national network. Although James is identified in part with a particular region, his career is not rooted in those local or regional markets, and he is not a "performer of place" like Newfoundlander Buddy Wasisname or Cape Breton's Jimmy Flynn: as such, it is not likely that his audience draws outside of the region can be attributed exclusively (or even in large part) to other transplanted Atlantic Canadians.

Rosenberg notes how a craftsman's repertoire "may include eclectic as well as unique elements for his audience accepts him on personal terms" (1986, 157). There are two consequences of this for James's performance. Firstly, as was discussed in the last chapter, he can assume his audience has some inkling of his biography, and he does not need to introduce himself cold to them. As such, the Maritime framing apparatuses are present to reinforce what is known of him already but are not as required as they would be were he a *tabula rasa*. Secondly, with the "personal acceptance" an audience has for the craftsman, James is able to not simply coast on that goodwill but capitalize on it, allowing himself to venture into riskier material knowing that the audience—however cautiously—will follow.

For Rosenberg, one of the distinctions between an amateur and a professional is the use of the media to aid in reputation cultivation, and James is adept at interviews. I sensed, in part, that he understood my request to interview him as being along these lines: as I have mentioned in passing, some of his answers were from a repertoire of answers to anticipated questions. He also had performative expectations of how he should answer: he wanted to get it right and answer them properly.

When I followed James on tour in 2005, his performances in Nova Scotia first and foremost provided an opportunity to see someone on their "home turf." Ron James was born in Glace Bay in 1958. His father (a Newfoundlander originally from Burgeo) worked for the phone company, and in 1967, when Ron was nine, he moved the family to Halifax. Ron attended Acadia University in the late 1970s and, in 1979, moved to Toronto to become a comedic actor, beginning with Second City. Although he has not lived in the Maritimes for over thirty years, his Maritimer persona is in part a strong residue and in part deliberately cultivated for the stage. His two Halifax shows and the performance in Glace Bay were, in their way, homecomings. The fourth, in Pictou, was nevertheless presented in the guise of one, and his identity was negotiated as a regional, albeit not local, figure.

Although Atlantic Canada, and especially Nova Scotia, is certainly part of his biography, it is not a persona he dons exclusively for Eastern Canadian audiences. I asked him about how and why his performed biography and his onstage persona as a Maritimer are effective (and affective):

Well I think we're part and parcel with the greater Celtic *diaspora* you know
and I think that ah . . . y'know
we're just *driven* by the wind
it's just our . . . our *nature* and I mean
the Scots have been *moving* since day *one* and . . .
so . . . y'know
I touch on that a little bit in my new special *Quest for the West* about Alberta that
y'know the uh . . .
| when the oil boom *hit*
and the clarion call was *heard*
the East hadn't seen an exodus in numbers like *that*
since Charlton Heston parted the Red *Sea*
only thing missing was a biblical *soundtrack*
fast-moving *Jews* and slow moving *Egyptians* |
so we do um . . .
I think that . . .
I think to answer your question it's a marriage of . . . um
necessity and *feeling*
it's a necessity because I have a certain Maritime persona on *stage*
and um I know that *people*
have certain *expectations* with that persona
that's not to say I won't grow *out* of it
but um . . . and in terms of . . .
ask me that question *again*
I want to get it *right*
I want to answer it *properly*
[. . .]
Well uh . . .
from a *stage* persona uh
I know that the country doesn't find Maritimers very *threatening*
we're *funny happy-go-lucky folks* the *life of the party* uh etc. etc.
and for a person whose job is to get laughs
that's uh
a *very* convenient place to come from

and we're also traditional *outsiders*
which is a place you want to come from when you're a *comedian*
you never want to be a card-carrying member of the *country club*[10]
I know shows are very *successful*
that cozy up to *politicians*
and have an almost *jocular affinity* with them
I think that's the last place I want to *be* you know
so I uh . . .
well I think that's an *advantage* for me as a
as a *comedian*
having contempt for the *status quo* and authority
is really *important*
and I think that *Maritimers* when they've travelled around the country
have traditionally been *hewers of wood* and *drawers of water*[11]
even though I'm university *educated*
I do have a working-class *background*
so I always do have a *soft spot*
for the perpetual *traveller*
and I'm *part and parcel* with the Celtic diaspora as well y'know
| driven to the far corners of the *worth* . . .
of the *earth* in search of a *better run* at a *new day* |
and I think that I've always been looking for my little *acre of green* y'know
my little *place in the sun* (James 2005a)

By explicitly invoking not only his Maritime provenance but also the stereotype of the Maritimer both as outsider and as storyteller, he establishes a trans-Canadian right to address an audience anticipating a comedic performance. As was suggested in the last chapter, as his reputation has grown he has dropped this intensity of characterization and has developed into someone more and more indistinguishable from his audience.

Atlantic Canada has always had an ambiguous relationship with the West. Starting in the early 1900s, trainloads of Cape Bretoners and other Maritimers would travel to the Prairie Provinces to work the land as seasonal farmhands. And with the oil boom of the 1970s—which coincided with the death knell of coal and steel in Nova Scotia—and continuing to this day, flocks of younger people moved to Alberta with the promise of middle-class salaries from working the oil fields, or even the promise of twice to three times the minimum wage to work the service sectors of donut shops, Home Depots, and McDonalds.

For James's *Quest for the West* special, the ostensive purpose of the performance was an effort at communicating the western experience to the rest of Canada. He explained it thus to an Edmonton newspaper just prior to the show's airing in December 2005:

"I guess I wanted to get a grunt's-eye view of the land and the people and embrace a sense of people and place and to basically pay homage (to a place) that I've grown to love over the last six years of touring through there. And I wanted to explain to the rest of the country what it is and what it was that appealed to me."

He says he almost ended up living out west in the '70s, when thousands of Maritimers fled "the grip of pogey culture. . . . The West has always been the land of the second chance for people from my neck from the woods, and definitely that's a theme that's always resonated for me," James says. (Rankin 2005)

James has achieved his rank as a craftsman on the national stage in part through his facility with the press. This "homage" to the West comes through in his interviews, which he adeptly uses to set up audience expectations and build goodwill. The following quote comes from an interview with the *Calgary Herald*, just prior to filming the special in September:

"Alberta's always been a golden beacon of opportunity," he deadpans in a sing-songy Nova Scotian lilt at a speed that makes Robin Williams sound lethargic. "It's the land of the second chance, promising release for we eastern bums and scums from our soul-sucking burden of pogey culture, where we can finally score big-time boons in the oil patch and shirk unemployment's Sisyphean lump of f..k." (James, qtd. in Moore 2005)

But contrast this with how James talks about the West in Atlantic Canada; this is from the St. John's *Telegram*:

In my Newfoundland show, I talk about the role of the Canadian West as a "land of second chances" for Atlantic Canadians. The enclaves of Atlantic Canadians in Alberta makes me wonder about other countries and peoples in the world—if they have the same phenomenon of people being in exile in their own country, the way Maritimers are in the west." (qtd. in Hayward 2005)

The metaphor of opportunity seems to be supplanted by one of exploitation when he shifts in audience from West to East.

A question remains where the non-performative James stands on the issue. From my interview, his sympathies for his home region seem to be challenged by what he sees as an inherent flaw in Eastern psychology. Ron's stand-up comedy career emerged from his one-man show, *Up and Down in Shakey Town*. Intensely autobiographical, its focus was on three years spent in Los Angeles. As already mentioned, he moved with his wife and child to Hollywood to be part of the cast of *My Talk Show*, a vérité situation comedy much like *Fernwood Tonight*. The show was abruptly canceled, and, having been a professional actor in Canada for almost fifteen years, Ron found himself looking for work. I repeat this episode, as it is foundational not only to James's career as a stand-up comedian but to his offstage narrative as well. It is a personal myth or testimony: had the events therein not occurred as they are related, he would be fundamentally different from what and who he is today. In this manner the narrative is not open for debate (not that I choose to debate it), although one can still examine it as narrative, as a deliberate reconstruction and representation of events. It was a watershed moment for him, as it caused him to move away from what he understands as the "company town" mentality endemic to the Maritimes:

I think that also plays into your Maritime *motif* that you're speaking of um . . .
because essentially Atlantic Canada is a *victim* culture
it's a culture of *woe is me*
it's a culture of . . .
it's a culture that lives in the *past*
it's a culture that feels its best day is *behind* it
[. . .]
But it's *very very* important for me to
have a *deference*
and a *respect* for the average *man*
and I don't . . .
I just can't *imagine* not ever *having* that
I mean that's in my *DNA*
that being said uh I'm . . .
on my *road*
far away from a victim culture of dependence on *handouts*
I've been self-employed
vigorously
for ten years
well I've been self-employed for *twenty-five*

but this *stand-up* thing
so that's kind of different than the traditional *Maritimer* going out looking
   for ...
see I think a *Maritimer* carries
especially guys that *hunt* for work
they carry a *company town* mentality
that they'll go out there they'll make the money and *somebody somewhere* will give
   them something for their hard work
they'll never really *get* their place in the sun
but it's worth the *struggle*
it's worth the *journey*
and I think as an *artist*
a *creator*
I'm constantly *aware* of that y'know
[...]
America taught me not to expect *handouts*
and it was a *hard lesson* to learn but the most *important* one I learned in my life
and I think that extinguished whatever ...
flame may have existed for a deference for the company town (James 2005a)

The persona James enacts on stage and in (most) offstage interviews is not wholly coincident with his own understanding of Maritime identity, and this understanding is not something he particularly broadcasts in his interviews. However, to suggest disingenuousness on his part would be to misapprehend both the professional necessity of the stand-up comedian and, more importantly, his own understanding of the comedian's role: as much as he is an outsider by virtue of being a Maritimer, which allows him to make general comments about the dominant culture, so too he has put himself outside of a synoptic Maritime worldview in order to make general comments about the Maritimes themselves.

The stand-up comedian is a solo performer who is making some claim to both difference, because he or she has something interesting and distinct to say to an audience (and will say it in a fluent way), and solidarity, because what he or she has to say is relevant to the audience as he or she is recognizably similar to the them. As a performance strategy, the stand-up comedian has to establish this dual persona of simultaneously insider and outsider, especially when he or she is expressly not of the same group as the audience. There is sufficient distance for a fresh perspective, but sufficient intimacy for a safe performance of that perspective. Viability in larger markets requires the ability to perform material that is not too particular to a smaller region: in stand-up comedy it is not simply the material and repertoire but the comedian's persona that must be adapted lest it be found iconoclastic.

For all the play that occurs in the stand-up comedian's performance and for all the validating laughter sought, there are moments in performance when the stand-up comedian's talk elicits applause unaccompanied by laughter. Jason Rutter identifies applause as "practically non-existent" in stand-up comedy (2000, 479). I would tend to disagree with this point, although it is certainly less common than laughter. Rutter does qualify this statement, however, by saying, "Applause during stand-up tends to follow non-comic events. These often include events such as the putdown of a persistent or aggressive heckler, the announcement of a competition winner *or the offering of an ideological statement*" (479, emphasis mine).

If the stand-up comedian's ultimate goal is laughter, why spend time on stage talking and not getting laughs? Why make these ideological statements? Part of the stand-up comedian's technique is not simply the stringing together of a series of artful revelations of discrepancy and inconsistency: for all the ambiguity as to the "truth" of his or her statements that allows for laughter to be released, this series must be interwoven with declarative statements or testimonial personal experience narratives that squarely locate the comedian as sharing a core of fundamental precepts with the audience. Much like the classic folkloristic formulae for what constitutes myth, these precepts are incontestable and, for lack of a better word, "sacred" to the group and are met not with laughter but with applause and calls of approval.

In his *One Man* concert, filmed in Augusta, Georgia, Steve Harvey makes the act of establishing a baseline of commonality explicit:

> Before I get *started* tonight
> I'd like to say that God *is* to me
> God is everything [C:A]
> everything I *have*
> and everything I *am*
> I owe to *God* [A]
> now that I done said that [L]
> going to be some times tonight when it'll sound like I don't know God [L]
> but I do
> good to be here in Augusta

> it was a hard fight for me to get HBO to go *along* with coming to Augusta they
>   said [C]
> that . . .
> they told me that Augusta was too small of a town to support five thousand
>   people for comedy [C]
> but here we are
> here we are [C:A]
> but I'd stop all that clapping 'cause they *was* right about one thing
> this *is* a little ass town [L]
> you can clap all you want to this a *little ass* town right here [L] (Harvey 1997*)

An expression of personal religious belief establishes a social identity beyond that of the stand-up comedian: the connotations of one who "knows God" need not be articulated but imply a shared system of ultimate values with others who know God. Judging by the applause this statement elicited, it is a social identity shared by many if not most of the audience, who individually bring their own interpretations of that identity. However much Harvey's comedy performance veers away from that implied value system, he remains committed to it. In the second phase of this introductory section, he identifies himself as opposed to and successfully rebuking the dominant culture—as manifested by HBO executives—which systemically and systematically marginalizes smaller cities (markets) like Augusta as nonviable. This in turn then allows him to mock the city for its size: the next few minutes build on this theme. Further along in the performance he makes similar testimonial statements, about how grateful he is to his parents and that they are still alive and about how racism is nonsensical and yet pervasive in contemporary America.

These ideological, testimonial statements need not come solely at the beginning of performances. Chris Rock's *Never Scared* (2004*), filmed in Washington, D.C., was his first tour since the attacks of September 11, 2001. He comments on the "acceptable racism"—racism that was acceptable to espouse—that emerged as a consequence. "You'd watch TV man / and you'd see these weird *white guys* / nobody here / you guys okay / but uh [L] / you'd see these weird *white guys* / getting *overly patriotic*." He makes reference to the invocation of "American" as an absolute category that permitted this racism to be made manifest.

> A lot of white people like to scream they American as if they got something to
>   do with the country being the way it is [A]

know what I mean

like they was on the *Mayflower* or some shit [A]

I mean when you *really* break it down

there ain't even many Americans in this *room* okay

contributing Americans

check this out

if you're a *veteran*

if you fought in *any war* for the United States

you are American [A]

God bless all the veterans

big up to the veterans

I can't say *nothing* wrong about the veterans *okay*

you American

now

if you *swam* here from some shitty *country* [L]

that didn't allow you *Bubbalicious* [L]

you too are American

because you overcame *obstacles*

and made *sacrifices*

to actually *get here*

you are a *true American* okay [A]

you really are

don't let nobody tell you no different

everybody else

you're just lucky

that's it

you're just lucky

all you crazy white | *"I'm an American"* |

all you did was come out of your *mother's pussy* on *American soil* [L:C:A]

that's *it*

that's *it*

you think you're better than somebody from *France*

because you came out of a pussy in *Detroit* [L] (Rock 2004*)

There is nothing much risky about praising the sacrifices of veterans or of refugee immigrants and validating their claim to the social identity of American, and the applause the comments receive affirms that validation. It is only by introducing this concept of "contributing" American that allows for the follow-up counter argument of "circumstantial" Americans, those who are "lucky." Furthermore, by attributing the overly simplistic appropriation of the "American" social identity to a non-present other, he can label everyone present as "just lucky"—explicitly using the second-person voice—without necessarily suggesting that they too were naïve appropriators. The "lucky" theme continues later in the performance:

> Now I *love* America I must say
> I *love* America
> I've got to say it is the greatest country in the world okay [A]
> the greatest country in the world
> in the whole world
> it's the *best* place
> there's no place I'd rather *be*
> there's no place I'd rather be *from*
> and we are *all* lucky to be here
> everybody in this room
> *lucky* to be here
> even *black* people
> *lucky* to be here [L] (Rock 2004*)

The "even black people" tag, which is met with laughter, qualifies but does not contradict his initial premise of luckiness by recognizing that the shared social identity of American does not wholly negate the consequences of the social identity of black. Lucky and marginalized are juxtaposed: they are seeming contradictions inasmuch as they are not reconcilable.

Harvey and Rock, returning to core ideological statements, provide an explicit contextualizing framework of commonality, which then provides them with license for expressing alternate viewpoints. They can then make similar declarative statements that are contested (or are contestable) by the audience. Other comedians might not make claims as explicitly as "God is everything to me" and "I love America," but applause at certain lines indicates that the audience recognizes that something has been said that is a shared sentiment of the plurality of its members.

One of the most dramatic instances of this testimonial phenomenon comes in *Richard Pryor Live on the Sunset Strip* (1982a*). Following a discussion of a trip he took to Africa, Pryor recounts the following:

> One thing I got out of it was *magic* I'd like to *share* it with you
> y'know it was like

I was *leavin'*
and I was *sittin'* in the hotel
and a *voice* said to me said | *look around*
what do you *see* |
and I said | I see all colors of *people* doing *everything* |
y'know
and the voice said | do you *see*
any *niggers* | [!L!]
and I said | *no* |
and he said | you know why
'cause there *aren't* any | [!A!]
and it *hit* me
like a *shot* man
I started *cryin'* and shit I was sittin' there I said
| yeah I've been here *three weeks*
I haven't even *said it*
I haven't even *thought it* | [<!that's right!>]
and it made me say | oh my god I've been *wrong*
I've been *wrong*
I've got to *regroup* my shit | I mean
I said | I ain't gonna never call another black man nigger | [<!yeah!>:A:C
    (sustained)]
you know 'cause we *never was* no niggers
that's a word
that's used to describe our own *wretchedness*
and we *perpetuate* it now
'cause it's *dead*
that word's *dead* we're men and women we come from
we come from the first people on the *earth* [<yeah>:C:A]
<u>y'know the first people on the earth were *black people*</u> [A]
'cause *anthropologists*
{emphatic} *"white* anthropologists" [L]
so the white people go {caucasian voice} "that could be true you know" | [L]
yeah Dr. Leakey and them found
people remains *five million years* ago in *Africa*
you *know* them motherfuckers didn't speak *French* [L]
so black people *we* the first people that had *thought*
right we's the first one's to say
{bemused} | "where the fuck *am I* [L]

and *how* do you get to *Detroit"* | [L]

so you can *take it* for what it's worth I know . . . I ain't tryin' to preach nothin' to
     nobody I'm just talkin' about *my* feelings about it

and I don't want them *hip white* people coming up to me calling *me* no nigger or
     telling me nigger *jokes*

{emphatic} "I don't like it" [L]

I'm just telling you it's *uncomfortable* to me

I don't like it when *black* people say it to me [<!yeah!>]

I *really don't* no more

it's *nothin'*

it don't *mean* nothin'

so I *love* you all and you can take *that* with you [C:A (sustained)] (1982a)

This confessional moment, a moment of apotheosis and apostasy for a
man who had released albums with titles such as *That Nigger's Crazy* (1974*)
and *Bicentennial Nigger* (1976*), is not without laughter, but for the first
fifty seconds there is none, save for one uncomfortable laugh at the first use
of "nigger." When the applause and cheers come, they are sustained, both at
his avowal to renounce the word and at the bit's conclusion. Laughter isn't
heard until eighty seconds in, with the "white anthropologists" line.

At the beginning of *Quest for the West*, Ron James (2005*), speaking to
his Calgary audience in the year of Alberta's centennial, makes introductory remarks that simultaneously refer to Alberta's humble beginnings, its
current wealth, his Maritime persona, and Ottawa and Toronto as the hegemonic powers.

There you go well well *Calgary* huh

pleasure to be back in the *red meat lands* of the west

to celebrate a hundred years made manifest huh

who'd a thought in the dusty days of turn-of-the-century *Calgary*

that a hundred years *later*

Albertans would be sitting in a multimillion-dollar *Epcor* Centre

watching a homegrown Maritimer

now living in *Toronto*

do a show about *them*

for a network owned by *Ottawa* [L→A] (James 2005*)

However one chooses to interpret this, and there are a number of possible interpretations, the applause appears to indicate that for the participants the context of this performance is indicative of a notable, unlikely,

and unifying confluence of events. A more explicit moment occurs a few minutes later, just after James makes light of then Leader of the Opposition Stephen Harper's immovable hair and his need for "a makeover from *Queer Eye for the Straight Guy*":

> Course he lost on the *same-sex* marriage thing
>
> oh glad *that's* over with
>
> about *time* huh
>
> *such* a fuss about that that it's gonna
>
> *destroy* the sanctity of the institution
>
> look
>
> if the sanctity of the institution can survive the 40 percent shit-kicking *divorce* rates gave it over the last fifty years
>
> surely two people *tying* the knot 'cause they *believe in it* sounds like a *vote of confidence* to me
>
> I don't know huh [A (sustained)]
>
> besides
>
> after *twenty years* together it all boils down to not passing wind in *bed* and who stole the friggin' blankets *anyway* [L] (2005*)

When I followed James around on tour, it was between the filming of this special in September and its airing in December. Much of his new western material was included, including the above routine. Although it went over well in the two Halifax shows and in Glace Bay, it did not work in Pictou. I asked him about it that evening.

IB The same-sex marriage joke works in a similar way in that you always have that sort of . . .

RJ went quiet tonight

IB yeah

and you comment on the quietness

RJ well

IB | ooh, a polite smattering of Maritime applause |

RJ oh great one good one

I think those are important things to say

I mean that's where you learn

that . . .

that's where you learn that it's more than *laughs*

to get back to your first question

you know you start *off* getting *laughs*

and then when you know that's ... *part* of it
you've actualized that part of yourself
that you can get away from a *kitchen*
or away from a *classroom*
and step up to stage and get *laughs*
then you realize
what are you going to get your laughs on
and that's what separates the men from the *boys*
you're going to content yourself with your forty-five minutes
like 85 percent of the comedians in the country do
and because they've been doing it for twenty years figure that the boons
are *theirs*
sorry man
not part of the *equation*
what are you going to *talk* about
what are you going to *say*
and I happen to think that the role of the comedian is to be *progressive*
not to be reactionary
some people support ...
some people *delude* themselves into thinking ...
I mean
there's a couple of comedians out there who are *very accomplished* comedians
but they're *intransigent*
not *progressive*
they're not moving history *forward*
not *proactive*
reactionary
I don't want to go there (James 2005a)

Until October of 2006, Nova Scotia was the only province in Canada that still had strict laws prohibiting Sunday shopping. James had developed a joke on the topic, one which again worked in Halifax and Glace Bay but fell flat in conservative Pictou. An addition to the joke, which reflected on the availability of casinos and video lottery terminals on a Sunday, went over reasonably well in Halifax but didn't work well in Glace Bay.

RJ You can be subversive here
I just think you *have to* umm ...
be uh ...

a little more *careful* how you do it

you've got to *run the ball* a little bit

and before you know it you're *throwing long* and they're *catching it* with you

I mean you know uh and uh . . .

I mean you know the Sunday *shopping* thing's pretty exciting I'm playing around

with these days you know

I mean that's my new favorite *joke*

| Sunday *shopping*

before you know it

the *coloreds* will have the vote |[12]

IB   Yeah that's a great joke

RJ   *thank you*

and it's *everything*

and I think that the Maritimes have been their own worst enemy

I've lived away for *twenty-five* years

and I *love* it here

IB   I think it was on the uh . . .

the *Saturday* show

where you took the Sunday *shopping* thing

and then you added the comments about

well they still have the *casinos* and the video lot . . .

the *VLTs*

RJ   Right

IB   and y'know people are spending the *money*

that they're not able to spend on *Sunday*

RJ   but that's a joke I *love* man

IB   well exactly but how . . .

RJ   but how 'bout *that* nine hundred people going quiet

don't you *think* about that

don't you *think* that y'know

you can't buy groceries for your family on *Sunday* but you can lose every fucking

penny on a *VLT*

IB   on Sunday

RJ   you can lose every penny on *Sunday*

don't you make the *connection*

and that's where I think Atlantic Canadians are *fooling* themselves

[. . .]

I was *surprised* that's why I stopped doing that joke I did it twice and I thought it was

an excellent *tag* a thinker's *tag* (James 2005a)

When a comment is not met with laughter, it is sometimes intentional. Silence can be a natural condition of a setup, such as the silence of the audience as they listen to Pryor's routine. Applause is a validation for something other than the humorous: it validates that what has been said is "true" and ought to be affirmed as such. On the other hand, something that is met with silence—when all cues by the stand-up comedian indicate that laughter was anticipated—calls the routine into question. For James, the problem was not the joke, it was an audience not prepared to listen, not ready to accept that the premise he was espousing was true.

Earlier I spoke of the benefits for the study of stand-up comedy of employing the contemporary folkloristic discourse surrounding genre and generic classification without engaging in a "genre-spotting" exercise. In the flow of talk that comprises the stand-up comedy routine, there are times when the talk is an incontestable truth, times when it is an occasion for questioning and engaging with the truth proposition, and times when it is not true, but in the sense of "fiction," not "falsehood."

Myths are incontestably true: they are foundational, and were they not true they would undermine the very constituency and existence of the group itself. To challenge them is to threaten one's continued membership within that group. Myths—the violence and ignorance of Americans, by contrast with us Canadians; the inherent selflessness of mothers; the legacy of slavery; that there are no better audiences than New York audiences—can elicit no reaction other than assent within that group context, and myths are met not with laughter but with applause and calls of approval. The performance context of the stand-up comedy venue, where amplification is provided to the performer, doesn't allow for much more nuanced response than this and, given the cumulative desire to maintain a framework of non-consequentiality, those in the audience who do dissent tend to do so more by keeping silent. In a different context, myths can be more greatly scrutinized. Whereas myths are third-person narratives, one can infer the same sense of incontestability when the narratives are in the first person (testimonies) or are non-narrative belief statements.

Having established him- or herself as operating within the worldview of the group by reference to myth, the comedian can immediately turn around and directly challenge myth, the deeply held convictions. At this point dissent is anticipated, but those who approve of the comedian's counter-position are able to vocalize it, so there is a mix of both approval and opprobrium. The talk has become dialogic insofar as it is dialectic: truth is now ambiguous and subject to negotiation, and we are entering the realm of legend. It is also deep play: as it is the most threatening to a sense of operating within the same or a contiguous worldview, it is the talk most likely to break the frame of non-consequentiality.

One of its features is how it assumes that the audience, the group, is not homogenous and that there are differences within the group can be explored. The most obvious example is pitting men against women, where a comedian, of either gender, makes a generalization, typically unflattering, about the opposite gender and immediately elicits an anticipatable response. One needs considerable expertise or considerable accumulated goodwill to keep a performance within or bring a performance back to a "talking shit" frame.

The comedian may also directly challenge other cultural assumptions, ones shared but less central, less integral or foundational, to the group's worldview. He or she is anticipating that some of these will be met simply with laughter, as a fresh perspective is provided on some of the group's peculiarities. Such is the domain of the observational comic, where there is a form of ethnography going forward, as manifested in one half of the ethnographer's adage: making the familiar strange. It still takes the form of the dialectic of legend, but less, it appears, is at stake. The second part of the adage, making the strange familiar, also is in play, as the comedian deliberately adverts to a different experience but demonstrates how it is the same in kind to that of the audience.

Locating in which modes the comedian is operating at any one time will only ever be an interpretation by the exegete. This judgment, however, can be informed by paying attention to the responses of the audience. The stand-up comedian, through his or her words, shifts between speaking for and speaking to the audience, and the performance depends on this risky negotiation.

Discussing each separately is a difficult task precisely because they do not often appear in total isolation: a declarative, testimonial statement is made, and quickly thereafter a more contestable one is made, or a fanciful one that is judged aesthetically. When statements emerge as isolatable—when they are performed distinctly enough that the audience has time to affirm them—they are nevertheless quickly qualified by a follow-up, and their presence only makes sense by virtue of them being qualified. They are setting up a comic moment or series of comic moments, but even though they have that instrumental purpose, they are not dropped once the comic moment has been attempted. Because stand-up comedy is a performance of self and the professional comedian has a professional need to make him- or herself known, these testimonial statements both contribute to the development of a comic persona and emerge from that persona's enactment on stage.

There are times when the comedian loses control over his or her story: something happens in his or her real life and there is both a professional need and, strangely, an obligation to the audience to address it and incorporate it into the narrative, thereby reclaiming control over the story and reassuming, or reiterating the claim to, the social identity of stand-up comedian.

An audience has a certain investment in the life story of someone it has gotten to know through intimate performances. When famous comedians' life events spill out into the public sphere, they are often revisited on the stage. This stems in part because the intimacy between performer and audience and the audience's investment in his or her life story imply a set of mutual rights and responsibilities. Further, the performer must edit the autobiography, providing a version of events over which he or she has greater control.

In effect, the comedian reframes the history as legend. Determining its truth, falsity, or mootness is the purview no longer of an indeterminate, uncontrollable public arena, but of the present audience.

On July 26, 1991, actor Paul Reubens, better known as the character comedian Pee-Wee Herman, was arrested in Sarasota, Florida, for public indecency, specifically, for masturbating while in the audience of an adult movie theatre. Although his critically acclaimed children's show, *Pee-Wee's Playhouse*, had stopped production, its episodes were immediately withdrawn from rerun and syndication, and he quickly became a ubiquitous punch line. On September 5 of that year, he made his first public appearance as a presenter at the 1991 MTV Video Music Awards. Met with a standing ovation, his opening line, "So, heard any good jokes lately?" addressed the issue sufficiently to move beyond it. "I was just hoping I wasn't going to get booed. I had no idea what the reaction would be. I was optimistic, but what was going through my mind was, 'I hope they like me'" (Reubens, qtd. in Horowitz 2007).

In May of 1996, Martin Lawrence was picked up by police for erratic behavior when he was found screaming in the middle of a busy street in the San Fernando Valley section of Los Angeles with a loaded handgun in his pocket (*Jet* 1996). In September of 1999 he fell into a coma while jogging in multiple layers of clothing in extreme heat (*Jet* 1999). Both episodes were revisited in *Runteldat* (Lawrence 2002*), his concert film. The concert began with a brief film about the incidents, with footage taken mainly from media outlets, and in the last third of the concert he addresses them directly, at first creating intentionally teary moments of faux-sincerity, which he then breaks by confessing to simply being high. The routine moves on to discuss how he was indeed carrying a gun and how, when he passed out and subsequently recovered, he was hallucinating so badly that he was taken to hospital rather than to jail, albeit to a padded and locked room.

> I couldn't believe all these things was *happening* to me you know
> my marriage was on the *brink*
> all *kinds* of shit after that
> but before I left the *hospital*
> I got your *love*
> and I *felt* your love
> and your *support* for me [A (sustained)] <u>you know</u>
> you know and it was a *beautiful thing*
> and I thank each and every *one* of you
> it meant a *lot* to me and uh
> it just it just truly meant a *lot* to me
> and I'm *forever* grateful (Lawrence 2002*)

The "facts" of the incident up for negotiation are presented through video evidence, along with the media's interpretation: Lawrence provides his own interpretation and a supposed justification and plea of innocence, and the deliberateness of his display of indignant self-justification is understood by the audience as a cue to take this interpretation as fiction so that his eventual confession and presentation of true events—even with the exaggerated and fantastic flourishes—is accepted. His moments of sincerity, including both the coda of thanking the crowd for loyalty and support and the proverbial "ride this motherfucker till the wheels fall off"—an expression he uses both throughout the performance and in the documentaries that accompany the DVD—are met with prolonged applause, indicating the audience's affirmation. By performing his own version of events, Lawrence assumes control over them, much as Richard Pryor did in *Live on the Sunset Strip* (1982a) after his self-immolation while freebasing, and as Lenny Bruce tried to do following his multiple obscenity convictions, as recorded in *The Lenny Bruce Performance Film* (Bruce 1992*).

When Tig Notaro was diagnosed with breast cancer in August of 2012—following a four-month period that also saw pneumonia, a hospital-contracted *c. difficile* infection, the end of a long-term relationship, and the death of her mother—she appeared on stage for her regularly scheduled show. As she told the audience of her cancer diagnosis, it was the first time many of her friends and fellow performers had heard of it. Her performance was built around two intertwining themes: first, if comedy is tragedy plus time, she was still at tragedy, not having had the time to process; and, second, how vacuous the joke she had been working on about a bee on the highway now seemed. Coming as it did between the diagnosis and the final tests confirming the full extent of the cancer, the narrative is inherently unfinished (mastectomies and chemotherapy have since made her cancer free), and yet the wry observation of her ordeal allowed for a similar reclamation of the experience, punctuated by the extremely positive reaction when she is encouraged to close with the bee joke. The venue happened to record the performance and it was released online within two months (Notaro 2012*).

I have tried to establish in greater detail that the stand-up comedian develops a persona onstage that is both in keeping with the social identity of "stand-up comedian" and recognizably of a particular place and time, so as to be found accessible and acceptable by an audience whether the audience be from his or her group or otherwise. It is adaptable, and what is brought to the stage is not going to be consistent from group to group. As the audience increasingly knows the stand-up comedian through cumulative reputation, the more "performance" aspects of the persona can be dropped, and the potential disjuncture between on- and offstage personality becomes lessened.

Both as a technique of building an identifiable persona and as a consequence of having been accepted as a legitimate voice, the stand-up comedian can also express ideas onstage that either are not said specifically for laughter or, if they fail to elicit laughter because they have transgressed in some manner, are not retracted. Like between intimates, differing opinions can strain but, with an overriding goodwill, can be typically expressed without irreparable damage to the relationship.

CHAPTER 5
What Is the Stand-Up Comedian?: Intimate Other

My job essentially is
thinking up *goofy shit* [L]
it comes right down to that
I mean *you* don't have time all week [L]
so
signing *checks*
going to the *laundry*
answering the *door*
| Herbie come *here* |
a *lot* of interruptions
[. . .]
so I think up the goofy shit and I come on the weekend and *report* it to you
—**George Carlin,** *Toledo Window Box*

Starting from the claim of being "a" stand-up comedian, and all that implies, a comedian locates him- or herself in a specific relationship with the audience, beyond that of the complementary set of comedian and audience. For the most part, these additional social identities are also complementary sets: comedians are presented as venue- or medium-appropriate based in large part on an informed perception of an aggregate of the social identities of the audience. When that complementarity is not self-evident—as when a white comedian performs at an ostensibly African American venue or a southerner performs in the urban North—the stand-up comedian, in collaboration with the emcee, will typically address the difference. This is developed into a persona, which builds on this initial effort at biography and creates a larger and more complex set of social identities beyond the "stand-up comedian" one. In this manner the stand-up comedian is seen as "inside" enough to be accepted as an intimate, as permitted to speak frankly with, to, and, to a certain extent, for the group—that what he or she has to say is relevant. Now I turn to what the comedian says, not in an effort at autobiography but as a detached observer: in this manner, the stand-up comedian is seen as "outside" enough that what he or she has to say is interesting.

As with most comedians, Ron James's skills at cultivating a national audience lie in most part on respecting the worldview of not one but a variety of particular local or regional audiences and, thus, having in his repertoire material that can fall into one of three categories: material that is more or less the same text irrespective of place, material that is adapted for use in a particular region or locality but can play more or less anywhere, and material that is specific to a region or locality. These categories are by no means absolutes, as repertoires are dynamic not static constructs, and the professional comedian's imperative for producing "new" material further exacerbates the need for interpreting repertoires as dynamic: region-specific material that has proven successful may be tried out and adapted in a new locale; adaptable material may find a variation that works trans-regionally and thus find a "fixed-form"; and extemporaneous material—that which is not yet part of a repertoire or that allows for the immediate and drastic reformulation of a set piece—is unclassifiable.

James begins his shows with some location- or time-specific material: in the first of the Halifax shows, for example, which was on Remembrance Day, he saluted veterans (which was met with applause from the audience) and spoke of people's spurious suggestions to him that he purchase painter Alex Colville's South Shore house, which had recently been put on the market. At the second Halifax show (at which I was able to take much more substantial notes), he began by saying that he bought three lobsters when he landed at Halifax Airport from the Clearwater store, which cost him $32.50: "Anything I can do to keep the Risleys in real estate," a reference to John Risley, president and founder of Clearwater Seafood. In Glace Bay, where he lived the first nine years of his life, his show began with a ten-minute reverie of his childhood, mentioning local businesses and pubs on Commercial Street, his own experiences going to movies at the Savoy Theatre (the show's venue), and the barrenness of the Sydney to Glace Bay highway. It ended with a query about luxury cruise liners' passengers docking at Sydney and being presented with the Sydney Tar Ponds, Canada's most polluted site. And in Pictou, he spoke about the emergence of the mile-long box-store strip in New Glasgow (a larger municipality on the main highway where his hotel was located) and the drive from Cape Breton (which allowed for a flurry of *blasons populaire*).

I asked James how he finds this material, especially in contexts outside of his regular, lived experience:

RJ Well . . .
    I read the *papers*
    talk to *people*
    and I go for a *run*
    I run 6 to 8 k every city I'm *in*
    and it slides into my *head*
    stays at the front of my *head*
    in fact my new special called *Quest for the West* was written just *as* that
IB one long run
RJ   well
    three different tours out to *Alberta*
    I'd accumulated enough *material*
    but the trick *is*
    how do I make that stuff about *Alberta*
    how do I make the specific *universal*
    and that's what we'll see in December with the *numbers*
    and uh yeah
    so that's how I do it y'know
    and I uh
    I *talk* to people
    I like to *engage* people y'know
    someone will tell me something I'll write a *word* down
    someone will tell me something else I'll write *another* word down
    and you start putting this *puzzle* together
    [. . .]
    I usually do make a concerted and serious effort to let these people know that they
    matter (James 2005a)

I was interested in how James framed this engagement as "letting people know they matter"; it was a theme he referred to throughout the interview:

I think they're going to come see *somebody*
who's going to take the time to *get them*
that's the *best* compliment I got out west
a transplanted Atlantic Canadian who'd been there for *twenty-five* years

and made his *millions*
Jesus
he said thanks for taking the time to understand us
it's one of the best *compliments* I ever got
you take the time to *understand*
and uh
it's getting *harder*
because I'm trying to rediscover a place again for the *third time* (James 2005a)

The personal relationship between performer and audience is established through this rapport, which can be deemed a sharing of worldview
or, more precisely, the performed demonstration of a shared worldview. In
the short term, there is an occupational advantage to establishing this rapport, pertaining to the techniques of stand-up comedy performance, for
within the performance context it provides an emic and esoteric framework
for the interpretation of what is to follow; in the long term, there is a professional advantage, for goodwill is cumulative. That a personal relationship
has advantages does not necessarily imply that it is somehow disingenuous,
a charge James is ready to defend:

but *every* town I go to
I *try* to . . .
I try to let them know that they *matter*
it's *important*
it's a *big* country
and it's *important* that they matter
it's *important* to me that
they know I *think* they matter
and uh . . .
'cause it was never about *fame* y'know
it was about doing what I'm *supposed* to be doing
and if
if people find that uh . . .
kind of . . .
dubious
fuck 'em
I know when my heart rings *true*
and that's one of the good things about *stand-up*
it *validates* the life journey (James 2005a)

Another long-term advantage of specific material is how it can, with time and thought, evolve into routines that work elsewhere. He often makes the claim that every visit to a place provides him with new material.[1] Presumably, the vast majority of that new material is never performed more than once, but that which lasts can be retained, honed, and developed into something more permanent in the repertoire.

There are two advantages to having routines that are "universal" (which means the broadest range of viable markets for the particular stand-up comedian). Most obviously, it prevents the comedian from having to write new material for every locality and region. It also forms the basis for material that can be mediated to a larger audience. This material will be performed before a situated audience when it is recorded for broadcast, so the imperative is to make it funny for them while simultaneously making it funny for an indeterminate yet historically situated listener, different in space and, most likely, time.

Universal material tends to fall into two categories: it is either rooted in a national or international participation in and understanding of mediated culture (politics, popular culture) that is not particular to a region or locality or rooted in quotidian living (bodily functions, the differences between men and women, generational differences), which may have local manifestations but tends to be recognizable irrespective of place. Because the universal is the material that makes it to the media, it is the most easily accessible to the student of stand-up comedy. A performance will often begin with localized material before launching into universal material: this holds true even for recorded and mediated comedy, although the "localized" will not be so esoteric as to not engage the indeterminate viewer or listener. Rather, it will more likely build on exoteric understandings about the region or its people, known to the locals and non-locals alike but not necessarily believed by the locals themselves.

Conversely, the issue of what is "universal" is a subjective one and, when the centers of media production are limited and the live audiences are drawn from that area, their particular culture is understood as normative.

I asked James about his universal material:

RJ Well my *universal* material
    computers
    Future Shop
    anything about people walking through the modern *world*
    that plays *anywhere*
    old ladies in church with the *hat*[2]

IB   yeah
RJ   *kills*
    never *didn't* kill
    but you know where it *doesn't* kill
    at a *corporate* function
    too *stuffy*
IB   do you think that's *why*
    I'm *interested*
    are the corporate *functions* too stuffy
RJ   *yeah*
IB   or maybe the context of *church* is too stuffy
RJ   *maybe* the context of church is too stuffy or they're too ...
    yeah I *think* that it's got to do with that
    farts are not ...
    farts are not material for a *corporate* crowd
    but farts are good to have in your *show* you know
    [...]
    yeah so there's some things that don't play *well* in certain *contexts*
    but *Future Shop* always works um ...
    did I do my *wave and boat* thing[3]
IB   not today
RJ   not tonight but I've *done it* you've *seen it*
IB   yeah
RJ   that *works*
    the things that usually work *anywhere*
    are things that everybody's *experienced*
    futility in the face of change
IB   computer crashing
RJ   all the *technology* stuff you know that uh ...
    I think that *red meat* joke is going to work anywhere
    I think the *smart car* is going to work anywhere
    I think that the *Greenpeace* people coming door-to-door is going to work anywhere
    hangover jokes
    sex works anywhere you know like that joke that I closed with tonight[4]
    you know *that* works anywhere
IB   Air *Transat* material
    Air *Canada* material
RJ   yeah
    you know I'll tell you
    aficionados usually say that um ... airplane food jokes

and we can't make Air Canada airplane *food* jokes anymore 'cause they're not *serving* it
they say that airplane material is the sign of the *amateur*
just like talking about *dogs and cats*
and I always say it's *how* you deliver it
and *how* you say it
and I think that's also . . .
something that separates me from the *pack*
is *how* it's delivered
IB yeah it's in the context of a larger *narrative*
RJ *larger* narrative
a *story* (James 2005a)

In press releases, it is the universal material that is mentioned, as in the following two examples, for his 2002 and 2005 fall tours of Atlantic Canada, respectively.

With intelligent observations and a Maritimer's folksy irreverence, Ron James skewers everything from American consumer culture and the mosquito-driven torment of a northern camping trip to the financial trials of aging Canadian baby boomers and his own growing uselessness in the face of rampant technological change. (*Halifax Daily News* 2002; *Corner Brook Western Star* 2002)

James calls the show a rocket-fuelled rant on a world out of whack, from a man in collision with cosmic forces beyond his control. In the show, James bounces from the war in Iraq to home renovations; mid-life meltdowns to airport security; family vacations to Future Shop "blue shirts"; flatulent elders in church to party-hearty camping trips of youth, cutting a wide swath from past to present and back again. (*Corner Brook Western Star* 2005)

The "universality" of universal material is a conceit. With respect to popular culture and politics, these universal materials are particular to larger markets as opposed to small ones, and they are perhaps thus less idiosyncratic, but, without being pedantic, they do not transcend language and largely do not transcend the nation. There are exceptions, of course: Billy Connolly and Chris Rock have each undertaken international tours, and Montreal's Just for Laughs Festival brings comedians from around the world. To take material that works nationally to an international stage, one needs to adapt it in a manner similar to how one adapts material when moving from a regional to a national stage.

Midway between the universal routines and region- or locality-specific routines are those with "replaceable" punch lines or tags: fixed routines with a local reference thrown in. In one example, James describes the carnival rides of his youth. In the Maritimes, he evokes the Bill Lynch Show, the travelling amusement company based in Mount Uniacke, Nova Scotia, which was greeted with applause. When I saw him in Newfoundland a few years previous, he did not use the Lynch name, and as it appears in *The Road between My Ears* (James 2003*), it is simply "the midway." He speaks of the fear instilled by the Ferris wheel:

> That midway *flaunted* safety standards
> the Ferris wheel had bit of flesh and *clothing* hanging off it [L]
> *still* the scariest ride of *all*
> the *Ferris wheel*
> when you're a kid they'd keep you in that *bucket*
> that's what the ride is essentially a *bucket*
> at the very star top
> forever
> jeez I'm watching *weather patterns* change over the *Gulf Stream* [L]
> family of cretins in the bucket in *front* of me
> rocking it *back* and *forth* [mimes rocking with a gormless expression] [L]
>   (James 2003*)

In a local performance in Glace Bay, he tags this bit by adding, "Easy to spot the folks from New Waterford" (a town between Sydney and Glace Bay on the old coastal road), while in Pictou it was folks from River John, a town on the Northumberland Strait a few kilometers to the west. In another example, he performs a routine that was written for *Quest for the West*:

> But I'm *told*
> the most *dangerous animal* in the parks hmm
> mother elk during *calving* season
> and they'll drop a calf *anywhere* too y'know
> makes no never mind to *nature*
> grocery *store* parking *lot*
> *bowling* alley
> Laundro*mat*
> *street* corner
> they'll just *have at her* huh

hard to make a deposit at the *ATM* machine when there's a
nine-hundred-pound mother blockin' the *doorway*
lickin' the placenta off her *spawn* (James 2005*)

In Halifax, on the second night, James tagged this with "it's worse than Spryfield" (a poor neighborhood of Halifax), while in Pictou he described it as "worse than an afternoon in Stellarton," another town just down the road.

I used to have a *joke*
when the people *beside* me
when I was camping were playing *splits*
Mum and Dad uh . . .
| Mum and Dad are playin' *splits*
kids are in the middle of the *road*
guttin' a squirrel on a *Ouija* board
easy to spot the folks *from*
blank |
[. . .]
but see those are *just*
that's certain tricks of the *trade* y'know ah
and it's *always* good to
take a shot at the town down the road or something like that
so I like that
and they like it *too*
and *they* like it and even the people from *there* like it (James 2005a)

The flexibility of such material is self-evident, and it allows for a reaffirmation of place without diverting too far from established routines. It also works without references, which allows its use in national broadcast performances.

Another routine, "Paid in Game," can serve as an example of a similar yet distinct flexibility. The routine runs roughly as follows:

Five hundred people in the town
two last names [L]
there was a couple in the front row
came backstage after the gig
handed me a brown paper bag dripping blood

put my hand in
pulled out a seven-and-a-half-pound sirloin tip moose roast
you know you've made it in Canadian show business when the locals are paying
        you in butchered game
don't get those perks playing Las Vegas
people give you a brown paper bag dripping blood there
probably has the head of a teamster in it[5]

Although the text is performed more or less verbatim from performance to performance, what varies is the setting for the anecdote: at the first show in Halifax, it was said to have happened only the previous week, following the show in Grand Falls Windsor, Newfoundland; at the second, it took place in the generic "North"; in Glace Bay, it was by Lake Superior, near Lake Kujjubujjibak (a made-up name reminiscent of communities such as Kashabowie and Shebandowan); and in Pictou, it was in the same Lake Kujjubujjibak, with proximity to Superior not noted. The variations were not dictated by the particular performance context but by where they could fall in a performance: as he spoke of travels in smaller communities, whether that be the interior of Newfoundland or Northern Ontario or Alberta or the territories, he could interject that routine without introducing a notion that clashed with the verisimilitude of that particular larger narrative arc.

When I asked him about this routine in particular, he at first dismissed it by saying,

That's just *laziness*
it's got nothing to do with actual *credibility*
it's all about um . . .
not *laziness*
but it's all about uh
where it falls *in*
it's a *technical* thing (James 2005a)

I am inclined to equate this "technical thing" with oral-formulaic composition, such as that suggested by Milman Parry and Albert Lord (see Lord 1960; Taft 2006), and how for comedians the "routine" is akin to "the formula" in a number of ways. Most particularly, for present purposes, with certain routines in hand, substitutions can be made on the basis not of syllabic but of conceptual similarity; the most stable routines will be those with the most common ideas; and the stability of routines is almost wholly a result of utility. Like formulas, a routine should not be considered as such until for the particular individual performer it is established through regular use in his or her performances.

The complementary issues of common ideas and of utility raise the question of why these routines work in different contexts. We can assume they are funny, insofar as they invariably get a solid round of laughter from the audience (which is the only measure we need ever apply). And routines that vary in response to a local *blason populaire* easily connect an observation with place. (One could argue that the "Paid in Game" routine at the first Halifax show, being as it was performed during the opening few minutes of the performance amid a larger routine on being in Newfoundland the previous week, may also work as *blason populaire*.) However, a formula routine that is employed variously from performance to performance and that is adapted not only for an audience but for use in different places within a larger routine indicates its utility in illustrating a specific theme about place, and its frequency of use indicates that the theme is one James wishes to apply to a variety of contexts.

So I was unsure of James's dismissal of the variations on the "Paid in Game" routine, and I pressed him on the point, going over how it was able to work not only in different settings but also shoehorned into or alongside different narratives. Why does it work?

RJ I think the *visual*
    I think the uh . . .
    the *wonderful* uh . . .
    truth about Canada that we're an *affable* country
    that somebody *would* walk backstage and give me a bag of meat
    and it's *true*
    they gave me a bag of *meat*
    [. . .]
IB does that joke play in *Toronto* the same way
RJ yeah it *does* it *does*
    it plays in *Toronto* in a different context than it plays here
    it plays in *Toronto* that
    | oh *wow*
    this guy has gone to the far points of *frontier* |
    'cause it goes back to that Atwood or Northrop *Frye* thing again
    that we know the North is *there*
    we know it *exists*

I mean I mean *Roots* [clothing] built its credibility up on

I mean it's become an urban *style* thing now but it

it did have the *canoe* for a long time

it did have that

that uh

that *fur trade* connotation the *warmth* the *fleece* . . .

the *hearken* back to an earlier day of y'know

of campfire *camaraderie*

I think that motif is really *strong* in Canada

I mean I'm talking to you now I'm looking at that *maple leaf* at the foot of that thing

[a small brochure display rack] you know

and these are motifs that are in our *DNA*

and I think

somebody providing a *traveller* with a bag of *meat*

must have a kind of *resonance* you know

and I just

I just know it as a *truth*

and I had to leave it outside my hotel room *door*

every *night*

when I travelled *Superior*

but *since* then

that's the *first* bag of meat I got

I've gotten meat *everywhere*

in fact my wife in *Toronto* said

| please don't bring any more wild *game* home |

and I was up in Cold Lake *Alberta*

and they brought me half a side of *elk*

IB   [L] how do you keep *that* fresh for the drive home

RJ   well it was all frozen so I flew home on the plane so that was *cool*

but it's, it's uhh

that's one of the *mysteries* of this country

why does that work in *Pictou* and *Glace Bay*

and *Alberta* and *everywhere*

why does it work in *BC*

why does it work in *Toronto*

it's because I think Canadians have a deference for the *wild*

which gets back to. . .

and I think we . . .

even though 80 *percent* of us still live in cities

and less than 5 percent have *seen* the North
I think that that *mythology* of drawing sustenance from the *land*
it still *holds* with us
and I think we're probably going to be reaching for it *more* as the twentieth century moves
on and technology *overwhelms* us
that's *my* call on it anyway (James 2005a)

James's major routines, the themes he appears to be exploring, are presented through a performed autobiography of an inveterate traveller moving through Canada's regions: the working comedian qua contemporary explorer, whose movements toward "the four points of frontier" (one of his stock phrases) is no different from that of either "the Great Celtic diaspora" or a pan-Canadian mythos.

As a working comedian, James has to strike a balance between artistic needs and audience expectations: one could reframe this by saying that what marks the difference between professional and amateur is precisely this ability to balance the two.

Like in conversation or legendry or any interpersonal exchange, a factor in stand-up comedy is the establishment of some form of relationship between teller and listener: the comedian needs to provide credentials that the audience will accept so that he or she may speak to this group on this subject. Some frame this permission-granting through the term "license" (Koziski 1984; Mintz 1998), but for our purposes, this concept is ultimately too rigid. Instead, the audience accepts the performer as an intimate and, as we do among friends, permits him or her a certain latitude in opinions and the freedom to express them, for the audience knows that, like our friends, the comedian means well.

Whereas when we speak of the stand-up comedian as a type we intimate a *general* permission, when we speak of a specific comedian, there is a process whereby a *specific* permission is sought and granted. It is granted by a two-fold expectation of both *relevance*—understanding the worldview of the group by demonstrating some shared participation therein—and *perspective*, having a particular insight into that worldview.

There are a number of strategies used to effect this permission. First of all, as was discussed in the two last chapters, by claiming the social identity "stand-up comedian," the performer anticipates that his or her talk will be interpreted in a particular way. By virtue of allowing him or her a space to perform, those who run the performance venue suggest to any potential audience that the claim to the stand-up comedian social identity is justified. Local media, if a possibility, can be used to communicate the stand-up comedian's persona and begin to frame his or her particular perspective. If media is not available, the introduction by the host, emcee, or compère extends whatever goodwill the audience has shown to him or her to the comedian. By the time a performer arrives on the stage he or she is, to some nascent extent, "known" by the audience, insofar as they have been provided with enough information for an initial framework of interpretation. Reputation is cumulative, so an established comedian does not need (although may avail themselves of) the assistance; an unknown comedian relies heavily on such assistance.

Once the comedian hits the stage, however, he or she cannot rely solely on the continued goodwill of the audience. The stand-up comedy performance is a process through which relevance and perspective are simultaneously and continually reaffirmed. Above I referred to stand-up comedy performances being met principally with laughter but also with solemn affirmation. To briefly reiterate, throughout a performance the comedian often intersperses declarative statements that are not meant to be met with laughter: they serve as small testimonial moments to explicitly and directly inform the audience of the comedian's worldview.

In this manner the comedian locates him- or herself (or, more accurately, locates the comic material) within an identifiable framework, within a worldview of conscience, and, by virtue of them now "knowing" him or her, is accepted (or not) by the audience members as an intimate. Another strategy the comedian employs is locating him- or herself within a worldview of historical space and place, becoming a chronicler of place that is recognizably that of, or consistent with the experiences of, the audience. In that measure I refer to stand-up comedy as occasionally engaging in "vernacular ethnography."

Having disparaged the "stand-up as . . ." genre of academic approaches to stand-up comedy and comedians, it may at first appear disingenuous of me to ascribe an implicit function such as "stand-up comedian as vernacular ethnographer." I do not want to suggest that the surface purpose of stand-up comedy—entertainment or amusement—is somehow subsidiary to a deeper purpose. I am more interested in the techniques stand-up comedians employ in order to effect amusement.

"Ethnography" is a term that should not be bandied about carelessly, so I wish to be cautious. However we choose to define ethnography, we can most likely agree that it is not only a focused experiencing with the aim of understanding but also, and more directly for our purposes, the representation and communication of that experiencing and understanding, typically through words. Furthermore, that representation implies a hermeneutic of honesty or authenticity or even objectivity, however futile or in vain we may perceive that ultimately to be as a goal.

The comedian in his or her vernacular ethnography is not subject to the same constraints and set of expectations as the academic ethnographer: he or she is subject, however, to a parallel set of expectations, that of ongoing relevance to the audience. "Verisimilitude" is the order of the day: the account is expressly subjective but implies a recognizable truthfulness therein. The comedian is judged relevant by the audience in part by the accuracy of the worldview presented: it needs to be credible. Even though they are trying for laughter, comedians often honestly render representations of a particular moment and place in time.[6] I suggest that this is the case for the stand-up comedian's text as well. I thus refer to "vernacular ethnography."

The ethnographic proverb of "making the strange familiar and the familiar strange" can certainly be applied to stand-up comedy.[7] The latter half of the proverb—making the familiar strange—should be virtually self-evident: observational comedy, wherein the everyday is subjected to scrutiny and questioning, is the basis of much contemporary stand-up comedy.

In *Hip Hop America*, Nelson George discusses Richard Pryor's "The Wino and the Junkie" routine and its depiction of "the wino as a city-living country wit and the junkie as a wasted young urban zombie. The split is significant in that Pryor, an artist/cocaine addict himself, provided nuance to the difference between addiction to heroin and alcohol and how it would eventually affect the entire black community" (1998, 36). In the conclusion to his liner notes to *Classic Gold*, a two-disc release of George Carlin's first three albums (*FM & AM*, *Class Clown*, and *Occupation: Foole*), Tony Hendra writes:

> What is striking about these albums twenty years on, are not just those things we have come to expect from Carlin . . . but their warmth and range. They teem with people, none of them good or bad, but simply authentic, the voices of kids, cops, priests, parents, old folks, barflies, the sounds of the street, blaring radios, tinny commercials, rinky-dink dreams, posturing gangs, in a word, the whole wonderful, lumpy, loony mess we call humanity. (in Carlin 1993*)

This observational role is used in the promotional materials for comedians, as evidenced by three examples taken from the back covers of DVD releases:

Whether suffering Lake Superior salt licking moose, the torments of home renovation hell, or brain bursting futility at the hands of techno-speaking computer geeks, Ron [James] keeps a comic's eye peeled for the absurd and a poet's ear tuned for the language. (DVD of James 2003*)

Ellen DeGeneres: Here and Now features the kind of humor that first made her a star, offering her offbeat insights into everyday life. (DVD of DeGeneres 2003*)

In this live performance before a sold-out crowd [Steve Harvey] continues to draw on his childhood experiences, observations about life and human nature. (DVD of Harvey 1997*).

This comprises the "universal material" as discussed above.

For the former, making the strange familiar, one can cite as extreme examples Richard Pryor's experience of setting himself on fire while free-basing (recounted in Pryor 1982a*) or Henry Rollins's near-molestation as a nine-year-old on holiday in Greece (recounted in Rollins 1992b*), both of which were represented on stage in routines that were ultimately accepted by the audience (inasmuch as there was laughter and applause). In my interview with James, he phrased it in terms of making the specific universal: the particular episode does not have to coincide exactly with the life experience of the audience, but it registers as a recognizably analogous experience.

Stand-up comedy audiences are historically situated. When the stand-up comedian is local, he or she builds on esoteric knowledge, demonstrating and reaffirming insider status. When the stand-up comedian is not a local, it is a standard technique to describe that place as he or she sees it, which both addresses "foreignness" or "otherness" and demonstrates an effort to make a connection with the day-to-day world of the local audience.

Furthermore, in the case of recorded or broadcast stand-up comedy, which is invariably a recording of a live performance in front of a specific audience, there is a qualification to the notion of "local": the performance cannot be so esoteric as to be incomprehensible to someone from outside if it is meant to be appreciated (found funny and thus commercially viable). The performance typically builds not only on esoteric knowledge but on reflective esoteric knowledge: not only what the group thinks of itself but what it supposes others think of it (Jansen 1959, 206). A related approach is to talk of themes that are not particular to the specific audience but are shared with the anticipated larger audience, which is regional, national, or international. This includes exoteric knowledge about the site of the recording, but also includes politics, popular culture, or—perhaps most universal—the differences between men and women.

For his *Kill the Messenger* special, Chris Rock (2008*) recorded performances in New York, London, and Johannesburg; these were then edited together into one contiguous performance. In each city he started with localized material, although only the South African narrative was included in the final product. The following is from the London show, where he expressly admits to doing something "ethnographic."[8]

> I've been here a couple of days man y'know
> and I had to study the *culture*
> of the people
> had to figure what makes *you guys* tick
> what makes *you guys* y'know feel good
> and I realized you guys drink a *lot* [l] of alcohol
> you drink a *ton* of alcohol
> you motherfuckers *draenk* [l]
> you don't drink you *draenk* [l]
> that's right 'cause you got to drink a *lot* of alcohol
> to think that *darts* is a *sport* [L] (Rock 2008*)

In Johannesburg Rock performs a routine about a photo safari, where his family's tracker is able to locate animals by their droppings, when a group of white tourists start taking photos of him, presumably because their tracker is able to locate his family from a pile of chicken bones. It is, for all intents and purposes, a joke: an isolatable unit that can be extricated from its performance context and still be rendered sensible with little editing. However, within the performance context, and through his use of the first and second persons, and the third-person use for *white people* ("they had a tracker") he plays on both esoteric and exoteric understandings of the South African context while simultaneously presenting himself as operating within it, however touristically (Rock 2008*).

As I have been framing the question, part of the stand-up comedian's craft is establishing a sense of contiguity between his or her worldview and that of the audience. Simultaneously, he or she presents a different perspective on that worldview. By the former, comedians prove themselves relevant; by the latter, they prove themselves interesting. The concern of this section is primarily with the former: it is a vocational necessity for comedians to depict a recognizable and realistic cultural backdrop against which the comedy can unfold. The process is similar for when the comedian is communicating to his or her "own" group (i.e., as has been discussed above, groups whose aggregate set of social identities is largely contiguous with the comedian's own and differences are, in the main, elided) and for when the comedian is communicating across "marked" otherness (when differences in region, ethnicity, sexuality, gender, or other social identities are adverted to and inform the insider/outsider perspective). In either instance, the depiction must be one that bears a great degree of verisimilitude to the audience's experience and expectations, which can then be flouted.

I can present one simple example of how the folklorist could use the work of a stand-up comedian as ethnographic material. The children's game Buck Buck dates back to Roman times: it is one of the depicted activities in Pieter Bruegel's *Children's Games*. In *The Folkgames of Children*, Brian Sutton-Smith provides this description from Adair, Canterbury, New Zealand, from 1890.

> The first boy leans against the school wall with his arms horizontal against the school and his head and face looking towards the ground and his back in an horizontal position. The next boy leans against him in the same way with his head down and his back horizontal, and so on back to the last boy. Then another [player] who is going to call the tune jumps on the back of the boy at the end of the row . . . and works his way along the backs of all the boys until he gets to the [one] against the school. (1972, 192)

In this next version, there is a guessing game, with the boy on top asking how many fingers he is holding up and the boy below guessing. Edith Fowke provides a similar description, although she notes that the guessing-game aspect is not common in Canada:

> This game is played by two teams of five or more each. One team forms a long back beginning with one boy, the "cushion," standing with his back to a fence or wall. One member of his team then bends forward from the waist and nestles his head and right shoulders in the side and belly of the first boy. The next boy also bends forward and leans his right shoulder against the rear of the second boy, and grasps him firmly by the waist. The others form up behind him, each placing his head on the side opposite to that of the boy in front, until the whole team forms a long back. When they are ready, they shout, tauntingly, "Buck,

Buck number one," The first member of the other team then races towards their backs from some distance away, leapfrogs over their endman, and lands as far along the backs as he can. The first team then calls for "Buck, Buck, number two," and so on until either all the Bucks are on top of the Backs, in which case the Backs are the winners, or the Backs break under the weight of the Bucks, in which case the Bucks are the winners. (1988, 76)

Complementing these two accounts is the following account from post-war Philadelphia, from Bill Cosby's 1967 album *Revenge*.

> Now
> I wanna tell you
> this story
> this is a game that we played when we were
> when we were kids and it's called
> *Buck Buck* we played it in Philadelphia
> Buck Buck
> now
> you people out here on the West Coast probably know nothing about it
> in New York it's called Johnny on the Pony and
> other things
> it's where fo[ur] uh five kids line up you see
> and they bend over
> they're in a straight line
> and they bend over
> and one kid grabs a fence or wall or pole holds onto that
> the next kid puts his right arm around his waist you see
> bends over tucks his head under
> and you've got five guys lined up exactly like that [whoosh sound]
> so they all look like a *long* horse
> now,
> the object of the game is that one at a time
> one by one
> kids come running up and they say
> | [high pitched, Lone Ranger voice] *Buck Buck Number One Come in* |
> and they run up leap in the air and land on the horse [pumph]
> and they keep going
> BAM BAM BAM
> until they collapse the horse you see

now

that's the object of the game then you count how many kids you held then you
        go back and forth you see

now

we had

the champion Buck Buck team of the world

when I tell you we played Buck Buck there was nobody that whipped us any-
        where man

and you can tell kids that play a lot of Buck Buck because

they're built like this [L] <u>you see</u>

and their legs are only four inches long [L]

that's all they have

'cause they've been *crushed* so much [pumph] [L] (Cosby 1967*, "Buck, Buck")[9]

It may not be immediately apparent, but not until the description of the "kids that play a lot of Buck Buck," over a minute into the routine, is there any laughter, which would seem an inordinate amount of time. Cosby has repeatedly been heralded as one who was able to communicate an urban, black, lower-middle-class childhood in a manner that made it recognizable to a broad swathe of his audience. In other words he made the strange familiar and made the specific universal, largely through an effort at authentic representation. That he could then build upon that ethnography and develop scenarios of appropriate incongruity—and that the ethnography was in place in order to develop said scenarios (and one could indeed argue that he was, in essence, making the strange familiar in order to thence make it strange)—does not undercut the utility of the description as potential source.

In March of 2003 I conducted an interview with Kelly Roubo, after she had informed me that, when she was a child growing up in rural Maine in the late 1960s and early 1970s, her family would often entertain themselves by sitting around listening to Bill Cosby albums. Over the course of the interview she expressed how much the appeal of Cosby—even for material that she had never listened to before—was in his descriptive powers and how his comments on the everyday rang true. As we listened together to *Why Is There Air?* (Cosby 1965*), an album she had never heard before, Cosby describes a silent crier, and she commented: "That's such an image!" She had strong positive reactions to several passages of material, which she either related to her own life or anticipated the punch line. At one point Cosby describes his mother's warning about what would happen if he continued to play with his navel, which would involve deflation and flying around the room. Kelly reacted, "Now my mom used to tell my brother that if he didn't stop playing with it, he'd unscrew it and all his arms and legs would fall off." At the very beginning of a routine on the difficulties of driving in different cities, she asks, "I wonder if he's ever been to St. John's" [Newfoundland, where the interview took place]. When Cosby speaks of taking Midol for a toothache and assures the audience that he had no side effects, Kelly suggests that he must have grown breasts moments before he says that every twenty-eight days he gets a little irritable. Much of the appeal of Cosby for Kelly comes from his skill at observing the everyday.

> IB What do you think it was that your family liked about it so much? If anything, if you could even answer that specifically.
>
> KR I think it's the familiarity of what he's talking about, that so many people just don't seem to comment on; they just live with these things as they happen to you . . .
>
> IB Sort of focusing on the everyday.
>
> KR Yeah, and it's almost conversational, so that if you were standing beside him it would be a conversation. (Roubo 2003)

Anticipating what he is going to say demonstrates one aspect of Cosby's appeal. This mix of conversational style and conversational content narrows the gap between performer and audience. Familiarity with the delivery is not necessarily the same thing as familiarity with the substance of what he is talking about. The delivery may become trite or stale and be seen as affectation more than novel style. "I wonder how funny I'd have found him if we had all his albums, y'know? 'Cause listening to this, you're hearing the same sort of thing over and over again " (Roubo 2003). Even with a new piece of material, as this album was for Kelly, the tension between convention and novelty, or tradition and variation, is nuanced: if it is too "familiar," for example, relying on tried and true formulas, the routine becomes mere rote. If, however, the material strays too far from a sense of a shared experience, which happens with dated or obscure references, it is only the formulas that can save it.

As Cosby refers mostly to his own experiences, with an emphasis on the ordinary, the everyday, the routine, he employs an assumption of shared experience. Some of Cosby's success may have been a result of the avoidance of the esoteric. An African American from urban Philadelphia could be understood by a white family from rural Maine by emphasizing common or parallel experiences. In this manner his potential "otherness" is obviated:

this is helped, of course, by the already distancing mechanism of the album itself.

> IB Did the fact that he was black ever sink in, or was it ever an issue? Was he just a funny guy?
>
> KR He was just a funny guy. And I don't know how much of that comes from where I grew up. I mean, he was a black guy on the cover of an album; he was not a black guy standing in my living room. I don't know how old I was when I first saw a black person. There aren't that many in Maine, or there weren't at the time, and so I think the whole civil rights thing was something that was distant, particularly as a child. You have some recognition, you hear it from the news, you know something is going on, but, particularly if you've never seen a black person and it's not happening where you are, you're not connecting with the relevance of it. I don't remember ever thinking about it, of him being a black person. That doesn't mean I didn't, I just don't have the recollection of it. (Roubo 2003)

Ron James describes his method in a manner that is very much that of the ethnographer, the "deep hanging out" of participant observation, while this understanding, this trying to (re)discover, seems to be the essence of the ethnographer's quest.[10] Each of James's specials is, for lack of a better term, an ethnography. His one-man show, *Up and Down in Shakey Town*, began expressly as a series of observations about Californian life as seen through the eyes of an Atlantic Canadian. A reviewer of the stage version mounted in Halifax (after the filming of the special) described it thus:

> The emotional heart of James's presentation, however, is the acute cultural difference he plays up as he describes everyday life in the imagined paradise of Southern California. From an extended, edgy sequence about being stuck for four hours in traffic with a tragically full bladder, to a series of hilarious comparisons between American and Canadian gun laws, James draws the line between the cold-but-civilized North, and the go-go craziness of Southern California.
>
> James's observations about arriving in Los Angeles are pointed and sometimes painfully funny. He got there just as an endless train of plagues (riots, floods, fires) afflicted a place that had formerly been defined by its 24-hour liquor barns and consistently hot climate. These extremes of human and climatic behaviour make ideal fodder for a comic such as James. (R. Macdonald 1999, 45)

In one passage (a favorite of his which he had until recently also streamed on his website), he describes the lure of American consumer culture for the Canadian, with particular emphasis on "the liquor barn":

> Down there the *consumer* was king
> *whoa*
> I used to *buy*
> *forty ounces* of Captain Morgan Dark Rum
> for nine ninety-*five* [L]
> at a place called the *Liquor Barn*
> the {slowly} *"Liquor* Barn" [L]
> a *theme park* to booze [L]
> and a temple of homage for *any* Maritimer [L→A]
> eh | what are you doing *today* Ronald |
> | nothing at all just perpetuating a regional *stereotype* [L]
> and dancin' on down to the *Liquor Barn* is all [L]
> {singing and dancing} "oh the Liquor Barn [L:A]
> <u>the Liquor Barn</u>
> <u>we're all going to the Liquor Barn"</u>
> sing along the lyrics are fairly simple hey [L]
> follow the bouncing pint [L] <u>"we're all going to the Liquor Liquor Barn"</u> (James
>   1997*)

The consequent proviso is that, as rich in ethnographic detail as the performer's text might be, the intent is ultimately not to be an ethnographer but to be an entertainer: the ethnography is at the service of the laughter. In his profile of comedian Eddie Izzard, John Lahr captured the following moment:

[Izzard] was talking about Guy Fawkes and how he was "hung, drawn, and quartered." At the word "hung," Izzard tilted his neck and mimed a noose around it. At "drawn," he stepped back and pretended to sketch Fawkes.

"No, that's not it," a man shouted from the audience.

Izzard's eyes twinkled as he peered into the murky room. "Have you only just worked out that that's the first lie I've told you all night?" he said. "As it happens, there's a constant lying that goes on through the whole show." Instinctively, Izzard did a little of his "positivizing." He put his hands on his hips and rolled his eyes to the ceiling, imagining the man's bad review of the show. "'The lies that were said in that room,'" he said. "'I wanted to go out for a good night of realism.'" (2000, 181–82)

Ron James made a similar point when he described the "Paid in Game" routine as having "nothing to do with credibility": stand-up comedy, as much as its vernacular theory refers to "truth," "honesty," and "authenticity," is not an exercise in objectivity or absolute veracity. It is forever and always a means to an end: laughter.

Throughout this book I have been suggesting that there is a professional obligation for the comedian to be outside his or her group or be from outside of the group that comprises the audience in order to have something interesting to say. The vernacular theory concepts of "holding a mirror up to culture" and "seeing things differently" demand it. This outsider status has a further implication of someone without express power or privilege, somehow disenfranchised: to find something amusing is to point out some of the group's internal contradictions, its flaws, or, at the very least, its difference from an esoteric understanding of "normal," and for someone to do that from a position of privilege is a breach of the compact that stand-up comedy is emancipatory.[11]

> like *fat girls* can say whatever they want to about *skinny girls*
> *fat girls* can talk about *skinny girls*
> *all day long*
> | fuckin' skinny *bitch* [L] fuckin' skinny *ass* anorexic bulimic fuckin' regurgitatin'
>   *bitch* [L] fuckin' cheerio belt wearin' *bitch* [C] *salad-eatin'* motherfucker
> I hope she chokes on a *crouton* | [L]
> but *skinny girls* can't talk about *fat girls*
> that's just *mean* [L] (Rock 2008*)

The idea of ethnography, particularly as expressed in the "make the strange familiar and the familiar strange" proverb, provides one lens through which one can view the stand-up comedian's act. Like the contemporary ethnographer, the stand-up comedian locates him- or herself within a particular worldview and then examines phenomena from that perspective. For the purposes of that performance, and within its non-consequential frame, that worldview is portrayed as normative, and the audience—again within the non-consequential frame—alternately agrees and disagrees with the normativity of that worldview. The comedian makes a concerted effort to ensure that the disagreement does not last for long and that most are reconciled to that worldview. A successful unknown comedian will not alienate his or her audience; a comedian with a more established reputation will have the benefit of both having already weeded out those who would be alienated and attracting those who share—or wish to experience—this worldview.

There is something a little grandiose, I feel, in some of the literature and rhetoric about stand-up comedy and comedians. There is an impetus for an explanatory model that rationalizes the appeal: it must *do something* other than merely entertain. I am not adverse to the suggestions that the stand-up comedian acts as artist, social critic, anthropologist, mediator of social morality, forger of an ethnic image, or even indeed ethnographer, but the emphasis is on the "acts" aspect. As George Paton (1988) notes, the comedian is a *portrayer* of these roles, not necessarily fulfilling the role itself. These are also roles that are assumed, briefly, in everyday talk, and they arise in the flow of everyday conversation, although we would hesitate to frame them as "roles."

Stand-up comedians, out of professional necessity, are focused on "otherness": whether as an observational comedian reflecting the culture of an audience back onto itself or as a chronicler of an experience foreign to their audience, they deliberately seek out the other as a source of material. They fix their "comic gaze" at difference. Comic gaze is invoked casually by many writing about humor and comedy. Sigmund Freud began the "Analytic Part" of his *Jokes and Their Relation to the Unconscious* by quoting Kuno Fischer:

> The subject-matter of comedy is what is ugly in any of its manifestations. "Where it is hidden, it must be revealed in the light of the comic gaze, where it is noticed but little or scarcely at all, it must be brought out and exposed in such a way that it stands open to the light of day." (Freud 1976, 1–2)

In his study of Richard Pryor and Eddie Murphy and "the cool pose," Herman Beavers notes, "To be cool is also to be mobile, free to aim the comic gaze outward in all directions" (1997, 266). Ron James uses the gaze metaphor indirectly, through his invocation of the "satirist's eye for detail" (Lisk 2005) or the "comedian's eye peeled for the satire" (Ward 2005), which he pairs with the "poet's ear for language" (James 2003*).

Inasmuch as stand-up comedians are engaged in a consideration of otherness, and inasmuch as they are doing something on a stage that is done in everyday talk, I would suggest that much of what one can say about the comic gaze can be equated to the "tourist gaze." A number of the routines already discussed in the pages above—both Richard Pryor and Chris Rock on Africa and James on the far points of frontier—explicitly refer to travels to exotic locations.

But to equate the stand-up comedian's project with that of the tourist appears, at first, to diminish it. We tend to hold the tourist at an arm's remove. Malcolm Crick suggests that anthropologists express a certain repugnance for tourists, in part stemming from a reluctant recognition of commonality (1985, 77–78). We may indeed identify our own leisure travel as precisely that—"travel"—something less a project of consumption and more of encounter, and leave "tourism" for others.[12] Ellen Badone notes how the boundaries between tourist, ethnographer, and pilgrim are blurry at best, as their ostensibly respective projects—leisure, understanding, and self-transformation—are shared by all three, with different emphases (2004, 182). Much of this hinges on the issue of "authenticity": the tourist is assumed to be seeing a constructed reality of signs prepared for him or her precisely in a system that benefits from accentuating difference as an object for the tourist gaze; the traveller (and the ethnographer) sees the real.

Among stand-up theorists there tends to be an implicit or even explicit hierarchy, a delineation between "true" stand-up comedians and others. Comedians themselves tend to distinguish good comedians (and implicitly themselves) from "hacks" (K. Moore 1997, 93–107) and "boat-acts" (Pulliam 1991, 166). The same issue of saying something real or authentic drives that division. So I would imagine an invocation of "tourist" as a blanket rubric would give one pause. However, they are comparable. John Urry (1990) describes several features of the tourist gaze that I believe have analogues in stand-up comedy. For example,

> The tourist gaze arises from a movement of people to, and their stay in, various other destinations. This necessarily involves some movement through space, that is the journey, and a period of stay in a new place or places. (Urry 1990, 26)

The very act of being a touring comedian, including the itinerancy that this suggests, is part of the comedian's story.[13] Life on the road is such an integral metaphor for Ron James (2003*) that it formed the narrative backbone of his second special, *The Road Between My Ears*. As discussed above, he specifically credits travels as the source of his material.[14]

Urry continues:

> The journey and stay are to, and in, sites which are outside the normal places of residence and work. . . .
>
>   Places are chosen to be gazed upon because there is an anticipation . . . of intense pleasures, either on a different scale or involving different senses from

those customarily encountered. Such anticipation is constructed and sustained through a variety of non-tourist practices, such as film, newspapers, T.V., magazines, records and videos which construct that gaze. Such practices provide the signs in terms of which the holiday experiences are understood, so that what is then seen is interpreted in terms of these pre-given categories. (1990, 26)

That the tourist gaze is directed at sites outside the everyday ones of residence and work and anticipates intense pleasures brings with it the notion that the gaze is deliberately directed at difference, and the different is sought out as such. But in addition to the ethnographic descriptions of otherness through travel or through personal experience, the stand-up comedian also turns to the immediate everyday world of the audience and, with an eye on noting difference, makes observations on it as well.

I think it's just the way you perceive things around you. You've seen the silliness, the absurdity, the craziness that goes on in the world and you jump on that and expand it. You look at things in a different light. That's what makes comedy. (Carson 1979)

The itinerant stand-up comedian is a tourist at the moment of performance, recounting his or her perceptions of otherness not only in places far-flung but in places immediate to the audience. The local material presented at the beginning of a performance is a demonstration of the local as perceived through the gaze of an interested, engaged other.

The gaze is constructed through signs and tourism involves the collection of such signs. When for example tourists see two people kissing in Paris what they are gazing upon is "timeless, romantic Paris," when a small village in England is seen, tourists think they are gazing upon the "real (merrie) England." (Urry 1990, 26)

"Signs" are also how the stand-up comedian uses the previously held assumptions about a place and frames his or her performances around those signs, either utilizing them directly, especially when communicating a far-flung experience to an audience, or setting them up as mere conventions to be discounted, when communicating a local experience to a local audience. These conventions—stereotypes, motifs, dites, units of worldview—are conventions the comedian can use in precisely the same manner as the tourist: they are known (or at least accessible) to the audience through the mechanisms of vernacular and popular culture (not only the same sort of "non-tourist practices" Urry alludes to above but also oral tradition), and through legend-like discourse their underlying truth or falsity can be negotiated, affirmed, denied, or left uncertain.

> The gaze is directed to features of landscape and townscape which separate them off from everyday and routine experiences. Such aspects are viewed because they are taken to be in some sense out-of-the-ordinary. . . . People linger over such a gaze which is then visually objectified or captured through photographs, postcards, films, models, and so on. These enable the gaze to be endlessly reproduced and recaptured. (Urry 1990, 26–27)

Urry's point concerning the souvenir seems at first glance the least relevant to the study of stand-up, but I would suggest, building on how others have built on his concepts, that it is the most critical. In addition to how the *site* is visually objectified or captured through photographs and models, the *experience* is "narratively subjectified" through the narratives that are formed there and become part of the teller's repertoire. The folkloristic approach would be to suggest that the souvenir, Urry's visual objectification, is a form of memory object that occasions narrative (Kirshenblatt-Gimblett 1989, 331): but even without an object to occasion it, narrative is also a product of the tourist gaze, and the telling and retelling of the narrative communicates and allows for reproduction and recapture—really, its re-creation. Narratively, that experience is re-created to audience members, who now experience it themselves, albeit vicariously. When they are presented with narratives of places far-flung, they come to know that place touristically, and when they are presented with narratives of their own locale, they experience that too through the lens of otherness and difference.

> Tourism is a leisure activity which presupposes its opposite, namely regulated and organised work. It is one manifestation of how work and leisure are organised as separate and regulated spheres of social practice in "modern" societies. (Urry 1990, 26)

I have been making the suggestion that stand-up comedy is the professionalization of everyday talk, small talk, "talking shit": talk that exists in the informal realm of play and leisure and is distinguished from serious talk. Professionalization brings heightened expectations of consistent competency, particularly stemming from the comedian's place within an exchange economy. Tourism is located in the leisure sphere, but stand-up comedy takes those activities that occur on that leisure sphere and professionalizes them. The stand-up comedian is, on one level, a professional tourist, perennially casting his or her gaze on difference, to communicate that experience of difference to an ever-new audience. The talk of stand-up comedy is no longer the leisurely talking shit of face-to-face interaction, "a leisure activity which presupposes its opposite, namely regulated and organised work": it is work. Michael Robidoux, in his study of professional hockey players, noted the difficulty in reconciling the cultural division between work and play when one speaks of someone whose work *is* to play:

> The dictates of play demand that participants comply with the structure (or world) of the game; otherwise, the game will not be successfully realized. Of course, play theorist Roger Caillois, in his description of play, referred to what is intended to be a momentary departure from "the rest of life." Individuals who play for a living, however, are forced to abandon themselves to this principle, to the extent that the realm of play becomes their way of life. For professional hockey players, the notion of leaving or entering this "enclosure" becomes a very literal function, in that the game is not temporary, but rather, their livelihood. (2001, 16)

Stand-up comedians cultivate the comic gaze by professional necessity: whatever peripheral stance they might have had prior to their engagement in the professional life of stand-up, and however much that peripherality and marginalization informs the content of their work, it must be continually reestablished both through the explicit identification of self as "othered" and, implicitly, through drawing attention to how their perception of difference is something worth listening to.

Ultimately, as far as the comedian aims at intimacy with an audience, he or she also is forever divided from it, as the professional obligation to remain an outsider is always in play. That profession, as George Carlin said, is to think up goofy shit.

When people go to a stand-up comedy performance, they expect to be hearing a form of talk that is more or less consistently funny. Stylistically, the stand-up comedian may not be substantially different from "good talkers" he or she may encounter in the course of everyday life, but by virtue of being paid for it, making a claim about his or her particular skill set, the comedian had better deliver. One way to accomplish this is to meet the audience's twofold expectation of both relevance, understanding the worldview of the group by demonstrating some shared participation therein, and perspective, having a particular insight into that worldview.

Stand-up comedians do this by cultivating a hermeneutic of marginality, of pointing to the center from its periphery. This lens of outsiderness fits in with the established cultural understanding of what the social identity of the stand-up comedian connotes. This outsider is a persona that is performed and enacted on the stage, and it is built around previously held assumptions about similar persons. When a reputation is firmly established and the comedian becomes known, this sketched persona can be dropped or, at least, allowed to recede to the background as a more nuanced stage persona develops. Specific statements may be made that are not meant to be understood as funny but rather as testimonials, explicit opinions, and belief utterances that serve to firmly locate the comedian within some form of framework. These appear (and are far outnumbered by) the more ambiguous statements that are—hopefully—interpreted by the audience as funny, insofar as they are open to some negotiation of meaning.

The stand-up comedian adapts material according to the audience: some material can more or less go unchanged from performance to performance, some can be easily adapted to local contexts, and some is wholly localized. This localized material, however, can be reworked into something more permanent when the comedian communicates that local experience in a different context, and the performance becomes an evocation of place in something similar to the project of the ethnographer. The comedian's need for new material brings a requirement for noting difference as a category for comic fodder.

Next, we turn to mediated performances, where the performance becomes adapted to the various media, where a repertoire becomes fixed, where canons are formed, where reputations cumulate, and where the stand-up comedian, in addressing two separate audiences—one at home and one immediately present to him or her—divines new ways for building intimacy across the spatiotemporal distance.

PART 3

The Headliner: Distance Increases

McLuhan-wise, I mean, it's . . . it's hot. It's a hot medium: it isn't a cold medium, because they're, they're involved, they're involved in the routine.
—**Bob Newhart,** *Button Down Concert*

This is the headliner. This is why you came, why you shelled out the ten or twenty bucks, why you got dressed up. You know it's going to be good, because if it isn't, why is he or she headlining? And you've seen the headliner before, in some form or another. But maybe he or she will just be sitting on laurels, and when it's over you'll think the middle was better.

As a dialogic form, stand-up comedy requires the reaction of an audience to propel itself forward: it does not "work" without an audience. At the same time, although much of the power in the performance context resides with the performer, and although the skills of the performer are measured in part by how he or she wields that power, the reactions of an audience can be anticipated but not predicted with certainty. For further mediations, the reactions of the audience, more accurately now rendered as "viewers" or "listeners," have no direct affect on the outcome of the performance.

In reality, however, there are (at least) two audiences. Just as the first few rows of an audience may be the proxy for the entire crowd, albeit with respect paid to the presence of the entire crowd, similarly, when combined they are the audience at the site of the broadcast or recording; this audience, together with the performer, produces the performance and acts as de facto "proxy" (a term I begin to discard in the next section) for the much larger audience at the receiving end of the broadcast or recording. Moreover, the broadcast or recorded performance is ultimately intended for that other non-present audience, and that audience outnumbers (and thus outspends) the audience present at the performance. One cannot, therefore, simply examine further mediations as simulacra or, at best, documentaries of live performance, as the media alter the performance itself, both in its production and certainly in its reception.

This is what happens when the audience and performer are not co-located, not present to each other. First, we examine broadcasts, both live, through which the audience is experiencing the performance at the same time but not at the same place, and prerecorded, through which the audience is experiencing the performance at a different time and place. Then, it is recordings, through which the audience not only is experiencing the performance at a different time and place but also has control over which time and place they are experiencing it. In some cases, these categories are notional at best, especially as the performances appear on multiple media platforms, but if one considers them separately as ideal types, they bring to the fore a range of complementary but distinct concerns.

CHAPTER 6
Stand-Up Comedy Broadcasts

Well, pure television to me is also immediacy. That's why I don't like to do *The Tonight Show* a week or two in advance, like a lot of shows do. I like to be able to go out tonight and talk about what's happening *today*. So the immediacy of doing this kind of show, I think, has a certain value in it. People *know* it's happening right now.

Sure, we're delayed on tape, but we don't edit the show; we don't shoot two hours and edit it down. When *Saturday Night Live* says, "Live, from New York!" it's live in the East but it's not live out here. Doing it the same day on tape is exactly the same thing as doing it live.

—Johnny Carson

Stand-up comedy emerged in the postwar period at about the same time as television was supplanting radio as the dominant broadcast medium. The perceived intimacy of television seemed to suit stand-up very well, and a performer could be seen by millions of people at one time. The inexpensiveness of stand-up suited television producers' budgets equally well. Several minutes of airtime could be filled without expending anything on sets, costumes, or staff writers, and while the comedian performed in front of a backdrop or curtain a new set could be arranged behind it. Wide-scale network broadcasting altered the form of stand-up comedy irrevocably, both for good and ill: it was the predominant medium for stand-up comedy in its early days and continues its influence.

Broadcasting in the United States, and elsewhere to a similar extent, has been affected by three interrelated limitations. First of all, as the airwaves are licensed from the government, they are subject to regulatory agencies, who act in the public interest, or their interpretation thereof.[1] Secondly, programming was largely sponsored by businesses through advertising: for material that was or is not considered legally obscene, indecent, or profane, individuals and groups with no recourse to complaints to regulators could nevertheless make their displeasure known to the sponsors through threats of product boycott.[2] Lastly, both the broadcaster and the sponsor are aiming at engaging as large an audience as possible—the latter for maximum exposure of their products, the former for demonstrating that a "public need" is being met, which is a condition of broadcast license renewal—and as such are invested in appealing to the broadest possible base. The issue of "acceptable" language and content, predicated less on proactively imposing a standard of propriety and more on proactively avoiding controversy and retribution, becomes a consequent limit on performance. Obscenity and other risky material are not inherently part of stand-up comedy, but their avoidance can require a self-censoring and circumnavigation of certain topics that might not be present in conversation among intimates.

We imagine that those present to a performance, certainly present to a light entertainment, are there of their own volition, that they can exercise the option of leaving or staying, and that they can give voice to a reaction, whether positive or negative. Together the performer and the audience negotiate what is appropriate and what is inappropriate. How much actual control any one member of the audience has over the performance may be negligible but not absent entirely. With a broadcast, however, that negligible control is not available to the listener at home. To maintain an appropriate performance, the performer needs to read the reactions of his present audience and anticipate the reactions of his distant one.

There is more to appropriateness, however, than the highly subjective albeit straightforward issue of what constitutes obscenity or indecency. Relevancy and topicality are also determined in intimate performances. What might make sense to a local audience—references to landmarks, local characters, *blasons populaires*—would likely not make sense to an audience distantly removed. In an effort to be relevant to a group not defined by locality, broadcasted comedy necessitates the establishment of a framework of common reference and thus leans in two directions: firstly, there is a move toward generality, in terms of making reference to popular culture, national politics, or observations on everyday life not bounded by place; secondly, the local culture of the broadcast centers—primarily New York and subsequently Los Angeles in the American context and Toronto in the Canadian—becomes dominant and, somewhat, normative.

What resulted was an intimate genre transposed to an open medium wherein the participants became engaged in a dialogue they neither actively initiated nor could respond to directly. The fear of a negative response would certainly have an impact on what was broadcast, and by that same token a positive response would be cultivated. The two-audiences concept rears its head once more, somewhat similar to how the audience in the first few rows of a live stand-up performance represent the entire audience. On one hand, the audience in the immediate presence of the performer is understood as being in a synecdochic relationship with the home audience, and the reaction of its small and finite number represents the reaction of the larger and indefinite number at home. On the other hand, there is something of James Frazer's "homeopathic magic" transpiring, where a performer directs him- or herself at one audience for a reaction, with the hope of engendering that same reaction in another. In both cases, the reaction of the studio audience *is* what the reaction of the home audience *ought to be*, whether in its representative or denotative function.

The studio audience not only shows the home audience what works and doesn't work but, by its response, tells it so. Another way of examining this phenomenon is through Max Scheler's notion of "psychic contagion," one of the means by which, as he understands it, masses operate in a way whereby the individual is lost. Manfred Frings, the Scheler scholar, makes a reference to this within similar contexts:

> The taped laughter used in commercials, for instance, infects their viewers who smile along, although what the laughter is about would, in realty [sic], hardly or not at all be even worth a chuckle. . . . The same holds for types of entertainment and activities as Mardi Gras, opera, rock concerts, parades, organized election gatherings. (2003, 34)

Less stridently, Sara Kiesler and Jonathon M. Cummings make a similar argument: "Members of the audience at a live performance enliven one another, an effect simulated in the television laugh track" (2002, 62). The audience is an integral part of the packaging of the performance and, although the reaction would be difficult to fabricate de novo, certain manipulations, such as careful microphone placement, warming up the audience with more direct interaction prior to broadcasting, and applause (and laughter) signs, are used.

The studio audience becomes the arbiter of "funny." Moreover, this audience may not simply be a representative sample of the audience at home but more likely comprises a particular demographic that connotes certain ineffable qualities: urban, sophisticated, adult, and so forth. If the audience is thus representative of a group to which one is meant to aspire, the performance serves to demonstrate the tastes of this particular group.

One can easily and accurately give examples of this hegemonic exercise as it relates to socioeconomic class, region, sexual orientation, and so forth, but a simpler demonstration can be given with reference to age. When a child hears an adult audience laughing at a particular point in a comedian's routine, the child reasons that he or she ought to find it funny as well. In my own experience, as a child I would often listen to comedy that, for all intents and purposes, I didn't understand; but knowing that there was something to understand, appreciating that people (certainly) older and (ostensibly) more mature than me did understand it, prompted me, first, to laugh without really actually getting it and, subsequently, to focus on coming to understand it. "Getting it" or "not getting it" becomes a marker for insider or outsider status, doubly problematic when "it" is a cultural product on the public airwaves.

With a live broadcast, the audience members are made aware that the performance is going forward in real time, that they are experiencing it as and when the audience present to the performance is experiencing it. Immediacy is central to the experience. At the same time, live-to-air broadcasting was the default broadcast form for variety shows until the late 1960s, so in the early days the audience wasn't necessarily perceiving this immediacy as anything special or unique. In recent years, the "liveness" of a live broadcast is emphasized as part of the spectacle.

Stand-up comedy emerged in part out of radio, insofar as the vocal techniques that were practiced by early radio hosts introduced an intimacy of voice that lent itself well to a conversational style. And as the light entertainment divisions of early radio would often use the extant variety show format and broadcast it to a larger audience, the amplified variety show emcee (host or compère) would be the immediate progenitor. In his preamble to a 1979 interview with Johnny Carson, Timothy White observes how "[Carson's] conversational comedic style, which he acknowledges as having been shaped by such early heroes as Jack Benny, Bob Hope and George Burns, has become the very paradigm of nonchalant patter for every aspiring young stand-up or sit-down wit" (Carson 1979).

Bob Hope—however much his stiff and cue-carded delivery was fodder for impressionists in the later years of his life—is the exemplar of this age of voice broadcasting. He not only took his cue from the crooners of his time—Frank Sinatra, Bing Crosby—and spoke rather than shouted into the microphone, but also was consciously aware of working to two audiences, that of the studio or theater and that of the home. Nowhere is this more evident than in his broadcasts from the armed forces camps in the Second World War, performed simultaneously for the servicemen and for a home audience.

The immediate limitation of radio as a medium for stand-up comedy is that it is exclusively auditory: the sensory data available to the listener are exclusively that of sound. As a consequence, in order to be understood by the non-present listener, the physicality of performance—slapstick, mime, facial expressions, gesture, costume, appearance—must be pushed to the margins in preference to the verbal. Characterization, if it occurs, must be done through voice alone. Writing on the radio preacher, William Clements notes how he "must employ a delivery style different from that used in natural church contexts. Gestures, facial expressions, and personal allusions—all valuable aids to the transmission of the sermon message—are useless for a radio audience" (1974, 324).

The conversational mode of radio stand-up comedy is thus not much different from the conversational mode of the telephone, a technology that was becoming more universally available at the same time as the rise of commercial radio. In this vein, it is perhaps not surprising that some of the earliest comedy recordings, albeit not stand-up comedy, were the "Cohen on the Telephone" series (R. Smith 1998, 90–92). The limitation to the aural and the conversational also meant the temporary absence of the more florid vaudevillians from the mainstream.

The demise of radio networks with a centralized source of programming largely meant the demise of radio variety and the rise of both talk radio and the disc jockey. By the time stand-up comedy emerged in its contemporary manifestation, radio was already being superseded by television as the primary variety entertainment medium. There were exceptions in local broadcasting. Robert Stebbins recounts how CFOX in Vancouver would broadcast open-mike sessions live from Punchlines comedy club. Ironically, the collaboration ended when the radio station's format was becoming too coarse for Punchlines, at a time when the club's managers were encouraging comedians to develop material that was more television-friendly (Stebbins 1990, 22). In Canada, stand-up comedy continues (or, rather, reappeared) on radio through recorded variety programming such as Lorne Elliott's *Madly Off in All Directions* (1996–2006), albeit not live.

Although never a huge medium for stand-up comedy, as an influence on voice performance, radio left a mark on verbal entertainment by virtue of it being a solely auditory medium, namely, the disappearance, more or less, of physicality—gesture, props, costume—for characterization and humor, and a consequent "naturalization" of the form. The intimacy of voice at its natural register, already a factor from amplification but more tightly focused through the absence of visual cues, moved content further away from contrivances to quotidian observations. Since it was broadcast into the home, rather than being a deliberate engagement by the listener, content was selected so as not to disengage the listener. Finally, an understanding of the relationship between the live audience and the home audience— whether that be representative, synecdochic, homeopathic, hegemonic, or all of the above—had its grounding in radio.

In recent years, Internet radio has allowed for live and uncensored comedy. Scott Aukerman's *Comedy Death Ray Radio* (2009–2011*) started as a live Internet program on Indie 103.1 in Los Angeles and was immediately redistributed as a podcast, following a format not dissimilar from Jimmy Pardo's *Never Not Funny* podcast (2006–*). However, although both starred stand-up comedians and featured comedians as guests, neither show ventured into straightforward stand-up performance, focusing instead on topical conversations and improv-style games.

Much of what can be said for radio can also be said for television. Radio laid the groundwork for variety entertainment programming and the relationship between the live and home audiences. However, whereas radio had not allowed for visuals, television obviously did. The use of nonverbal cues was a possibility again.

In one perspective, television could be understood as a transposition of a theatrical stage, with the audio and visual technology merely mimicking the experience of the theatergoer. Physical comedy and the work of the more florid vaudevillians (who were left out of radio) were thus able to find a home on television. Television performance was directed at the live audience, with the home audience as bystanders.

But the camera allowed for the close-up. Already understood through the medium of film, the close-up allowed for a natural physicality much as the microphone had allowed for a natural voice. The intimacy of the clubs and coffee shops where stand-up comedy was brewing could be emulated through a close-up that virtually represented someone in your living room, just as the radio replicated someone on the other end of a telephone.

> The TV producer will point out that speech on television must not have the careful precision necessary in the theater. The TV actor does not have to project either his voice or himself. Likewise, TV acting is so extremely intimate, because of the peculiar involvement of the viewer with the completion or "closing" of the TV image, that the actor must achieve a great degree of spontaneous casualness that would be irrelevant in movies and lost on stage. . . . Technically,

TV tends to be a close-up medium. The close-up that in the movie is used for shock is, on TV, a quite casual thing. (McLuhan 1964, 276)

The static (or mostly static) single-shot allowed for further impressions to be made: although the studio audience could be heard—and, as in radio, remained an integral part of the performance for the home audience—it would not be seen, and attention was more closely pulled to the performer. So too would the use of overhead boom microphones, which hid the intermediary technology and reinforced that sense of naturalness. A static shot framed the performance space in such a way that for the duration of the performance the space off-screen could be re-imagined as something other than a television studio: that space includes not only above, below, and to the sides of the performer (the *x* and *y* axes of the two-dimensional frame of the camera), but also behind and, most importantly, in front of the performer, behind the camera, the *z* axis of face-to-face orientation.[3] That the comedian does not stare at the camera directly is not a contradiction of this intimacy, as the diegetic sound still betrays that an audience is present within that space: the audience at home, however, is amongst it. At times, the comedian does turn to the camera directly and establishes a further intimacy with the audience at home.

> Well, television is an intimate medium. I'm not conscious when I use the camera. I know it's there. I use it like another person and, do a reaction at it—lift an eyebrow or shrug or whatever. I'm conscious of it, but I'm not conscious of it. (Carson 1979)

Mort Sahl was an earlier exponent of this naturalism. He brought from the coffeehouses his habit of wearing a cardigan and a shirt with no tie, which broke the conventions of the suit-and-tie or tuxedo. He would also have that day's newspaper as a "prop," using its headlines as an entry point for political satire. When he attained a Hymesian "breakthrough into performance" (Hymes 1975), it was after much intentional delay: the stuttering, false starts, and trailing-off sentences that marked his talk at the beginning of his routines, together with flipping through the newspaper and some vague gesticulations, would eventually give way to a freer flow of talk, in a deliberate effort at emulating face-to-face interaction. That this was "a Performance" was obfuscated by an appeal to naturalism and intimacy (Nachman 2003, 50–51).

Speaking both of radio and of television, Gunther Anders had this to say in 1956 about the idea of intimacy as created by these media:

> [To] enable the program consumer to treat the world as something familiar, the televised image must address him as an old chum. In fact, every broadcast has this chummy quality. When I tune in on the President, he suddenly sits next to me at the fireplace, chatting with me, although he may be thousands of miles away. (I am only marginally aware of the fact that this intimacy exists in millions of copies.) When the girl announcer appears on the screen, she speaks to me in a tone of complete frankness, as though I were her bosom friend. (That she is also the bosom friend of all men is again only a marginal realization.) (1957, 365)

Stand-up comedians appeared alongside other forms of variety entertainment: shows were not dedicated to comedy exclusively, and the comedian would be one of a number of acts, interspersed between commercials. This had two immediate consequences. First, the length of time allowed for performance was restricted, typically from about five to eight minutes. Much like how the cylinder, the 78, and the 45 recording formats each restricted the time available to a song text and thus had an influence on how long a song could be, so too would a five-minute time slot foreshorten a routine from the longer or undetermined lengths in a club context.[4] Open-mike nights at comedy clubs typically limit performances to five minutes. However, in addition to being a concession to the number of performers wishing to take the stage, the timing is partly based on the standard set by television convention.

> Bill [Hicks] was not really coming across on television. What the audience saw was a smooth, intelligent act by anyone's standards, but with only six minutes Bill lacked time to build momentum or really work an idea and it robbed him of the fiery crescendo so critical to his act. The demand from network television for a quick witty spray of set-up punchline fare seemed designed, however insidiously, to abbreviate anything approaching actual social commentary. Just as Bill started to build, one sensed him halting as he shifted down, changed gears, moved to the next bit. (True 2002, 91)

Second, these short units needed to be immediately accessible to an audience that was likely not in attendance expressly to see this particular comedian. Routines were self-contained and discrete, ones that work with virtually no further contextualization needed. "With TV, it was quick minutes and scram. A comic did not have the time to woo an audience with the cumulative rhythm of his act. The café or coffeehouse gave him up to an hour, long enough to live or die grandly" (Berger 2000, 168). The host of the program, like the emcee discussed above, might give a brief introduction, but this would be little more than a sentence or two. Otherwise, the routine needed either to be on a topic immediately accessible to both audiences— politics, popular culture, history, or the prejudices of the general population—or, if they were presenting a perspective that might be different from the general population, to include a short autobiographical statement that contextualized what was to come. Robert Klein puts it succinctly:

> Television presents a very unique problem. The audience didn't pay to see you. They may have sent away for tickets to the Johnny Carson Show nine months ago and there could have been anybody on that night. They are fairly conservative, middle of the road audiences, not particularly hip or educated, and usually of one mind. The most crucial thing about television in addition to language and other restrictions is timing. Six minutes, which is a long stand-up period for T.V., is a lot different than an hour and twenty minutes. You must be funnier in a hurry. You must be extremely economical and very universal. You must use material that doesn't require an awful lot of explanation. You have so little time and it requires a special kind of preparation. (1977, 8)

Finally, and most self-evidently, content is restricted: both language and premise need to be meet a standard of acceptance by the network. In the interview prefacing George Carlin's first HBO special, he is asked about how he alters his performance for television:

> The most important alteration is that you can't use the body of language that's generally called "dirty" or "bad" or "filthy" language. And that's not a bad restriction if you have something to say: obviously you don't need a series of street terms to make your ideas clear. But they're very useful at enhancing ideas and enhancing characters and in giving the element of reality to speech that you want. You can suspend that for six minutes on television. I wouldn't want to suspend that for two hours on the stage because I think it would take something away from it. . . . But you don't go in there to try to change their system, usually: you go in there to fit within it for your own narrow purposes. (Carlin 1977a*)

As Carlin's "for your own narrow purposes" suggests, television—despite the restrictions and limitations imposed on content—was the easiest way to reach a vast number of people: far more might see you in one appearance than in a lifetime of working clubs. Comedians' biographies and autobiographies are replete with narratives about television exposure. In *Pryor Convictions*, Richard Pryor recalls his first television performance:

> On August 31, 1964, I made my TV debut on Rudy Vallee's summer variety show, "On Broadway Tonight." Rudy himself, over the producer's objections, insisted on putting me on the show. I considered it a stroke of luck, my first opportunity at nationwide exposure. Back then, Cosby, Dick Gregory, and Nipsey Russell were among the few black comics who appeared on TV. I was happy to join them. (1995, 80)

An appearance on network television variety programming was and continues to be one of the most important stepping-stones in a comedian's career, as it not only provides immediate exposure to the largest possible audience but, as he or she can now be introduced as having appeared on a particular program, reclassifies the comedian as having been deemed worthy by a respected authority. One can move from a middle act to a headliner, demanding higher pay and longer time on stage.

> The best part of getting on the Tonight Show was that I was able to go directly from the clubs in Denver to a concert tour. I never had to really work the clubs and be ground down; they would have killed me, I would've never made it. (Barr 1989, 185)

> Being on *The Tonight Show* presents more problems than solutions after the initial flurry of excitement wears off. You begin the process of getting the hell over it. Right after my appearances, I was trying to book myself as usual, and what I was hearing was, "Just because you've done Carson doesn't make you a headliner." I would reply, "I know. Just keep me middling." Then they'd give me another Catch-22. "Well, we can't middle you if you've done Carson, either." (B. Butler 1996, 237)

With television being so pervasive a medium, television exposure allows for the comedian to enter a larger market, while repeated exposure allows the comedian to develop a reputation, to create both a cumulative repertoire, with which a personal, idiosyncratic style can be developed, and cumulative goodwill, for which expansions within that repertoire and style are warmly anticipated.

This expansion of repertoire is also expected. One further downside to television appearances is how widely disseminated one's material becomes, with the attendant need to create new material for a subsequent appearance.

> I soon realized that I'd made the classic mistake among comedians. My first
> shot [on *The Tonight Show*] had been a compilation of my very best mate-
> rial—and it had gone extremely well. The second shot was okay, not as funny—
> because I used the best of what I had left over. And the third shot, all in all,
> wasn't very good. The real trick is to get hot and then keep coming up with new
> stuff at this incredible pace. If you continue to take from the well, eventually
> the well runs dry. (Leno 1996, 192–93)

Live television eventually gave way to shows being prerecorded; this is discussed below. *Saturday Night Live*, the obvious North American exception to this trend and a deliberate throwback to the potential for spon-
taneity of early television, also subverted the variety format by having a revolving host from week to week. Stand-up comedy was not part of the regular rotation of variety acts: following a cold opener and the credits, each show began with a host performing a monologue, whether these hosts were stand-up comedians or not. With some notable exceptions (Andy Kaufman's regular appearances in the first season, appearances by Sam Kinison, Damon Wayans, and Stephen Wright in season 11), stand-up comedy has never been part of the variety format outside of the monologue.[5]

When a stand-up comedian was the host, the monologue would be an opportunity to do a part of his or her regular act. Richard Pryor, hosting the seventh episode on December 13, 1975, was legendarily put on a ten-
second delay lest he say something offensive (Shales and Miller 2002, 64): this despite no similar delay for George Carlin, host of the first-ever episode (October 11, 1975) and no stranger to strong language. Andrew "Dice" Clay, the host for May 12, 1990, had already been rebuked by cast member Nora Dunn, who refused to appear that week, and the scheduled musical guest, Sinead O'Connor, followed suit by refusing to perform alongside him: his was the only monologue where security needed to throw out hecklers and metal detectors were in place at the entrances (Shales and Miller 2002, 337–
41). Martin Lawrence, hosting on February 19, 1994, went off-book and per-
formed a monologue about declining women's hygiene: he was banned for life from the show and was, for a time, banned from NBC altogether. When his episode was rebroadcast, this section of the monologue was replaced with a voiceover.[6]

In July of 2006, Comedy Central began broadcasting *Live at Gotham* from New York's Gotham Comedy Club, following the format of other stand-up comedy anthology series. Language restrictions on cable are loosened as the evening progresses: the initial evening broadcast was live but censored, with rebroadcasts left uncensored depending on the broadcast time.

Television, with its broad reach, was what often introduced stand-up comedy to both fans and future performers in the first place. In addition to accounts of the first television performance, biographies often speak of first encounters with stand-up comedy as viewers, which inspired them either as children or as adults to become comedians, often in an emancipatory way:

> "Mama," I ask her again, "why you cryin'?"
>
> "It's nothin', Bean. Sometimes I think sad thoughts."
>
> "What thoughts?"
>
> She didn't answer. She was lookin' at the TV. Black guy's talkin' to Ed Sullivan, I look at him, but I don't hear but a few words. And I can't make them out anyway, see, because suddenly my mama's laughin' to bust a gut. Her whole lap's shakin'. I got to hold on tight or get thrown clear across the room.
>
> I turn to look at her—this is the same woman that was cryin' a second ago?—then turn back to the TV. "Who that man, Mama?"
>
> She's still laughin'. Takes her a while to catch her breath. "Bill Cosby, son. He's a comedian."
>
> A comedian?
>
> "What's that?"
>
> Now she's laughin' harder. Tears still comin' out of her eyes, but she's happy. She's slappin' the arm of the chair, she's so happy. She's lettin' it out.
>
> I look over at this Bill Cosby again. I don't know what he's talkin' about—something's going on in his bathroom—but I know that whatever it is, it's got *power*.
>
> "That's what I want to be, Mama. A comedian. Make you laugh like that, maybe you never cry again." (Mac 2003, 7)

In the main, broadcast television has moved away from live stand-up comedy just as it has moved away from live television in general, in part because it allows them to record at a time and pace not dictated by the broadcast schedule, in part because the technology of recording allows them a better, more polished product, and in part because they have greater control over the product as content.

Although live radio and television variety broadcasting ceased to be the norm, programming that is close to live continues. Variety programming—especially shows such as *The Tonight Show* and *Late Night with David Letterman*—is often used as a vehicle for promoting other appearances, new movies, and so forth. To serve its promotional function its moment of broadcast cannot be too far removed from its moment of recording.

> Towards the end of his great run as a talk show host, Merv Griffin taped his shows on a six-week delay. Of course, this made it difficult to keep a daily show current. And sometimes it made for surreal situations. Once, I was on the show with another guest who was a well-known television actor. A few weeks after we taped the show, he accidentally drowned in his swimming pool. But our show aired a couple of weeks after that. And there he was telling Merv, "I just put a pool behind my house. Boy, Merv, it's the best thing I ever did! I love that pool!" (Leno 1996, 239–37)

Typically, filming will be the day of (or, in the case of daytime programming, the day before) the broadcast. The style of the program often emulates a live performance at that time of day: the backdrops behind the desk of *The Tonight Show* represent the Los Angeles skyline at night, a technique copied on virtually all successor and imitator programs. Shows are also recorded in real time, to set the proper pacing and, presumably, to emulate somewhat the frisson of a live performance. But the hours between filming and broadcasting do allow for a certain flexibility: if needed, a performance can be edited.

> How the joke ended or who that televangelist might be remained a mystery to TV viewers watching Bill [Hicks] hours later that evening. In post-production, *Late Night [with David Letterman]* cut into the joke, interrupting Bill mid-sentence with canned applause. Meanwhile, the camera awkwardly cut to the studio audience (too brightly lit and from what appeared to be a different part of the show) smiling blankly. The edit was so crude that not only was the punchline buried but Bill was not even shown saying thank you or goodnight to the crowd. The next bizarre shot was of Bill walking over to Letterman's couch for some stiff patter. (True 2002, 94–95).[7]

The continued emulation of a live broadcast, despite the awareness by the audience (both in the studio and at home) that it is a conceit, appears to speak to the impression of immediacy needed for the "proper" appreciation of stand-up comedy, specifically, and the contemporary variety talk-show, in general. The casual conversation with the host at the couch—frequently as planned and structured as a solo performance and providing opportunities for performing further material—is a further performance that seems to demand immediacy. Although shows that are recorded as live are repeated, they are typically no more than a few weeks old when rebroadcast.

However, although audience reaction continues to be a key element in the success or failure of a specific performance, and although half a century of television means that North American audiences are comfortable with its conventions and do not have their illusions shattered by being aware that the performance is taking place in a television studio or that a microphone is in use, studio-based variety program rarely if ever show audience reactions to a comedian's routines. It would take a new form of televised stand-up comedy to more fully incorporate the audience.

In December of 1975, HBO aired *An Evening with Robert Klein*. Broadcast live from Haverford College and filmed with multiple cameras, it shows the audience waiting for the performance to begin and then reacting throughout. He begins with a comment on getting to Haverford (a suburb of Philadelphia) from New York via the New Jersey Turnpike; the crowd applauds and laughs when he mentions the section between Newark and Elizabeth: "the *oil* refineries there / you get a smell of / universal *fart* [L] <u>for about 20 minutes</u>" (Klein 1975*).

It was the first HBO comedy special, a format that would become the dominant medium and revolutionize stand-up comedy, much as the LP did fifteen years prior. The move to presenting stand-up comedians was an effort by HBO at expanding its audience through diversifying its programming, heretofore based mostly on airing unedited and uninterrupted films. Original programming that it would own and not have to license and that was inexpensive to produce—like stand-up comedy specials, documentaries, and reality television—soon proved to be if not more lucrative then at least successful enough to use as a bargaining chip with film studios (Berger 2000, 381–82).

With cable television specials, three factors that alter television performance in general—namely, issues of appropriateness in regards to indecency or obscenity, a highly restricted or segmented allowable performance length, and that comedians are not performing to an audience who is there to see them specifically—are absent. "[Viewers] saw comics do their acts as God intended—not as five-minute excerpts but as the full-length unexpurgated performance that previously only cabaret or concert-hall audiences glimpsed" (Berger 2000, 381). The subscription-based nature of cable television in the United States, particularly in regards to broadcasters like HBO that do not supplement with advertising revenue, means that broadcasters are not making use of the public airways and therefore are not subject to the same federal regulation.[8] Nor are they subject to pressure from sponsors, as their revenue comes from subscriptions and not from advertisers.

"Appropriateness" is still in place, however, in the sphere of market viability: the performers who appear would typically be understood as having reached a significant plateau in their careers to warrant the investment in the broadcast, with an anticipation of subsequent recoup of expenses through rebroadcast, syndication, and, in recent years, repackaging as audio and video recordings. The almost invariably mandated one-hour limit is approximating the typical performance duration while headlining on tour: the performance needs to be worked out to fit the time more exactly, but the televised performance would be constructed more or less along the same lines as an untelevised one.[9]

Although the specials are not always live, live broadcasts of stand-up comedy specials carry with them the specter of being an "event." Paul Rodriguez's *Behind Bars and Live in San Quentin* (1991*), Jerry Seinfeld's *I'm Telling You for the Last Time* (1998a*), broadcast live from Broadway's Broadhurst Theater, Robin Williams's *Live on Broadway* (2002*), broadcast from the Broadway Theater, and George Carlin's *It's Bad for Ya* (2008a*), from the Wells Fargo Center for the Arts in Santa Rosa, were all preceded by much publicity concerning the potential rawness of the performance. Although they were sure to be rebroadcast and available on recording formats, to watch them live is considered akin to having "been there."

The quasi-ephemerality of live broadcasting brings to mind the social dimension of broadcasting itself and an aspect of ritual. Building on Georg W. F. Hegel's suggestion equating newspapers with prayer—"Reading the morning paper is the realist's morning prayer" (qtd. in Rosenkranz 1977, 543)—Benedict Anderson suggests that the exercise in orientation is shared with others:

> [Each] communicant is well aware that the ceremony he performs is being replicated simultaneously by thousands (or millions) of others of whose existence he is confident, yet of whose identity he has not the slightest notion. (1991, 35)

Similarly, particularly with comedy performances like the host's monologue on late-night variety shows—less a routine and more a series of jokes whose directive is topicality—there is an awareness that, as one listens and (presumably) laughs at one person's perspective on recent events, a large section of the nation is doing likewise. Participation in a broadcast performance by virtue of being a member of the viewing audience is a shared experience that bears similarities to the shared experience of live performance.

Live broadcasting of stand-up comedy performances continues to this day, but by its nature it is ephemeral. When it is broadcast it is with the intent of some form of redistribution in order to maximize the investment, and the redistribution—now temporally distant as well as spatially—orients the form.

If the physical distancing of performer from audience introduces some limitation on the pool of common referents that a group immediately present to each other would share, the temporal distancing does likewise. But the audience is still bound temporally to the scheduling of the replayed performance and watches or listens to it in real time: it is a homeostatic phenomenon, not to be repeated until its next availability, control of which lies outside the control of the audience.

Cable television had started a greater interest in comedy, but it was still absent from network and basic cable television save for on variety shows. In 1981, Canadian investors looking for a tax shelter funded *An Evening at the Improvisation* (later shortened back to *An Evening at the Improv*) (Berger 2000, 450). Filmed at Budd Friedman's Improv club in Los Angeles, a celebrity host (Louis Gossett Jr., Andy Kaufman, Mark Hamill) would introduce three or four comics over the course of an hour. The fifty-two episodes were syndicated to the A&E Network, which commissioned new episodes in 1987, which ran until 1996.

An Evening at the Improv introduced some new facets to televised comedy. Performances were longer, often ten or twelve minutes. By virtue of being shot on location, the "natural" context of club performance was restored, as the audience was seated, not in the risers of a television studio or at the theaters typical of cable television specials, but at tables. Multicamera shoots would allow for more than simply the sound of the audience: audience reaction could also be shown. Performers would walk through the audience when getting to and from the stage. Unlike in the studio, specific members of the audience could enter into exchanges with the performers, and cameras would capture that interaction. Finally, a cutaway to the audience—and to specific members of the audience—could be employed by the producers to frame and encourage a reaction for the home viewer.

Alison Kibler (1999) discusses audience response in great detail in her article on *Evening at the Improv*: the show's use of close-ups is integral to these processes, although it does not explicitly constitute the focus of her argument. However, in passing, she notes the techniques employed by the show directors:

> The basic unit of this congenial Improv audience is a man and woman laughing as a couple. Audience close-ups most often capture laughing pairs of men and women. Performers ensure that couples in the audience will be coded as heterosexual. . . . These portrayals of men and women laughing together reassert the predominant mode of the consumption of leisure—heterosexual romance— and also attempt to guarantee that the common laughter of the Improv is, above all, not divided by gender. (Kibler 1999, 50)

The imperative of "congeniality" (using Kibler's term) is achieved, in other words, through demonstrating that, however discordant the performance might become, however divided the audience might be, the comedian always works toward a resolution that the group collectively enjoys, and the congenial, communal, intimate atmosphere is restored.

> [Bobby Collins's] response to his wife, "Shut up. Shut the hell up," brings a mix of boos, catcalls, and cheers from the audience. While the camera maintains a close-up on Collins during this volatile and obviously divided audience reaction, Collins quips, "On the inside," thus upsetting the gender expectations and his gender alliances with the audience. Following his confession that his verbal subjugation of his wife was merely an unexpressed wish, the camera captures a laughing woman, a patron who may have been booing when he told his wife to "shut the hell up." Located just behind the pleased woman are laughing men. (Kibler 1999, 52)

The question of why the sight of discordance and not the sound would disturb the sense of congeniality and the related question of why the sight of congeniality serves to reinforce it so effectively are perhaps best left to a different analyst, but televised stand-up comedy outside of the studio context continues to use the audience as a visual prop, following *Evening at the Improv*'s format.[10]

By framing the series by the venue, the show's producers were also able to demonstrate that, unlike the audience for a variety broadcast, the audience members here were deliberately present to observe a stand-up comedy performance, although not necessarily a performance by any of the particular comedians on stage that evening. They were fans of stand-up comedy as a form, if not of the individual comedians. They had come to the venue with the expectation that they would be presented with a stylistic form that could conceivably offend them, and, although they would still judge the individual comedians according to their respective merits, they were there with the expectation that they would be entertained by this particular form. The performances were still constrained in that they needed to conform to broadcast standards, but they didn't need to be so generic in content that they would be palatable to the non-fan.

Other shows would follow. *Caroline's Comedy Hour* (also an A&E production) debuted in 1989, running for five seasons. Virtually identical in format, it differed in part by being explicitly located in New York City. Following a number of annual specials that started in 1985, CBC began an eponymous series filmed during the Gala shows at the *Just for Laughs* festival in Montreal. This was followed a few years later with the *Halifax Comedy Fest* (1994–present) (which was filmed since its inception) and *CBC Winnipeg Comedy Festival*. *Just for Laughs* would be interspersed with host segments taken from backstage or the streets of Montreal but avoided an onstage host. *Halifax Comedy Fest* would have no host and would be filmed in a variety of venues, ranging from auditoriums to pubs, throughout Halifax. *Winnipeg Comedy Festival* varied further, in that the gala events were specially commissioned material on a given theme—"Sleeping with the Elephant," "Turtle Island—North America's Best Aboriginal Comics"—which would have a well-known theme-appropriate host. In the United States, HBO and Russell Simmons started *Def Comedy Jam* (1992–1996; 2006–2008), which used a similar format—an established comedian introducing a number of less well known acts—but without the censoring restrictions of basic cable or network broadcasting. BET's *ComicView* (1992–2006; clip show 2006–), launched the same year and equally an example of "narrowcasting" (see Schulman 1994), did have to abide by those restrictions.

In 1989, HBO introduced *One Night Stand* (1989–92; 2005). Whereas the anthology-style shows that preceded it relied on a group of performers and—typically—the mediating presence of a host, this show was a half hour devoted to a single performer who at that point in time in his or her career might not have been able to sustain an entire special. It was filmed in the studio, the audience was not typically shown, and the backdrop was unusually elaborate.

CBC's *Comics!* (1993–99), HBO's *Comedy Half-Hour* (1996–2006), The Comedy Network's *Comedy Now* (1997–), and *Comedy Central Presents* (1998–) each follow the same format: with relatively few exceptions, they are in stylized venues, without a host, and with standardized opening credits. Because the shows take place outside of a comedy club, outside of a "natural" venue, the audiences are specifically invited to participate in the taping of the show, whether or not they are fans of the specific comedian.

In the unedited footage for Mitch Hedberg's (1999*) episode of *Comedy Central Presents*, Hedberg makes frequent references to the audience clearly having no idea who he is and having no familiarity with his material, delivery, or background:

> Thank you
> hey
> welcome to my *half-hour special*
> does anybody know who I am? [I]
> Why did a bunch of people who don't know who I am show at my special? [I]
> That's *bullshit* [L]
> alright everybody
> this will be *fun* (1999*)

Unlike the variety-show comedy performances, there is not the presumption with series that they are recorded in a timely fashion: there may be a significant distance in time between the performances and the eventual broadcast. This is further the case when shows are continually rebroadcast in syndication, and the span becomes not weeks or months but decades.

> HOMER: Oh, I like it better when they're making fun of people who *aren't* me. [*gasps*] I know, "Evening at the Improv." They never talk about anything beyond the 1980s.
> COMEDIAN (ON TV): See, I think about weird stuff. Like, what would happen if E.T. and Mr. T had a baby? Heh, well, you'd get Mr. E.T., wouldn't you? And you know, I think he'd sound a little something like this: "I pity the fool who doesn't phone home." [*audience laughs*]
> HOMER: [*laughs*] Ooh, I wouldn't want to be Mr. T right now. (Daniels 1994*)

With the proliferation of specialty cable channels, both those specializing in comedy and those whose focus is classic television, the continual rebroadcasting of stand-up comedy series as part of their regular line-ups means the increasing distance in time between the original performance and today. However, given the nature of their original recordings, although the precise distance could not be anticipated, that there would be distance was a known factor, and the material either avoids the intensely topical or aims at what is believed at the time to have greater time depth (as the E.T. quote suggests).

Already discussed briefly above, the one-hour solo stand-up comedy special is a lucrative goal for the comedian. For one thing, merely having the opportunity to do a special is an indication by a media outlet that one has reached a certain level in one's career. Unlike the half-hour specials discussed in the previous section, the comedian's name is included in the title.

Specials would have had their origin with variety specials—one-off versions of variety series—which like their forebears incorporate solo performances, sketch comedy, and musical guests. The Bob Hope television specials, starting in the 1950s, set the template. Notable specials with stand-up comedians as the host include *The Alan King Show* (1969*), *The Richard Pryor Special?* (1977a*) (later spun off to the four-episode *The Richard Pryor Show* [1977b*]), and Andy Kaufman's *Andy's Funhouse* (1979*). The requirements of commercial broadcasting—the strictures imposed on performance content and the interruptions of advertisements—did not allow for extended performances, nor was it thought that the single performer could sustain the interest of the audience at home without either the support of some featured artist or a variety of content styles.

It was cable that introduced the long-form special, building on the precedent of comedy feature films. An hour of uninterrupted and uncensored airtime allows for an approximation of the rhythms of a live performance. As it is original programming, cable channels heavily promote this, emphasizing how this form of programming is unavailable on regular broadcast networks.

They also replay them frequently and for long after their original airdate. For example, in July of 2008, on HBO Comedy (the comedy specialty network), David Cross's *The Pride Is Back* (1999*) was scheduled for broadcast four times, Dennis Miller's *They Shoot HBO Specials, Don't They?* (1994*) three, D. L. Hughley's *Going Home* (1999*) three and his *Unapologetic* (2007*) twice, Martin Lawrence's *You So Crazy* (1994*) five, Dana Carvey's *Squatting Monkeys Tell No Lies* (2008*) five (in addition to four showings on other HBO networks and availability through the On Demand service), Larry David's *Curb Your Enthusiasm* (1998*) four, George Carlin's *Playin' with*

Your Head (1986a*) twice and his *It's Bad for Ya* (2008a*) four times (plus On Demand), John Leguizamo's *Freak* (1998*) twice, and Robert Klein's *The Amorous Busboy of Decatur Avenue* (2005*) twice (with one showing on the main network). This is in addition to multiple showings of episodes of *One Night Stand* and *Comedy Half-Hour* and anthology shows such as Rodney Dangerfield's *Nothin' Goes Right* (1988*) and the 1995 *Young Comedians Special* (Shandling 1995*).

In Canada, CBC has been the sole progenitor of the independently named comedy specials. (CTV and the The Comedy Network still use the *Comedy Network Presents* and *Comedy Now* format.) Mike MacDonald's *On Target* (1991*) was the first stand-up comedy special on Canadian television, followed in quick succession by two more (1992*, 1993*). Although cleaned up for television, the less restrictive broadcast standards in Canada and the need for programming content that is both Canadian and inexpensive to produce have allowed for the special to flourish on regular network television: Ron James had one special every year between 2005 and 2008.

One of the real draws of the comedy special is the flexibility of the content. Following the effort involved in its production, the comedian or the network can subsequently redistribute the performance in other media. The same performance can become an audio or a video recording (or both) and thus become a specific durable good that the comedian can sell, as happened when home video became a viable market in the early 1980s. Furthermore, unlike live broadcasts, specials are often recorded over the course of a number of performances: the comedian wears the same outfit and largely keeps to the same order of material. This allows the opportunity to present a smoother program. Unused footage can also be added to subsequent mediations—albums or videos—in "director's cut" versions. For Ron James's *The Road Between My Ears* (2003*), two nights were filmed at the Elgin Theatre in Toronto. For the television broadcast a twenty-minute bit about an Air Canada flight went unaired, having been too long to include uninterrupted by commercial breaks or within the allotted hour, minus commercials. It is restored in the DVD.

In total, there have not been a large number of mainstream stand-up comedy films. They were originally a way of circumventing the economics of touring and promoting a comedian whose material excluded him or her from mainstream media. They tended to be remarkably low-budget independent productions when gauged by today's standards and would not get the major theatrical releases of standard cinema. If one discounts *The Lenny Bruce Performance Film* (Bruce 1992*), which was filmed using a single camera in an effort at documenting his act to use as evidence in his obscenity trials, Richard Pryor's *Live and Smokin'* (1971*) is perhaps one of the earliest examples of a film created for commercial purposes, although it maintains a documentary feel, using a three-camera shoot and capturing much of the feel of a live performance, with walkouts, false starts, and running commentary on how well the performance is going. Rudy Ray Moore's *Rude* (1978*), on the other hand, acts as an extended commercial, replete with breaks wherein he looks directly at the camera and encourages the audience to purchase his album.

By the time cable television came into full swing, the potential market for full-length comedy was now recognizable, yet film remained the exception rather than the rule. It was an expensive proposition, requiring the support of distributors, and needed to be of sufficient technical quality (i.e., filmed, not recorded on video) if the comedian wanted distribution to theaters. The incentive for going through such a process was that a film could generate an enormous amount of revenue if the comedian was of sufficient stature. Whereas the cable companies themselves owned cable specials, comedians owned the films and would be directly entitled to that revenue. Richard Pryor made three more concert movies, through small independents and later through his own production company: *Live in Concert* (1979a*), *Live on the Sunset Strip* (1982a*), and *Here and Now* (1983a*), each of which grossed over $15 million. Each also generated its own LP (Pryor 1979b*, 1982b*, 1983b*).

In 1983 Bill Cosby wrote, directed, produced, and self-financed *Bill Cosby: Himself* (1983*), which in turn generated its own album of the same name, released six months prior to the film's release (1982*). The film resuscitated public interest in Cosby at a time when his comedy was seemingly out of synch with Pryor, Eddie Murphy, and Robin Williams (R. Smith 1997, 160). Some of its routines on family life were direct inspirations for the pilot episode of *The Cosby Show*, which started in 1984.

As Eddie Murphy's *Delirious* HBO special (1983a*) had been one of the first to have a significant impact through video sales and rentals, he also wrote and executive produced *Raw* (1987*) while at the height of his film career. It remains the top-grossing stand-up movie of all time and held the record for a concert movie until it was eclipsed by the *Hannah Montana* concert film (Hendricks 2008*). Unlike in some of Pryor's films, the camera never leaves the stage in *Raw*, and the filmmakers maintain throughout the illusion that the film audience is no different from the live audience. Although no album came from it (unlike *Delirious*, which produced *Comedian* [Murphy 1983b*]), portions of the performance were included on Murphy's *Greatest Comedy Hits* CD (1997*).

When Andrew "Dice" Clay sold out Madison Square Garden, the event was filmed and released as *Dice Rules* (Clay 1991*): in part because the venue and the frenzy of the event did not lend themselves to a particularly good performance, the film did poorly at the box office, earning only $600,000. For the album that emerged, *Dice Live at Madison Square Garden* (1994*), half of the tracks were taken from a club recording in October of 1991.

For most of the 1990s stand-up comedy films seemed to disappear. The dynamics of home video had shifted from primarily renting to buying, and cable channels proliferated, including comedy-only channels. But since 2000 a number of comedians have returned to film as a potential vehicle.

Margaret Cho has made three theatrically released stand-up comedy films, *I'm the One That I Want* (2000*), *Notorious C.H.O.* (2002*), and *Margaret Cho: Assassin* (2005*), through her production company Cho Taussig. Without having achieved the mainstream success of Murphy or Pryor, she has an intensely loyal fan base, particularly among gay men, which has enabled her to continue making films, albeit with limited distribution (only *Notorious C.H.O.* played on more than twenty screens at the same time). They have all fared well as home videos.

Martin Lawrence's *Runteldat* (2002*) was his first recorded performance since his HBO special *You So Crazy* (1994*). Opening in over seven hundred theaters, it went on to gross almost $20 million in its thirteen-week run. The next year Eddie Griffin released *DysFunktional Family* (2003*), which interspliced his full-length performance with footage of him walking through the streets of Kansas City, Missouri (his hometown), and interviews with his family. With a similar opening of just over six hundred theaters, it was pulled after only four weeks, having failed to recoup its $3 million budget. However, it produced an album and a video release, which became Griffin's first consumable products, and perhaps not coincidentally, his HBO special (1997*) had its DVD release in 2005.

Perhaps more than any other mediation, the stand-up comedy performance film is best able to emulate the dynamic of live performance inasmuch seeing a movie in a theater is a collective and ritualized activity. "People go to movies in groups. . . . People do not read in groups" (Riesman 1970, 256). The potential people in the audience at a screening are closer in number to that of the audience at the filming, and far more than would be possible at a home viewing. Simply put, unlike television watching or radio listening, there is a specific effort, outlay, and risk required for attending a film. As Bruce Austin states,

> Movies are a consumer product, unlike many other products, that do not offer "trialability." Also, the film consumer typically enters into a "consumption agreement/situation" with little precise knowledge of the commodity itself; while the form is perhaps familiar, the exact content remains enigmatic. Further, with movies, unlike other consumer products, few "repeat purchases" (i.e., attendance) of the same product (i.e., movie) are likely to occur. Additionally, movie selection and attendance is a costly commitment in terms of time, finances, and effort (i.e., one *goes* to a movie as opposed to sitting down to watch TV). (1982, 22)

An audience member needs to leave the house, go to a specific, specialized venue, purchase tickets, sit in fixed seating alongside both intimates and strangers, and, as decorum dictates that focus be on directed toward the screen, keep the interaction with each other to a minimum in favor of the reaction to the comedian. The decision to do so is predicated on the expectation of seeing something worth the effort. Prior to the advent of cable television and, subsequently, home video, the only other way for an audience to experience and actually see a full-length, unexpurgated stand-up comedy performance was live, which requires a similar effort. The extraordinariness of film as a stand-up comedy medium turns the films into events. (When Eddie Muphy's *Raw* [1987*] premiered in Los Angeles, fights broke out at three separate theaters, resulting in the shooting death of one man and the stabbing of another [United Press 1987].)

I remember going by myself to see *Raw* in January of 1988 (it had been released in late December). It was in the wake of my father moving out and, fourteen though I might have been, I was able to disappear from home on a weeknight for a few hours and get into a restricted movie. The sense of occasion in the theater was palpable, with laughter, catcalls, and applause coming both from the recorded audience and the one of which I was a member. Outside of live performances, it is perhaps my most palpably focused stand-up comedy audience experience.

With the rise of digital filmmaking and an expanded film and comedy festival circuit, some comedians have produced stand-up performance films that premiere at film festivals and circulate to independent cinemas before entering into more typical distributions channels. Sarah Silverman's *Jesus Is Magic* (2005*) opened in eight theaters and expanded to fifty-seven cities, whereas Louis CK directed *Hilarious* (2010*), which had its premiere at the Sundance Film Festival and a one-day, eight-city theatrical release prior to being shown on the Epix channel. However, performance films remain an unusual forum, given the increasing ease of access audiences have to comedy programming.

Network broadcasting is the most pervasive medium for stand-up comedy; it is the one through which most people—fans and non-fans alike—have been exposed to it. It cannot offend, it cannot be too esoteric, and it must be aimed at appealing to the non-fans present at the site of performance. As one moves toward narrowcasting—stand-up-comedy-specific programming, specialty cable channels, films—the performances begin to more greatly reflect the interest of the audience, in part because they are being specifically sought out and in part because they are not at pains to be wholly inclusive of those who are not seeking them out.

For the audiences of stand-up comedy on radio, television, or film, the experience is homeostatic: its scheduling is beyond their immediate control, and there is a certain ephemerality to it, for re-experiencing it is either at the whim of the broadcasting programmers or, in the case of film, involves a return to the cinema. But there is a desire to re-experience a stand-up comedy performance and to do so at one's own leisure.

CHAPTER 7
Stand-Up Comedy Recordings

> Have they told you enough
> that we're . . . we're recording a *CD* [A] [!<Yeah>!]
> so you might pick it up
> and not recognize your *laugh* [L]
> you may not want to *buy* it
> 'cause you've already *seen* it [L]
> this is not the *target market*
> —**Mitch Hedberg,** *Strategic Grill Locations*

We have been examining how various media—from such simple things as the elevated platform of the stage to modern contrivances like video projection—affect the stand-up comedy performance itself, discerning what each new mediation allows and proscribes, whether it be a consequence of the medium itself or of its control by owners. In this chapter, on recordings, we turn to formats where the media still have their limitations and contributions, but the audience has more or less total control over the experience of the performance. Recordings allow performances to travel beyond the confines of a live performance and a broadcaster's prerogative of retransmission.

When thinking about stand-up comedy in recorded media there are a few things to consider. Firstly, it is with recordings that stand-up comedy becomes a merchandisable product. Comedians certainly get known through media exposure on radio and television, and they are paid for it. Typically, the benefit comes from the exposure more than from the remuneration, as being able to identify oneself as having appeared on a particular program can change the comedian's professional status for live venues. A recording, however, becomes a tangible product that not only serves as exposure but can produce ongoing revenue for the comedian directly. Furthermore, as recordings progress, the comedian has a developing and accumulating back catalogue that allows for a cumulative reputation: for an established comedian with a number of recordings, new material can be introduced in the context of past material and performed with the expectation that the audience is for the most part familiar with his or her work.

186

Building on this, because a recording can be stopped and started and replayed, the recorded performance need not be experienced in a homeostatic way. The listener can go back and listen to a section again and again, if he or she desires. In this manner, the performance becomes something like a printed text: parsable, revisitable, reviewable. It also becomes fixed and, just as certain versions of fairy tales become elevated to canonical status when fixed in print, when a comedian commits a routine to vinyl or binary it becomes the de facto canonical version. Moreover, with recordings forming a part of the comedian's natural and professional landscape, that recordings are canonical is a given: when new comedians wish to learn the craft, they turn to recordings as much as they turn to live performance.

That being said, humor theory tends to indicate that part of the way humor works is the revelation of the unexpected or unanticipated. This demands the question as to why anyone would *want* to experience a comedic performance—the exact same comedic performance—a second time. Either humor theory is wrong, or there is more to stand-up comedy as a content than humor alone, or each re-listening brings something new.

As we have been proceeding along a spectrum of ever-increasing distance, recordings have been placed at the end of this discussion of mediation. But comedy recordings predate radio. Roland Smith notes how, during the "classic age" of the 78 rpm records,

> comedy records flourished. One reason was that record companies found it economical to hire comedians. Unlike singers, they didn't require expensive backup musicians. Primitive technology was well suited to simply reproducing the sound of a person talking. (1998, 3)

Records were often used as a form of parlor entertainment when, in lieu of having a member of the party perform a monologue or poem, guests would listen to a recording instead. Although musical comedy and duos were the norm, these recordings would often be a short monologue by a solo comedian, recorded in the studio. Major labels were releasing these discs, including Columbia, RCA Victor, and Okeh. With the advent of radio and the proliferation of comedy freely available through broadcasts, recording sales slumped. The 1950s saw the advent of "party albums," recordings of live performances, which availed themselves of new LP technology. These party records, however, tended to be released through smaller independent labels and were performances of artists who couldn't attain mainstream success, excluded from broadcasting largely from the (tautological) perception that they would not appeal to a large enough audience (Del Negro 2010).

In 1959 the jazz label Verve released *Inside Shelley Berman*, which became the first comedy album to sell 100,000 units: encouraged by the possibilities, major label Warner Brothers began its own comedy imprint, starting with Bob Newhart's phenomenally successful *The Button-Down Mind of Bob Newhart* (1960*).

Newhart's comedy principally revolved around one half of a conversation, most famously half of a telephone conversation, the other end of which was only ever implied by his straight reactions. It was a technique he borrowed from Berman, and it in turn dates back to Joe Hayman's "Cohen on the Telephone" 78s from the 1910s and '20s (R. Smith 1998, 90–92). A typical bit involved an introductory premise, sometimes rooted with a passing autobiographical note ("I was in the army," "I used to work as an accountant") and then the portrayal of a character. These characters were either identifiable types (a man returning a toupee, a driving instructor) or tangential witnesses to history (Abraham Lincoln's public relations man, Sir Walter Raleigh's agent). As such, although Newhart was recognized as the artist behind the material, it was not inextricably linked with Newhart's own biography, as he was not engaged in a performed autobiography. To put it another way, a fan might look forward to hearing Newhart's material, but it is equally accessible to a neophyte.

An early artist to the Warner Brothers roster was Bill Cosby. His first album, *Bill Cosby Is a Very Funny Fellow, Right*, was released in 1963. Recorded at the Bitter End in New York City, it consists of 12 tracks, only one of which is longer than five minutes. It is similar in style to Newhart's: some tracks are character monologues of a recognizable type (the football coach in "The Pep Talk"), a few are observations about everyday life (eccentrics on the subway in "A Nut in Every Car"), again often rooted in a passing, albeit generic, autobiographical note ("I played football at, uh, Temple University," "I am not from New York City / I was born in Philadelphia / raised in Philadelphia / educated in Philadelphia"). The most famous tracks are the three about Noah ("Right!," "And the Neighbor," and "Me and You, Lord"), explicit conversations between Noah and either God or a nosy neighbor, in which Cosby performs both roles.

For the modern listener, what is striking about these tracks (and others on the album) is the use of non-diegetic sound: the voice of God is introduced with a bell and is distorted with reverb, and there are sound effects added of rain and thunder. A YouTube search reveals his only (surviving) televised performance of this routine, and the non-diegetic sounds are indeed absent. What worked on television was thought to not work unaided on record.

Cosby's next album, *I Started Out as a Child* (1964*), had 15 tracks, five of which clock in at under a minute and a half. However, several features distinguish this album from the one previous. For one, there is an absence of non-diegetic sound. Furthermore, he begins to introduce autobiographical and ethnographic details that do not speak to a pan-American experience. In his liner notes to the album, comedian Allan Sherman puts it thus: "This is the world that you and I live in, turned inside out so we can see what *really* makes it tick, and laugh till we hurt." With this album we are first told of his poor Philadelphia background. As for ethnography, the first track, "Sneakers," involves a long description of how worn-out dress shoes would be resoled with tacked-on rubber and become shoes for playing street football, in the absence of real sneakers. Beyond the description of a street life that fell outside a mainstream American experience, Cosby also used some of the biographical detail about home life, specifically, a drinking father ("The Giant").

One very striking difference is how, whereas *Funny Fellow* fades to silence between tracks, *Started Out*'s tracks blend into one another, and the division of the performance into tracks is, albeit not arbitrary, certainly a matter of judgment. The first five tracks in *Started Out* are all about his childhood and, although the specific topics and themes do indeed vary, could just have easily been one larger track. Following these tracks and their personal, idiosyncratic content, the rest of the album has more universal material: "The Lone Ranger," "Half Man," "The Neanderthal Man," and "Seattle" each build on premises that are not anchored in some form of performed autobiography. Others are purportedly first-person narratives, some of which ("My Pet Rhinoceros") are more tall tale than personal experience narrative, while others ("Oops!," "Medic," "T.V. Football") have the same grounding in only the most superficial autobiographical detail as *Funny Fellow*.

The album's penultimate track, "T.V. Football," is of particular interest as it is revisited, with much expansion, in "Hofstra," the last track of *Why Is There Air?* (Cosby 1965*). In the latter, which is almost seven times as long, he extends the anecdote by providing further detail about his football days, including an introduction that begins with the insistence that it is indeed true that he played college football. Below, the two tracks are transcribed next to each other, "T.V. Football" in full and "Hofstra" with the additional material summarized.

"T.V. Football" (Cosby 1964*) 1:14	"Hofstra" (Cosby 1965*) 8:02
	[0:00–0:58] True that he played football at Temple University; not good team at the time, played mainly weak teams, and Hofstra, losing to all.
[0:00] The first time ever televised . . . we ever had a game that was televised we played against a school called *Hofstra*.	[0:58] We were going to play against Hofstra which is a really *terrible* school they *killed* us every year, boy
	[1:04–2:28] Time spent in locker room, praying not to be hurt. Description of second team as "nut squad," trying to avoid going on field by acting crazy. First team getting last rites. Coach diagramming trick plays.
[0:04] The athletic director came into the locker room and he says	[2:28–2:56] The athletic director asks to speak to the team, is introduced by coach as the person responsible for scholarships.
	[2:46–3:44] Gives long pep talk, how Hofstra consistently beats them 900 to nothing, how Hofstra's players are even bigger than last year, how there are twelve people in the stands despite homecoming.

[0:08]
now listen fellas he says
you guys are on television he says
and this is a first time for ya, he said
	[3:44]
	| This is our first game on television [L]
	we want to *keep* this television contract
	    going because this is the only way we
	    can make some *money*
	to buy little scuba diving suits [L]
	and snowshoes and ice skates for all the
	    weirdo squads here [L]
	so we're going to *say* to you please
	remember that you're on *TV*

I am *not* really concerned with *winning* as I am with the fact that you guys are *on* television and there are *certain* areas of your body that you *shouldn't touch* because it's *embarrassing* to the people watching *TV*	by that I mean don't worry about winning the game as much as we want you to be concerned with the fact that while you're out there on the field we're going to ask you *please* do not touch certain areas of your bodies while you're [L] out there on the football field because if you're out there diggin' and scratchin' people at home are going to turn you right off and we're going to lose the contract so *please* do not [L] touch certain areas of your bodies while you're out there on the field
[0:25] so the guy says yeah okay *we* know what you're talking about	
[0:27] so he made us sign an affidavit promising that we would not touch certain areas of our body	[4:36] Now we're going to pass out these affidavits and I want you to sign 'em saying that you will not touch [L] <u>certain areas of your body</u> while you're out there on the football field alright	
[0:33] So we ran out on the field . . .	[4:34–6:30] Players sign affidavits and run onto field. Hofstra players are described. First and second teams run around petrified. Entire first team injured in first play. Second team takes field.

[0:34] I don't know *why* it happened to me first time I carried the ball	[6:30] | Alright run the kamikaze play on one, alright [L] kamikaze *Cosby* up the middle *whole team* off the field *break* | [L] [6:36–7:10] Play is run. There is a hole, which he has never seen. Rumination on the anomaly of hole in opposition defense.

[0:37]
I went up to this *hole*
and I *saw* this guy on the ground, the
    defensive man
he was down
and I started to step over him
and just as I raised the left leg
he came *up*
and really *hit* me {WACKO!}, y'know
in the worst place
	[7:10]
	There was a big hole
	with a defensive man on the *ground*
	I planted *one foot*
	stepped over him
	when I did he stood up and hit me
	    {POOM!} [L]
	and the *pain* [L]
	<u>was</u> tremendous [L]
	and I threw down the ball [L]

[0:51]
and I said | ohhhhn! |
and I started to grab it and
| You'd better not touch any areas of
    your body |
	[7:28]
	and I said {very calmly} | oh | [L]
	{urgent} | <u>I've been</u> hit in the |
	| You'd better not touch [L]
	<u>any areas of your body</u> while you're on
	    the football field | [L:A]

[0:58]
So I grabbed my *head*
And I went into the huddle guys said
    what's the matter
I said | [series of groans] |
and to make it look *good* they ban-
    daged up my *head* [L]
	[7:42]
	<u>So I</u> grabbed my head [L]
	<u>and went into</u> the huddle guys say
	    what's the matter
	I say I can't say nothin' 'til they bring
	    the commercial on alright? [L]

[1:09] That's the truth. That's the truth	[7:50] Thank you and good night.

Already, by this third album, Cosby is moving away from the staccato rhythms of segmented routines and being more languorous, more descriptive, more discursive, and more prone to tangents. He is availing himself of the freedom the LP allows. There are only 8 tracks on *Air*, averaging five minutes apiece, and the material, for the most part, avoids the universal material of the first two albums. Absent altogether are pieces about popular culture or historical persons, and none are character monologues. The patterns continue over the next few albums: the routines become longer and less constrained—as they emerge out of a flow of longer material rather than as isolatable units—and the material becomes more rooted in autobiography, with characters and family members introduced in earlier albums revisited and, as his children are born and age, developed.

In a more or less steady progression from *Funny Fellow* onwards, Cosby's routines grow longer and fewer per album. One could even argue that tracks could have been fewer and longer were they not divided up at all: when they are all on a similar theme one could just as easily have left it as one large track, eschewing the thought of the album as a compilation of smaller units and moving toward exploring the possibilities of long play.

It is with the two albums from 1968, *To Russell, My Brother, Whom I Slept With* and *200 M.P.H.*, that Cosby fully takes advantage of the LP format. In writing about the phonograph in general, Marshall McLuhan has this to say about the LP:

> With regard to jazz, l.p. brought many changes . . . because the greatly
> increased length of a single side of a disk meant that the jazz band could really
> have a long and casual chat among its instruments. The repertory of the 1920s
> was revived and given new depth and complexity by this new means. (1964,
> 247–48)

Both *To Russell* and *200 M.P.H.* are structurally similar: four shorter tracks on the first side and then the second side taken up by one long eponymous bit. "To Russell, My Brother, Whom I Slept With" begins with a polling of the audience about who in the crowd is an only child, then a brief restatement of how being the oldest by seven years made him take revenge on his younger siblings. He then describes his apartment and his family's sleeping arrangements growing up in the projects. There is then a three-and-a-half-minute diversion, wherein he speaks of pranks he used to pull on his father and the bemused "that child is not right" reactions they would engender, and then of the differences between mothers and fathers with respect to their ease of manipulation and how seriously they are taken as figures of authority and threat. He then pulls back to the original thrust of the sketch, setting the scene for a twenty-minute reenactment of a discussion between the two brothers, regularly interrupted by their father bursting in with threats of punishment. It contains whispers, lines mumbled, and long stretches of silence.

"200 M.P.H." is the first routine on record that makes mention of the fact that he is not only a celebrity but also a wealthy one. Although it is very much in keeping with his delivery and basic style, there is something fundamentally odd about the routine. On the other hand, Cosby had reached a level of fame and wealth, and to avoid that as a topic would have started to sound disingenuous. He was by this point a celebrity, famous for being famous, independent of his ability. In his final album for Warner Brothers, 1969's *It's True! It's True!*, Cosby continues touching on narratives that are from his current position as wealthy celebrity, such as a fear of helicopter travel (in "Helicopters").

Over the course of these eight albums, there is a shift from small self-contained, discrete tracks that could essentially be performed by anyone to longer routines that are self-referential, cumulative, and inexorably linked to Cosby's autobiography. There is a stark contrast between the zingers of *Funny Fellow* and the languorous descriptions of *To Russell*, but when one looks at the intervening albums one sees an artist honing a craft to a specific medium and, just as importantly, an audience following along. In one development, the possibilities of the long-play format are explored more fully, and the performances are geared toward those possibilities, rather than the album being a compendium of material better suited for radio or television. In a second development, with each new album the cumulative body of work reaches a critical mass, not only listened to but *re*-listened to, and this informs the audience's expectations for each subsequent album. Cosby's fame as a performer begins to impinge on the everyman persona, and he must at least begin to address the fact that he has had several years' worth of life experiences in the public eye and that the audience is familiar with him as much for that as they are for his comedy and his performed autobiography.

Cosby effectively transformed the stand-up comedy album from a compilation of pieces best suited to another medium to one that needed to be seen as wholes and, ultimately, parts of an oeuvre and, consequently, helped to move the understanding of the stand-up comedy performance from a series of small routines to a contiguous whole.

If by 1969 Bill Cosby had firmly ensconced himself in the established culture, in 1970 George Carlin was working to remove himself from it. For ten years he had been a stand-up comedian in an older sense of the word, doing characters and monologues. He had recorded the album *Take-Offs and Put-Ons* (Carlin 1967*), which had been nominated for a Grammy. With characters like the hippy-dippy weatherman and the disc jockey at WINO radio, he had become a television favorite, mocking the beatnik and hippie culture. However, with the foment of the end of the 1960s, he had become disaffected with the middle-class expectations of his audience. In the liner notes to *Classic Gold*, Tony Hendra traces the "epiphany" to a show at the Lake Geneva Playboy Club on November 27, 1970:

> He could play it safe, stick to the officially approved noncontroversial material that has made him a rising star in the mainstream media. But because deep down he is more than a play-it-safe happy clown he is torn. He is aware vividly that he is entertaining the parents of the people he sympathizes with, whose point of view he shares. He is living a lie. He feels he is nothing less than a traitor.
>
> . . . Carlin goes out to perform. Instead of the material his audience expects—the hippy-dippy weatherman they've seen on Ed Sullivan and the Tonight Show—he tries to share some of his misgivings with them, some of the changes he feels taking place. (in Carlin 1993*)

Over three nights in June of the next year, at the Cellar Door in Washington, D.C., Carlin records the album *FM & AM* (1972a*), a deliberately transitional album. The "FM" in the title refers to the more experimental material of the first side, while "AM" refers to cleaner sketches and characterizations. On both sides he often roots the performance of the routine in some form of autobiography. The opening track, "Shoot," is a rumination on the word "shit," which begins with a brief narrative adverting to the hypocrisy of his previous show business life, while "The Hair Piece" is a poem to his long hair and then to his beard. It again refers to this transitional period in his professional life. The tracks on the rest of this side are observational pieces, but dealing with topics ("Sex in Commercials," "Drugs," "Birth Control") that had not been fodder for mainstream comedians on record. Although it is the first side, at the end of the last track he thanks the audience as if it were the end of the performance.

By Carlin's next album, *Class Clown* (1972b*), his counter-cultural credentials had been firmly established. The first eponymous track is over sixteen minutes long, although it is divided into three sections. The first four tracks on the second side return to childhood, but, as opposed to the more universal experience of "Class Clown," this time it is the distinctly New York Irish-Catholic schooling that informed his early life. Finally, the last track is the infamous "Seven Words You Can Never Say on Television." Much like "Shoot" at the beginning of *FM & AM*, it continues the theme of how certain euphemisms are branded profane while their synonyms are deemed acceptable. When he finally lists the words, over a minute into the seven-minute routine, it is the first use of profanity on the album, which aids in both their shock value and, conversely, their neutralization.[1]

Six months after recording *On the Road* (1977b*), his last album of the 1970s, Carlin did his first HBO special, *On Location: Carlin at USC* (1977a*). When it aired, it was prefaced by an introduction by Shana Alexander, then one of the "Point-Counterpoint" debaters on *60 Minutes*, followed by an interview with Carlin where he speaks to both influences on his comedy and the limitations of broadcast television. The concert begins by Carlin adverting to the fact that the performance is being recorded, which will constitute the first time he will have had the chance to actually see one of his own full-length performances. In later interviews, he would describe this performance as "very tentative" (Carlin 2007), which is a fair assessment. At one point he looks exceptionally nervous, holding his hand to his chin, as he struggles to remember or think of what to say next, and soon thereafter, when a technician interrupts as his microphone needs to be replaced, it takes him a moment to regroup and return to his routine.

Most of the concert is comprised of either old material or subtle variations thereon. There are a few new routines, but the value in watching the performance stems from being able to see him. Although the albums suggested a certain amount of gestures and facial expressions, and his earlier television performances made use of them, a segment on "walking" would be one of his first opportunities to do an unexpurgated recording of a visual routine. Furthermore, during a version of "How's Your Dog?" that is remarkably similar to the version from *On the Road*, he spends more time on (or, just as likely, does not edit out) the nonverbal reactions of guests at a dinner party sharing a room with a dog licking himself. A rendition of "Headlines" shows that he uses cue cards, although whether it is as a prop or genuinely as a mnemonic is unclear.

Prior to his most recent incarnation of "Seven Words," the screen freeze-frames and a message appears: "The final segment of Mr. Carlin's performance includes especially controversial language. Please consider whether you wish to continue viewing." As the screen unfreezes, he begins, "There is left that word . . . that group of words that we uh—" He stops to finish his glass of water, and the crowd begins to applaud and cheer loudly. The documentary feel of the special appears to suggest that they are creating something more like an artifact rather than a unique creation unto itself. There seems to be little impetus for new material despite that it would be broadcast so widely (albeit HBO's subscription base at the time was still very small). In fact there is something of a "greatest hits" feel about the piece, and the applause that met the introduction to the "Seven Words" material—like an opening guitar riff to a well-known song—obviously meant that it had excited the crowd. Lastly, Carlin's nervousness might have been more a consequence of him having limited control over the final product, unlike with his albums. He is not listed in the show's credits.

Carlin is more confident in his next special, *On Location: George Carlin at Phoenix* (1978*), over which he had greater control: his wife was associate producer. It varies little from *At USC*: it begins with a strong language warning, albeit without the additional apologia of a trusted third party; much of the material had already been released on album; he ends once again with a variation on "Seven Words," which rouses the audiences to cheers. The special had yet to become a forum for new material.

Carlin returned from a self-imposed exile in 1981 with the album *A Place for My Stuff* (1981*). What is most striking is how it is the only album that contains studio material as well as live performance. This allows for some strange dissonance to the tracks. For example, the first track of the second side, "Abortion," is essentially a one-liner. "Have you noticed that *most* of the women who are *against* abortion are women you wouldn't want to fuck in the first place man [L:A (17 seconds)] there's such *balance* in nature [L]." The track following is a studio piece, so "Abortion" sits outside of a regular flow of performance. In previous albums, even when the tracks faded to silence in between, one was never taken out of the performance per se. Although the intrusion of non-performance material would reemerge in specials such as *Carlin on Campus* (1984a*), it was an experiment not repeated on album again.

Carlin at Carnegie (1982*) was the last special not to be an album as well: it is also the first that was released as a home video and the first to be a product of his own production company, Cable Stuff Productions. At that point the home video market was almost exclusively perceived in terms of video rentals: the tapes themselves were often prohibitively expensive, as they were not meant to be purchased by the regular consumer. The alignment of video with sound recording as an equivalently consumable product had yet to take place.

That started, more or less, with *Carlin on Campus*, which produced both an album (1984b*) and a concert special (1984a*). The special incorporated some additional material, including a filmed vignette revisiting of "Class Clown" and three animated shorts. Although there are discrepancies between the album and special, suggesting certain performances were better for one medium over the other, what is clear is that a new strategy had emerged: not to view the albums and the specials as distinct avenues of performance, but rather to have two products emerge from the same performance. The *Playin' with Your Head* concert is more closely aligned on the special and album (Carlin 1986a*, 1986b*). In the closing credits, it is noted that the "soundtrack" is available on Eardrum Records, implicitly suggesting the album is a spin-off product: it may be at this point that we begin to see the special become the primary medium and the album secondary.

In January of 1990 Carlin recorded his seventh special, *Doin' It Again*, and his performance continues the more strident political elements that began with 1988's *What Am I Doing in New Jersey?* recording: his comments are frequently met with applause rather than laughter. He has also started to perform using an angry, New York Irish "accent" rather than the non-inflected neutral voice of his earlier work, from which he would occasionally venture into accent. The album it produced is the only album with a name different from the special: *Parental Advisory—Explicit Lyrics* (1990b*).

Jammin' in New York (Carlin 1992a*) is the first special to be broadcast live: two were recorded, but the show on April twenty-fifth went out live to air. With the exception of a thirty-second stretch in the last routine, the album (Carlin 1992b*) uses the same performance version as the special. It is also the last time that a concession is made to an LP having two sides: although there was no break in the broadcast performance, "Airline Announcements" fades out and "Golf Courses for the Homeless" fades back in.

Carlin's *Back in Town*, from 1996, is the first time that there was no LP release: the CD (1996b*) was the principal audio medium, which meant that the performance could be presented uninterrupted. This relationship between special and CD continued to Carlin's final special, *It's Bad For Ya!* (2008a*, 2008b*).

If we take his early specials as an indication of what his live performances were like at the time, new material could always be supplemented and complemented by a return to his filthy-language routines. His break from performance in the late 1970s engendered a creative realignment toward a "third career":

> By the time this interview appears, my first album in seven years will be out. I'm also working on a series of Home Box Office specials, a book, and a motion picture. . . . I hope I'm now beginning a new cycle of energy and creativity. If so, it'll really be my third career. The first was as a straight comic in the Sixties. The second was as a counterculture performer in the Seventies. The third will be . . . well, that's for others to judge. (Carlin 1982)

This realignment meant in part the embracing of the special as an impetus for new creativity, not an incidental snapshot of a career. This only emerges with the advent of home video, which allows for the special to be revisited at the whim of the viewer, much like the album did for the listener. Although the early days of video were largely rental driven, the market for personal video libraries soon meant that there was also created a market for a tangible product, and thus another revenue stream. Although Carlin started experimenting with the special as a form, his new material was lacking either the counter-cultural credibility or the language play of his earlier work. By the later 1980s, just as he was at risk of becoming stale, he began to move away from the random one-liners on a goofy theme and began longer routines, linked together less with narrative and more with a sense of arguing a particular viewpoint.

> Right around 1990, 1992 the writer took over and the pieces became more thoughtful and more extended and more like essays. . . . I discovered around that time that there was something I could do with an audience that didn't involve getting a laugh every 20–30 seconds, and that was to engage their imaginations and hold their attention with ideas and language. (Carlin 2007)

More importantly, by actively working to have new product available, reissuing older product in more era-appropriate media, and launching an online store where his products were prominently featured, Carlin was able to have his cumulative repertoire accessible to a potential public.[2]

As Cosby did for the LP, George Carlin more or less honed the stand-up comedy special as a type: a long-form performance that was also the opportunity for new material, with an eye for it being redistributed in other media. The special didn't simply become a new medium: it became the primary medium for stand-up comedy.

Starting with *The Road Between My Ears*, Ron James has used the special as his primary medium, and each has been made available as a DVD (save for *Manitoba Bound* [2008*]). Although they are also available through retailers and the CBC online store, he sells the DVDs off of his website and in the lobby at his performances. At the shows I attended the merchandise table saw casual interest before the performance but was swept clean afterwards: in Pictou, where he has also set up an autograph table after the performance, recently purchased DVDs were what got signed.

With the advent of performers developing websites as promotional vehicles, stand-up comedians have used the Internet to distribute and broadcast their performances. Dane Cook has pioneered this technology: samples from virtually every track of his albums and DVDs, with expletives bleeped out, are available through his website as streaming audio on the home page's media player. He has also produced podcasts with exclusive content ever since RSS distribution protocols have been in place. HBO and Comedy Central have each started audio and video podcasts of their own, featuring two- to three-minute clips from current specials. Comedy Central and its Canadian counterpart, The Comedy Network, also have archives of entire comedy performances on streaming video if they had originally been broadcast on their networks. Video On Demand services feature recently premiered stand-up comedy specials in their offerings.

Carlin's "Seven Words" was the first routine broadcast on XM Satellite Radio's "XM Comedy Channel," which allows for "uninhibited and uncensored standup comedy." The digital radio service maintains two other stand-up comedy channels on both its American and Canadian line-ups: "Laugh USA," which is marketed as "a good hearty laugh minus the crude or offensive," and "Laugh Attack," whose "spotlight is on Canada's rich pool of extraordinary comedic talent" (XM Satellite Radio 2001–2008; Canadian Satellite Radio 2005–2008). The other satellite radio service, Sirius, has four channels: the southern comedy themed "Blue Collar Radio," the uncensored, self-professed, uninhibited "Raw Dog," Jamie Foxx's "The Foxxhole," and the family-friendly "Laugh Break" (Sirius Canada 2008).

Satellite radio has two advantages over terrestrial radio: it allows for narrowcasting and selectivity and it is unfettered by broadcast regulations or deferral to advertiser concerns. A channel may choose to restrict content to appeal to a broader audience, but that is both an explicit choice and one made in the context of other channels having unrestricted content. Typically, these channels orient themselves around the routine rather than the entire performance: much like a music radio station, they will cycle through cuts from albums rather than listen to an entire album from beginning to end (there is programming on several of these stations that is devoted to entire performances, but it is the exception rather than the rule). As such, there is a potential curtailing of pieces that do not operate as "stand-alone" tracks, nor does one have the opportunity to see how a routine works within the context of an entire performance. In exchange for variety, listeners experience the same ephemerality and lack of control as listeners of conventional radio and television. However, as variety is the appeal, even within a framed parameter such as "urban" or "southern," it seems a fair exchange, and the exposure for comedians, to both their current repertoire and their back catalogue, is useful for reputation building.

As for streaming content and podcasts, the propensity is for short clips: the HBO and Comedy Central podcasts average two to three minutes, and the samples from tracks that Cook and others have on their sites are often under a minute. The draw therefore comes from highlighting the easily isolatable, shorter bits of a comedian's repertoire. Although I don't think it harbingers a return to the shorter material of, say, Bill Cosby's first album, it may have some impact on what is understood as the normative form of stand-up comedy: the bit, the routine, or the performance. Chris Rock was asked a similar question in a *Rolling Stone* interview:

Do you agree with Jerry Seinfeld that an iPod screen is a perfect venue for stand-up?

It depends. Me and Jerry are like Miles and Monk, always arguing about shit. And our internal argument is, Is it the show or the joke? Jerry's all about the joke and I'm all about the show. And if you're talking about just seeing a joke or two, the iPod is great. But the show probably needs to be seen on something a little bigger. I don't really want to watch *Richard Pryor: Live in Concert* on an iPod. (Rock 2007, 156)

Websites and digital media have also allowed for labels and artists to sell out-of-print material, whether through sites such as iTunes or through their own websites. Through dolemite.com, most of Rudy Ray Moore's back catalogue, none of which was ever available on a major label and rarely carried in stores, is available uncensored for streaming and for purchase through an affiliation with amazon.com's online music sales, either as a CD or as an MP3 download.

In 2011, Louis CK self-financed the staging and recording of his *Live at the Beacon Theatre* special (2011*), paying for the $170,000 production cost out of his own pocket (and from the ticket revenue from the two shows filmed). He then sold it exclusively through his website for five dollars. Within four days sales topped half a million dollars, and within twelve days they had reached a million (CK 2011a, 2011b). Encouraged by this model, other comedians followed suit: Jim Gaffigan's *Mr. Universe* (2012*) and Aziz Ansari's *Dangerously Delicious* (2012*). These experiments have demonstrated that if content is inexpensive and available in a preferred format, audiences don't mind paying for it. Similarly, streaming distributors like Netflix and Hulu have become lucrative venues, skipping both tangible distribution and potentially redistributable downloads: specials such as Rob Delaney's *Live at the Bowery Ballroom* (2012*), Moshe Kasher's *Live in Oakland* (2012*), and Marc Maron's *Thinky Pain* (2013*) were produced for Netflix distribution.

Conversely, like in music and film, much content is made freely available through torrents or by uploading to YouTube. While efforts are made at pulling these distributions down for copyright violations, the exercise is often fruitless. While "piracy" has made recordings potentially less lucrative, it has made it all the more important for comedians to ensure that recordings reflect how they want to be represented online, as—whether or not they are fairly paid for them—recordings still contribute to the development of a reputation and persona.

Whereas the LP, CD, video, and DVD were tangible marketable goods, digital distribution has removed the tangibility: there is a distribution network that does not require the infrastructure of handling actual physical content. Although there is the need for some form of intermediary like amazon.com or iTunes, there are no costs associated with storage, freight, or reproduction when supply runs out. But it would be unlikely for the tangible recording to disappear completely: like musicians, many comedians bring their physical recordings with them to concerts and sell them at merchandise tables, and the recording becomes a souvenir of the event (albeit not a recording of the particular performance the purchaser had just seen). Tig Notaro's *Live* (2012*) proved such a strong seller digitally that a physical version was made the following year. Such considerations are not particular to comedy, but tangible reissues of comedy albums have proven difficult: much of Cosby's back catalogue after the Warner Brothers albums is not available on CD; Carlin had to purchase the Little David label to get his reissues started; and many other comedians, whose works were never on major labels or imprints to begin with, will likely never have the option of physical reissue.

One further form of mediation, and one that a number of comedians have embraced, is print. In the last twenty years there have been several books written by stand-up comedians that, essentially, transliterate their onstage performances to print. This is not a wholly disingenuous exercise, as most comedians profess to writing routines prior to testing them in performance rather than to having them emerge in performance contexts. But these efforts are often largely unsatisfactory in that, on the page, despite whatever insights they may contain, the routines lack a certain rhetorical flourish. The distance and unidirectionality of printed text creates a relationship with the reader that is literally less engaging and more authoritative: the comedian is speaking *to*, not *with*, the reader.

There is a tradition of jest books and mass-printed texts of humorous narratives that extends back to the fifteenth and sixteenth centuries (see, inter alia, Holt 2008; Hutchinson 1963; Speroni 1965; Zall 1963), and similar anthologies date back to Roman times. These jest books were often associated with or attributed to particular characters, such as Italy's Poggio Bracciolini or England's Joe Miller. However, although they may have been texts that were also part of oral tradition, and although they may have been deliberate and performed creations of the person to whom they were attributed at the time of printing, we can only speculate as to what transformation they may have undergone between orality and literary manifestations. With the stand-up comedians of the twentieth and twenty-first centuries, who practiced in a mode of talk that implied broadcast and recorded mediation of their spoken performances in front of audiences, we need not resort to speculation on the form of their "natural" oral performances.

After his death, many of Lenny Bruce's performances were transcribed and published as *The Essential Lenny Bruce* (1967): edited and compiled by John Cohen, the emphasis was on Bruce's social commentary, so much so that it makes for a rather torpid and solemn read. Although Woody Allen and Steve Martin had each written comedy, they did not make a habit of translating their routines from the stage to the page.[3]

In 1986, at the height of his *Cosby Show* success, Bill Cosby released *Fatherhood*. It was written in part as a guide to parenting, and it incorporated many of his routines on parents and children. This opened the floodgates, and successful comedians were offered book deals.

What is found funny in performance does not necessarily translate well to the page. It needs to be reworked to accommodate the absence of an audience. This is a transcription of a Chris Rock performance from his 1994 HBO episode of *HBO Comedy Half Hour*, "Big Ass Jokes":

Alright

things are going *alright*

I can not *complain*

doing my *special*

doing a new *movie*

got a new *TV show*

successful black man [A:C]

so you know you know what's next right

white girl [L→B]

<u>got to get a white girl</u>

can *not* be a successful black man without a white girl [L]

they won't even let you buy a mansion without a white girl

| here's a million dollars | | {nasal} "where's your white girl [L]

we *have zoning restrictions"* | [L]

you know what's funny

you know what's funny

if you're black and you go out with a white girl

everything that goes wrong in your life

people blame it on the white girl [L]

everything

it's like | yo man I heard Chris got hit by a bus |

fucking around with them white girls | [L]

| yeah I hear Chris broke his leg | | white girl [L]

that's what he gets |

people are bugged man

there's like you know

there's white girls who only go out with black guys

there's black girls who only go out with white guys

I *met* a black girl like that

did *not date black men*

I said girl how come you don't date no black men

she said | *no reason*

no reason |

no reason

so I punched her in the face [L]

now she got a reason [L] (Rock 1994*)

It is the first bit of the performance. Rock anticipates and builds into the text the interaction with the audience, and the audience not only recognizes his "successful black man" claim but praises it and reaffirms it. Note also how the laughter following the "got to get a white girl" turns to (good-natured) dissent, in that the audience actively boos him. This is the corresponding section from his book *Rock This!*:

Yes, things are going great. I do comedy specials. Movies. Albums. Got a new TV show.

You know what's next?

Right. White Girls.

Got to get a white girl. You're not a successful black man without a white girl. They won't even let you buy a mansion without a white girl.

Black Man: Here's your million dollars.

Real Estate Agent: Where's your white girl? We have zoning restrictions.

You know what's funny? If you're black and you go out with a white girl, everything that goes wrong in your life gets blamed on the white girl.

"Hey man, I hear Chris got hit by a bus."

"Going out with a white girl."

"Yeah, I hear Chris broke his leg."

"White girl. That's what he gets."

. . .

People should date who they like. I believe in chemistry. If it works, go for it. But there are white girls who only go out with black guys. And there are black girls who only go out with white guys.

. . .

I once asked out a fine sister: she turned me down.

Her: Sorry. I don't date black men.

Me: Girl, how come you don't date black men?

Her: No reason.

Me: No reason?

So I punched her in the face. Now she's got a reason.

Okay, I didn't really do that. I'm not really violent or intolerant. (1997, 107–8)[4]

Contrasting the performance with the version from the book highlights the absence of the qualifying "people should do what they like" preface to the seeming diatribe against miscegenation, and the need to qualify his most outrageous claim—the punching of the woman in the face—as an explicit fiction. In other words, the text requires the resolution, the return to equilibrium that—in performance—the audience provides with its laughter. The audience determines the alleged truth of the punching incident to be false or, rather, fiction.

Ellen DeGeneres has also transliterated her routines into book form. One example appears in *My Point . . . And I Do Have One*:

> I went camping recently for the first time. It was a fantastic experience. I went to an amazing place: Montana. I don't know of you've ever been there, but it is gorgeous. I've never seen any place so spectacularly beautiful as Montana. Or was it Maine? It *was* Maine. Anyway, it is beautiful, and I've never seen any place like it. It is so special.
>
> The important thing is that I went camping. Now, I normally don't wake up that early, but I woke up to watch the sun set. I was sitting in front of my tent, and eating breakfast—some type of Mueslix, or some other outdoorsy stuff, just eating it right from my hand. I didn't even have a bowl. I just had milk and the Mueslix and my hand.
>
> Anyway, so I'm enjoying my Mueslix (That may be an exaggeration—let's just say I was *eating* my Mueslix), when suddenly I hear some kind of noise. Since I'm alone in the middle of the woods, I'm a little bit scared. But I gather my courage, look up, and . . . Awww, how cute! Only ten feet away from where I'm sitting there's a family of deer drinking from a little, babbling brook thing (I'm not sure of the technical outdoorsy term). Just the mother, father, and two little baby deer lit by the reddish glow of the setting sun. It was so beautiful, so perfect, so wonderful, and I though "Oh, I wish I had a gun." I could've just . . . BANG BANG BANG BANG BANG! I could have shot 'em, gutted 'em, skinned 'em, then sprinkled 'em on my cereal.
>
> Actually, none of that story is true. Well, some of it is true. I did go camping in Maine.
>
> No, that's not true either. The closest I've come to camping in Maine is spending a few nights at the Hilton in Maui (come to think of it, that's not very close). My point . . . and I do have one, is that I was being sarcastic. I don't understand hunting at all. (DeGeneres 1995, 145–46)

But this is how it was performed in a 1994 concert recording, released in 1996 on her *Taste This* CD:

> So and you know I'm back on tour which is *fun*
> but I took a little time off between shooting the show and then coming out on
>   *tour* I went um
> *camping* which was I hadn't ever done that

which was an *amazing* experience

I went to an *amazing* place which

Montana I don't know if anyone has been to *Montana* but . . . [C:A]

it is gorgeous I have never seen anything like it

and um . . .

[bashful chuckle] I'm sorry

Maine I was in *Maine* [L]

<u>it is *beautiful* and I've never seen any place like it</u>

it is so

special

anyways the story still applies I'm camping and . . . [L]

<u>I *woke up*</u>

and I *never* wake up this early

but I *woke up* to watch the sunset I'm sitting in front of my tent . . . [L]

and uh . . .

eating some just *breakfast* some type of *Mueslix* or some kind of *outdoorsy* just
    healthy and . . .

just from my *hand* I didn't even have a *bowl* I had *milk* . . . [L]

<u>and the Mueslix and just a *spoon* made from wood</u> anyways so I'm [L]

<u>I'm having my Mueslix</u>

and I hear some kind of *noise*

and of course I'm kind of *scared*

and I look and I'm *telling you*

like *right*

well like ten feet away from where I'm standing there is a family of *deer* drinking
    from a little babbling brook thing that was there

just a mother father *two little* baby deer and I thought

| oh I *wish* I had a gun | 'cause it's right . . . [L]

BANGBANGBANGBANGBANG! <u>I could have just *shot* 'em</u>

and *killed* 'em

gutted 'em

skinned 'em

sprinkled 'em on my cereal

I just had them . . . [L]

<u>*so* close</u> . . . to be able to . . .

just *no gun*

I had a *spoon* so I *hit* 'em just as hard as I . . . [L]

just over their little *head* . . . 'cause the baby can't run as fast

so I had that, just [L]

> *ungh ungh ungh* [sounds of intense rhythmic effort] like that
> and it *cracked* but I was just . . .
> 'cause the baby is so *tender* and *juicy* they're *little* so . . . [L]
> and he just *looked* and *scurried* away he just . . . [L]
> <u>got away</u>
> that's sarcasm I don't understand hunting at all (DeGeneres 1996*)

In both instances, DeGeneres negates the episode by framing it as sarcasm, and each is a prelude to a bit about hunting. In the live performance, however, it is framed in the very recent and specific past (just before going on tour); Montana is affirmed as a place of beauty through cheers; the seemingly incidental spoon returns later as a club; the clubbing interlude is not only present but fairly gruesome; and the negation, when it comes, is sotto voce. Conversely, the back-pedaling of the printed version is quite elaborated and prolonged, even though it is retreating—reestablishing equilibrium—from a claim not nearly as brutal as that of the performance. DeGeneres, whose persona is nice and optimistic, plays against type to such an extent that the audience can easily make the truth/fiction judgment. Rock, on the other hand, walks a thinner line, knowing the successful black man persona still carries the perceived threatening presence of the violent black man (Bryant 2003). By building a bit around it he, in collusion with a sympathetic audience, inverts it.

Text is absent an audience: to quote Riesman again, "People go to movies in groups. . . . People do not read in groups" (1970, 256). But stand-up comedy recordings have groups "built-in," as it were: books do not. The sound and occasional sight of an audience is integral to a stand-up comedy performance not only because stand-up comedy is a dialogic form, a dialogue between performer and audience, where one half shapes the responses of the other and vice versa, but also because that sight reaffirms, by and large, what an authentic response to a performer's efforts *ought* to be. For text, comedians do not have at their disposal the collective audience actively engaged in the realm of play, and the judgments and frameworks for interpretation of their words need to be articulated.

Furthermore, stand-up comedy, as it is performed and as that performance appears on recordings, is a homeostatic phenomenon: the listener experiences it at a set pace, unlike the reader of a text, who proceeds at his or her own pace. There are performative qualities extrinsic of—albeit determined by—the audience's reaction, like timing. Johnny Carson made this same observation, building on the role of timing in performance versus text.

Yes, it's all in the timing, as far as I'm concerned. Humor is so much timing, and that's why, as we talk here for reproduction in print, I know that you can never make that transference from the audio sound of a joke or delivery, with all the nuances, to paper. That's why some funny people who can write very well—for example, S. J. Perelman's a good writer; H. Allen Smith had a brief flurry where he was funny—never fared too well when they tried to do it in person. (Carson 1979)

In the past few years, Twitter has become a regular forum for comedians. Even though the form is limited to 140 characters of plain text, the potential to reach an immediate audience and the dynamism of an instant response are sufficient temptations for many to transcend those limitations. Patton Oswalt, who came late to Twitter, has called it "as restrictive as haiku, and because of it, I think it really frees people up" (2011). Twitter was initially used as a tool primarily for appearance promotion, but now comedians will occasionally test out new material or engage in public conversations cum repartee with fans and other comedians. It can be used as a virtual workshop:

[Aaron Glaser] began filing the sort of one-liners that punctuate his stand-up. "If the Beatles were founded today," went one Tweet, "Ringo would be a laptop." He developed a system: tap out a joke on Twitter, then monitor the reaction. "I'm sure no one will admit it," he said, "but it's nerve-racking when you think a joke is great, and no one responds to it."

If followers do react, though—with retweets, "favorites," or "likes" on Facebook, to which his Twitter feed is linked—Mr. Glaser will drop the line into his stand-up material. Such was the case with the Ringo joke, which killed in performance after earning online kudos, and now it's part of Mr. Glaser's regular set. "Generally if it works on Twitter, it works onstage," he said. (Angelo 2011)

The options of noting re-tweets, favorites, and likes, of re-tweeting positive responses (or histrionically negative ones, as Neil Hamburger often does), and of blocking negative comments allows for a comedian to get an immediate reaction while simultaneously maintaining control over the performance. Moreover, as comedians can recommend others to follow, whether through the follow Friday hashtag (#ff) or through regular interaction, they can extend the extant goodwill of their followers to lesser-known twitterers.

One of the offshoots of recorded stand-up comedy is how it fixes the performance, for good or ill.

On the one hand, what is recorded is but one version of a routine: the version that gets committed to a medium becomes privileged and elevated, much as particular versions of other folklore types become the de facto canon. One may lament about what never made it to record, that the act of canonization excludes performances equally if not more vibrant and interesting. In a review of the inaugural CD releases from the Canadian comedy chain Yuk-Yuks, Andrew Clark writes, "Ideally comedy CDs should offer the live experience that fans missed, such as seeing Mike MacDonald circa 1982" (1996b). However, recordings are not accidental or incidental to performance: they are not (typically) documents of a random evening in the performance life of a comedian. They are deliberate creations, with care taken to produce the best performance from the perspective of the performer and producer. The liner notes for Bill Cosby's *To Russell, My Brother, Whom I Slept With* (1968a*) indicate that the performance was two and a half hours long, but the resultant album is just over forty minutes. In Jeff Rougvie's liner notes for Bill Hicks's *Love Laughter and Truth* (2002*)—which is a compilation culled from Hicks's personal recordings for self-study—he notes:

> In 1997, Bill's *Arizona Boy* and *Rant in E-Minor* were posthumously released by Rykodisc. Although completed after his death, Bill had both meticulously plotted out and left detailed instructions on how to edit and sequence them. Those four albums [*Dangerous* and *Relentless* were released prior to his death] are the official Hicks canon; the releases that he oversaw, were created to his specifications, and released as he envisioned them. . . . When Bill stepped out on stage the nights of those performances the mics were prepared and the levels were set. Bill knew he was recording an album and performed accordingly.

Even when the performance is also a live broadcast (as in the case of George Carlin's final releases), it comes at the end of a long process of honing material into a routine precisely to culminate as that broadcast and recording.

On the other hand, there is now a "canon," as there is an available body of work that can be revisited and learned from. Audiences can listen to them, but so too can other performers. In this way, recorded comedy fuels and perpetuates the art form.

In his study, Robert Stebbins noted how "a large proportion of the respondents said they were fascinated as children and adolescents with either recorded comedy or televised comedy or both" (1990, 62). Biographies, autobiographies, and even performed autobiographies are rife with comedians telling of the importance of recording:

Herb [Gart, an early manager] encouraged [Cosby] by playing him some Lord
Buckley records. Buckley was an underground legend, well known for his cool
storytelling. Buckley's "hispomatic" rendition of "Jonah and the Whale" was
a classic back in 1950 and audiences were with him when he'd spin away from
one-liners and riff through five- and ten-minute tales. The joy was as much
in Buckley's delivery and characterizations as in any jokes along the way. (R.
Smith 1997, 39)

A friend lent me some comedy records. There were three by Nichols and May,
several by Lenny Bruce, and one by Tom Lehrer, the great song parodist. . . .
Some people fall asleep at night listening to music: I fell asleep to Lenny, Tom,
and Mike and Elaine. These albums broke ground and led me to a Darwinian
discovery: Comedy could evolve. (Martin 2007, 71–72)

> Richard [Pryor] is the *rawest* motherfucker in show business
> Richard's the one that *made me* want to do *comedy*
> when I was little I wanted to be Richard Pryor *so bad*
> I used to *read lips* with . . . listen to . . . sneak into
> remember you'd *sneak* into the basement
> put his *albums* on
> and just *listen*
> your mother ain't supposed to hear
> so you'd *listen* | {stifled giggle} |
> and *listen* to this shit
> and I *turned* into . . .
> I wanted to be Richard *so bad*
> I used to go out on *stage*
> when I was *fifteen*
> and *talk* and *act* and *walk* and do *everything* like Richard Pryor (Murphy 1987*)

The most artfully rendered illustration of this understanding of canonic-
ity and the role of recordings might well be the opening footage of Chris
Rock's *Bring the Pain* concert (1996*). As the camera follows his feet as he
walks from his dressing room to the stage, the covers of comedy albums
are flashed in time to the music: Bill Cosby's *To Russell, My Brother, Whom
I Slept With* (1968a*), Dick Gregory's *In Living Black and White* (1961*), Flip
Wilson's *Geraldine: Don't Fight the Feeling* (1972*), Richard Pryor's . . . *Is It
Something I Said?* (1975*), Steve Martin's *Comedy Is Not Pretty* (1979*), Pig-
meat Markham's *Tune Me In* (1968[?]*), and both Woody Allen's (1964*) and

Eddie Murphy's (1982*) eponymous albums. In this manner, Rock identifies influences both obvious and surprising and locates himself not only within an ethno-social group—African American—but also within the occupational group of stand-up comedian, by placing himself at the confluence of his predecessors.

This phenomenon does not exist in isolation. Kenneth Goldstein has noted how a folksong revival seems to have followed each technological innovation (printing press, phonograph, radios, etc.), making the observation that, rather than "[freezing] its form and content so that it ceases to be folksong, . . . each successive communication revolution has speeded up its circulation through space and time" (1982, 4). As to the role the tape recorder and phonograph played in the folksong revival, Goldstein writes:

> Now the tools existed, not only for the recording of the much needed new repertoire of the burgeoning revival, but also for the issuance of those recordings in a compact and relatively inexpensive form. Instead of being heard only on radio programs, performances could be copied on tape recorders from those programs or could be issued on records. The would-be folksinger could then learn songs at leisure through repeated playbacks of the tapes or records. (1982, 6)

Goldstein also notes, almost in passing, how the songs also served as models for the inspiration of songwriters (1982, 8). When one speaks of the canon of stand-up comedy, one is primarily speaking of those routines of particular comedians that serve as exemplary executions of the comedian's art. To not know them is to not know the tradition in which one is operating. But stand-up comedy, being a contemporary, popular genre—which implies a model of a specific creator and "ownership" of material, as opposed to a folk genre that, loosely, implies a model of communal creation and "proprietorship" of material—is a genre of novelty. One does not learn the canon so much as learn *from* it. One locates oneself within a tradition not simply to continue it but to develop and add to it.

What the stand-up comedian is doing for professional development, the fan does in a less deliberate but equally focused way: contemplating comedy as craft, developing a sense of connoisseurship. Furthermore, through recordings creations by particular performers can enter the vernacular tradition: routines by the African American vaudevillian Bert Williams were in active circulation in the white folklore about blacks thanks to his consenting to be recorded for phonograph records (Rosenberg 1972, 148).

Lastly, it should be noted that, without making live performance peripheral, the exigencies of live performance—and the restrictions placed upon recording these performances by performers who wish to retain control of their output—make recordings the de facto primary data for anyone studying stand-up comedy.

One of the seemingly self-evident features of humor and comedy is that there is an element of surprise: a situation is set up and there is an outcome that is unanticipated, although it "makes sense" in retrospect. When folklorists study joke tellers, they may hear the same joke again and again, especially those jokes firmly ensconced in the teller's repertoire. But with each retelling, the context of performance means a new version, however practiced and deliberate the performance may be. With a recording, however, the text is fixed: surely, if the "value" of comedy is the unanticipated resolution, there is little need to hear it more than once. Why then is there a viable market for comedy recordings, going on fifty years, in the case of major labels? I would suggest three possibilities, which are non-exclusionary.

Firstly, we must distinguish between first and subsequent listenings. In his article "When Is a Legend?" (1989) Bill Ellis suggests that a legend is, principally, a narrative that does not return to a stable situation: it ends at disequilibrium. The legend process continues after the narrative is ostensibly over, however, as participants in the telling—performer and audience—engage in negotiating the possibility, credibility, and viability of the underlying propositions. ("That couldn't happen." "Yes it could." "Well you know how people from there are.") In Ellis's phrasing, "a legend is a narrative that challenges accepted definitions of the real world and leaves itself suspended, relying for closure on each individual's response" (34). But when the legend is told again to the same audience, "the narrative now becomes in re-performance an aesthetic event, during which we appreciate the methods of narration instead of falling under its spell" (35). Ellis is grounding this approach in the work of Tzvetan Todorov and his work on the fantastic novel, which held that for any reading subsequent to the first reading, it "inevitably becomes a metareading, in the course of which we note the methods of the fantastic" (Todorov 1973, 90).

So too is it with stand-up comedy: on its first listening, we react with surprise at the appropriate incongruity. "Getting it" is the more or less spontaneous act of retroactively reinterpreting the narrative now that we can grasp it as a whole, discerning the process by which the conclusion was inevitable yet obscured. On subsequent listenings, our reaction is more one of delight, as we retrace (in real time, as it were) that same process. In this

manner, what the fan listener is doing is, to some extent, what the professional comedian is doing when listening to canonical recordings: it is an
appreciation of technique.

My second possibility as to the "re-listening" of comedy performances
is borne out more by ethnography than by any theoretical perspective. In
my fieldwork, and in my own experience, I have been surprised to note how
the listening to (or watching of) comedy performances is done as often in
groups as it is done singly. Kelly Roubo told me how, in rural Maine in the
1970s, her family would regularly sit together and listen to Cosby's *Funny
Fellow* album: it was a family activity, not something she ever did by herself.

> Listening to the radio and listening to albums was something we did a lot more
> when I was young. We had a black and white TV and three channels, two of
> which came in, so it wasn't like now where you've got so many choices and so
> many media. It was fun on Saturday night, they'd have fifties music and we'd all
> sit around and, y'know . . . it sounds really like, Happy Days kind of crap but . . .
>
> We were too rural, so there wasn't neighbor kids to play with: there was just
> us four kids. (Roubo 2003)

Another colleague told me how, when living in an Atlantic Canadian university residence in the mid 1990s, bootleg copies of Adam Sandler's first
album, *They're All Gonna Laugh at You!* (1993*), were made and circulated
throughout the resident population. As an adolescent in Ottawa I would
go to friends' houses and would often be told, "You have to listen to this":
they would watch me in my surprise (my Todorovian "first reading") while
they were simultaneously experiencing their own delight (their Todorovian
"subsequent reading"). My own students at Cape Breton University have
sent me comedy MP3s that they wish to share with me. This is less an explanation so much as it is the articulation of a phenomenon, which somehow
speaks to a level of commensality involved in listening to comedy. *Toronto
Star* columnist Andrew Clark noted the same phenomenon:

> Those who wished to enjoy the live comedy experience in the comfort of their
> very own polyester decorated basements listened to comedy albums. Records,
> such as the *Button Down World of Bob Newhart*, George Carlin's *Class Clown* and
> Steve Martin's *Wild and Crazy Guy*, got played until their grooves wore out.
> More often than not, listening to a comedy album was a group activity, you,
> your friends, some mood-altering substances.

In the 1980s, this breed of comedic entertainment began to go extinct. A new beast loomed on the horizon. Someone you knew . . . purchased a newfangled invention called a Video Cassette Recorder (VCR). . . . Then, in 1984, you watched purple-leather-clad Eddie Murphy's standup concert *Delirious*. It was excellent. Watching comedy videos was just like listening to an album, only better. Your friends came over, you partook in mood-modifiers. Who knew, maybe something cool would come of it, man. (Clark 1996b)

Moreover, without wishing to push the didactic function of stand-up comedy too hard, watching a performance that covers certain topics can lead into a discussion on that topic. At one "Boy's Night," in St. John's, friends and I watched Chris Rock's *Never Scared* DVD (2004*), which culminates in a long routine on marriage. This led—awkwardly for the rest of us—to a rumination by one of our lot on his significant other and to the question both rhetorical and desperate, "What does she want?" James Lull has written on the social uses of television as it promotes conversation within families or among strangers, providing "conversational props":

To turn on the set when guests arrive is to introduce instant common ground. Strangers in the home may then engage in "television talk"—verbal responses to television programs which allow audience members to discuss topics of common experience which probably have little personal importance. (1990, 37–38)

My third possibility is closely related to the second. With the recorded comedy performance, we have not only a performer and his or her funny text, but also the reactions of an audience. As I have written above, the comedian performs to the specific and finite audience in front of him or her but cultivates the indistinct and (potentially) infinitely vast audience at home. The former acts as the latter's surrogate, and each time we listen to a recording we experience their surprise, a reaction as fresh and absent of any meta-reading as it was the time prior. Through a form of psychic contagion, we participate in their surprise.

This appears to merge two approaches: the idea of listening to comedy as ritual and the notion of "vicarious audience play" (Sutton-Smith 2001). On the one hand, as an audience member listens or watches recorded stand-up comedy, space and time are transcended, and they are at the original performance. On the other hand, the audience is participating in the original performance, experiencing it anew through the reactions of the crowd.

In all instances, there is a sense of familiarity—with technique, with the topic matter, with the vicarious thrill of hearing it anew. One listens to these again in much the same manner as, in folk societies, one listens to the same stories time and again. They become part of the audience's collective experience: they are something that now informs their worldview, no longer simply interpreted through it. These performances are part of a shared experience, and the stand-up comedian is part of that experience, as an intimate.

TIP YOUR SERVERS
The Validation of Laughter

I have no *ending* for this
so I take a small *bow*
—**George Carlin,** *What Am I Doing in New Jersey?*

Throughout this book I have been making the argument that the form of talk that occurs on the stage at a stand-up comedy performance is coincident with the forms of talk that occur in informal, day-to-day, face-to-face communication among intimates, which is the object at the heart of folklore studies. Stand-up comedy is an intimate, interpersonal genre. However, the realities of stand-up performance—a stage introducing an explicit distinction between performer and audience, an itinerancy that brings the stand-up comedian in front of groups outside of his or her own, and the realities of broadcasting and recording, which separate in space and time the performer from the audience—define it as a form of talk different from informal talk. How does one reconcile the distance of stand-up with the intimacy it requires and implies? Hopefully, this book has set out answers about technique and about the vernacular theory of stand-up comedy that both comedians and audiences can implicitly bring to the moment of performance.

But how do we know when the stand-up comedian is *successful* in bridging the distance and establishing a connection between him- or herself and the audience? The answer is laughter. By virtue of one taking up the mantle "stand-up comedian," the presence or absence of laughter is the standard by which you measure a comedian's success or failure. He or she may bring a place and a time to life through his or her evocative descriptions, or share brilliant insights into the nature of the culture, or make startling, unsettling, yet profound critiques on a state of affairs and how that state of affairs ought to be, but if his or her talk is not met with laughter it is not, as it were, "good." The audience expects to laugh, and the comedian has a professional obligation to effect that laughter. Conversely, if the stand-up comedian is interpreted as funny, he or she has a right to hear laughter in response and the audience has the obligation to laugh.

ROCK: Dane Cook's funny.

FRIEDMAN: I can say this because I'm not you, but he's not funny.

ROCK: Anyone who can keep an audience is funny. Dane Cook's for college girls. So if you find college girls who don't think he's funny, then he's not funny.

(Rock and Rickles 2008, 130)

Laughter demonstrates that whatever has been said on stage has been interpreted as simply an intimate momentarily interrupting the flow of conversation with a startling observation that is immediately judged as playfully testing the group's worldview. We are all friends here: I not only permit you to say that but I encourage it, because I know at heart you are talking with me on our own terms, with an understanding of my group and my concerns as I understand them. Whatever other identities we share or do not share, at this moment we are close to each other. It does not matter that you cannot hear my nuanced response; it does not matter that you cannot see me because I am not in front of you; it even does not matter that you are long deceased. This is a new moment of performance, and I appreciate your talk, and I laugh.

In the introduction I asked the question of whether what I was writing is or is not "not folklore." I suggested that it was not "not folklore," in the sense of "as opposed to a popular study," as it was grounded in a disciplinary perspective with attendant theoretical and methodological concerns, and that it was also not "not folklore," in the sense of "as opposed to anthropology, sociology, history, communications, and so on," as the disciplinary perspective it was grounded in is folklore. I would not go so far as to suggest that it was definitively not "not folklore" in the sense of its focus being small-group, informal, interpersonal, artistic communication, although neither would I suggest that it was definitively "not folklore," as this same small-group, informal, interpersonal, artistic communication is omnipresent in stand-up comedy.

The folklorist would be interested in the study of stand-up comedy—whether he or she is engaged or amused by the content of any particular performance or not—because it is always an interaction between a performer and an audience. At its core is this face-to-face interaction, the same encounter that is at the core of folkloristic study. No other popular cultural product emerging from vernacular practices retains that tie to its originating performance context as strongly or as necessarily.

NOTES

Welcome to the Show

1. Robert Stebbins cites the ninth edition of *Webster's Collegiate Dictionary* and designates the origin of the term "stand-up" at 1966 (1990, 5), while John Limon, without citation, assigns it to "in or around the year of Lenny Bruce's death," again 1966 (2000, 126). Willis Russell and Mary Porter provide a citation from the August 6, 1961, edition of *Parade*: "A stand-up comedienne is a female who stands in front of an audience and tells jokes at which the audience laughs, but *laughs*" (1973, 140). Interestingly, George Carlin himself referred to "the stand-ups" to designate an older form of comedian, different from contemporary performers like Mort Sahl, during an appearance on the television show *Talent Scouts* dating from 1962: "The old school is largely made up of the fast-paced stand-up comedians, the one-liner comics who came from vaudeville and burlesque, and they comprise the insult school of humor" (archival footage in Carlin 1997*). An article in *Time* from 1960 gives weight to this meaning: "Always Garry considered himself a stand-up comic. But by 1949, when he started the Garry Moore Show on CBS Radio, he had learned that he got a bigger response simply by playing himself" (*Time* 1960a).

2. Bill Ellis, writing from within the context of September 11 jokes, notes that humor following disasters arises after a latency period, at which point the "making and passing on of jokes provokes laughter and provides social rewards that outweigh the social risk of being thought sick or insensitive" (2003, 41). Ellis's comments are directed at the process of informal joke telling, but, clearly, professional stand-up comedians faced similar challenges of timing and perception following the tragedy.

Chapter 1

1. Patrick Mullen as early as 1970 draws comparisons between it and the improvisatory nature of a street performance, noting how it "places [the performer] closer in style to improvisatory stand-up comics than to any epic tradition" (1970, 97). Norine Dresser cites comedians Sam Kinison and Charles Fleischer as both building routines around a 1990 variant of the colo-rectal mouse (1994, 232). Kay Stone mentions it briefly in passing when she writes of the vagueness of the term "storyteller," listing it among forms ranging from reading aloud from books through mime to puppetry (1997, 234). Peter Tokofsky, in a discussion on the concept of "communal creation" in folk drama (specifically, *Moritat*, specially composed songs performed during *Fasnet*, a carnival in Elzach, in southwestern Germany), concludes with the following: "The combination of spontaneous inspiration and deliberate tinkering with texts characterizes the author-function of *Moritat* authors

and other folk artists, scholarly and other elite writers, as well as stand-up comedians and other popular figures" (1997, 229). Susan Rasmussen draws parallels to how one of her informants in Tuareg blacksmith theater understands himself: "A smith friend once remarked to me that he felt 'like a journalist for women' and 'advertised' this feeling in his jokes and songs, thereby suggesting a proximity to our own media specialists, stand-up comedians, and talk-show facilitators" (1997, 9). DoVeanna Fulton's (2004) article on black female stand-up comedians is significant in that it applies Gary Alan Fine's "folklore diamond" model (Fine 1992, 5) to stand-up comedy, but it does not bring much fresh insight otherwise. Anne-Karin Misje (2002) brings a folklorist's sensitivity and sense of group identity to her analysis of stand-up performance as a negotiation of identity. Giovanna Del Negro has done extensive research on Jewish women's stand-up comedy (2005, 2006, 2010). Susan Seizer (2011) has done work on the uses and strategies of swearing in stand-up, along with producing an ethnographic film on road comics (see Clift and Demmon 2012*).

2. In "Differential Identity and the Social Base of Folklore," Richard Bauman makes the argument that, whereas traditional folklorists, and even his contemporaries, argue for folklore being a phenomenon that exists "within groups," there are numerous examples from the work of folklorists themselves that evidence folklore occurring between groups, and the folklore performed is expressly adverting to the differences between the groups. He presents the immediate counter-argument to his statements, which he has illustrated through the example of storytelling sessions between the Tahtlan and Tlingit tribes of northwestern Canada: "[It] would be perfectly consistent with group theory to view the Tahtlan and Tlingit storytellers as jointly constituting a group in their own right, by virtue of their interaction in face-to-face trading-storytelling relationships. . . . This is not the sense, however, in which folklorists (and I, at times, following their usage) have used the term 'group,' that is, for a set of people with shared identity" (1971, 35).

3. William Hugh Jansen makes a similar point in "The Esoteric-Exoteric Factor in Folklore" (1959), wherein he describes not only how part of a group's folklore concerns its perception of itself and its perception of others, but also how it is aware that it is in turn "othered," so that its folklore also reflects what it perceives the other thinks of it, and what it perceives the other thinks the group perceives of the other. How one chooses to identify the self is often predicated by how one identifies the other: commonality is sought, as is difference.

4. In his study of British monologue traditions, Kenneth Goldstein notes how the performer depends "upon the empathic identity of this audience with the material he performs, and through it with himself" (1976, 20).

5. Carl von Sydow (1948) referred to non-narrative verbal traditions as "dites," while Gary Butler (1990) borrowed the term "traditum," from the work of Edward Shils, as he struggled with how to refer to a "belief" that no one believes. Barre Toelken used a similar approach to Alan Dundes in his term "multiform folk ideas" (Toelken 1979, 171–81). Toelken was, in the main, writing about elements that appear across genres, and not explicitly about how they constitute units of worldview. Nevertheless, his definition of

worldview is predicated on the notion that "the members of any given culture perceive reality in terms of culturally provided sets of ideas and premises" (226).

6. Radner and Lanser write of strategies of coding in women's folk culture. One strategy is "trivialization": "Trivialization involves the employment of a form, mode, or genre that the dominant culture considers unimportant, innocuous, or irrelevant. When a particular form is conventionally non-threatening, the message it carries, even if it might be threatening in another context, is likely to be discounted or overlooked" (1993, 19).

7. Goonie-googoo, GI Joe, and Mr. T are references to routines from earlier in the performance.

8. Although she does not call this an esoteric assumption on behalf of the audience, S. Elizabeth Bird makes this point in relation to problems with much audience research (1992, 110).

9. This is not to suggest that stand-up comedians make more money through sales of recordings than they do through live performances: however, mass-mediation, whether it be through albums, television appearances, radio appearances, or websites, or through appearances in other performance genres (notably, television and film), leads to a greater name recognition and potentially larger audiences and markets and higher ticket prices.

10. Ron James's *Quest for the West* (2005*) was filmed over two nights (September 19 and 20, 2005): it aired as one performance, and there was an extended "performer's cut" of the same show created for when it was released on DVD. Mitch Hedberg's *Comedy Central Presents* (1999*) performance was 22 minutes, edited down and rearranged from the 45 minutes originally filmed (both the released version and the unedited performance were released on Hedberg 2003*). Such is not always the case: as often as not, the performances that are mass mediated are based solely on one live performance. They are also sometimes explicitly marketed as such: Jerry Seinfeld's *I'm Telling You for the Last Time* (1998a*), Robin Williams's *Live on Broadway* (2002*), and George Carlin's *Life Is Worth Losing* (2005*) were all broadcast live on HBO: each was preceded by an extended tour to hone the act (see Ressner 1998).

Chapter 2

1. Such a distinction is the catalyst for I. Sheldon Posen's "cultural schizophrenia" when he reflects on the "authenticity" of the folksong revival of the early 1970s and his own involvement in the Mariposa Folk Festival (Posen 1993, 128, 134). In a different context, Dick Hebdige notes how the ideology of professorial authority and the hierarchical relationship between teacher and taught is naturalized through the layout of the lecture theater, wherein the unidirectional flow of information is dictated by "benches rising in tiers before a raised lectern" (1979, 12).

2. The staging for D. L. Hughley's *Goin' Home* concert (1999*) is essentially a recreation of a southern black home, and for his final routine ("Come Home with Me") he provides a vernacular ethnography of the home, using the set as referent. For the first five minutes

of Damon Wayans's *The Last Stand?* (1990*)—during which he performs a routine about the danger of doing comedy for the money and about becoming "safe" for white audiences—there is a mural suspended from the rafters that depicts other African American comedians, both contemporary and forebears. The mural is withdrawn at the end of the routine, although no explicit mention is made of it.

3. For an interesting parallel, see Gelo 1999 on the role of the master of ceremonies at intertribal powwow events.

4. See also Everett (2003, 343) for a discussion of the "earthy, casual look" in the folk revival scene. Dress is discussed in chapter 3.

5. For the brick wall as used in *The Simpsons*, see, for example, Daniels 1994*; Cary 1988*; and Frink and Don Payne 2002*.

6. Both Lockheart (2003) and Narváez (1986) have written on the use of the microphone by politicians to create an intimate connection: Lockheart wrote on the "Fireside chats" of Franklin Delano Roosevelt, and Narváez wrote on Newfoundland politician Joey Smallwood and his ability to address a crowd through the public address based on his experience as a broadcaster.

7. "The Huns" refers to a routine set in "the round Church" (Saint George's Anglican) in Halifax, comparing the flatulence of the old Anglican ladies with mustard gas in the trenches of World War I.

8. "[The microphone] can be removed from its stand to serve as a rope, a club, a penis . . . , an electric shaver, and so on. Kenny Robinson, a Yuk Yuk's headliner, briefly performs fellatio on it as part of his impersonation of Margaret Trudeau applying for a job" (Stebbins 1990, 43).

Chapter 3

1. The concept of "vernacular theory" was proposed by Houston Baker (1984) and developed by Thomas McLaughlin (1997). Insofar as the task of critical theory is "the uncovering of cultural assumptions that dominate in a society" (McLaughlin 1997, 4)— the identification and thus challenging of ideologies—the task is not critical theory's exclusive domain. McLaughlin makes the claim that "individuals that *do not* come out of a tradition of philosophical critique are capable of raising questions about the dominant cultural assumptions. They do so in ordinary language, and they often suffer from the blindness that unself-conscious language creates. But the fact that vernacular theories therefore do not completely transcend ideologies does not make them different in kind from academic theories. They manage in spite of their complicity to ask fundamental questions about culture" (1997, 4).

2. Lombana was writing a paper for Henry Jenkins's Media Theory and Methods graduate pro-seminar, which explicitly uses the lens of vernacular theory.

3. This is frequently how performers do take to the stage in club situations: waiting at the back of the room or exiting a backstage room that opens up into the back of the room and walking through the crowd and onto the stage.

4. In his discussion of the zoot suit, Stuart Cosgrove writes, "The zoot-suit was more than the drape-shape of 1940s fashion, more than a colourful stage-prop hanging from the shoulders of Cab Calloway, it was, in the most direct and obvious ways, an emblem of ethnicity and a way of negotiating an identity. The zoot-suit was a refusal: a subcultural gesture that refused to concede to the manners of subservience" (1984, 78).

5. In a CBC marketing practice of having a performer "host" an evening of programming, introducing the individual program while promoting a future broadcast, Ron James hosted the evening of December 6, 2005, the Tuesday prior to the airing of his *Quest for the West* special (2005*): in the course of his introductions, he made explicit reference to the rare occurrence of seeing him in a suit.

6. However, Jay Leno, for his first *Tonight Show* appearance in March of 1977, famously wore a bright green suit. "Years later, the only thing that people remembered about my first appearance was the green suit. On his anniversary shows, Johnny [Carson] would play the clip—which I came to call the *blackmail tape*—and unfailingly remark on my sartorial style. I was always secretly thrilled to be comic fodder for him. Once, he described the suit as 'a used clown outfit.' Another time, he said that I looked like an Italian elf" (Leno 1996, 190).

7. Molly Shannon created the character of Jeannie Darcy for *Saturday Night Live*; Darcy was similarly attired, replete with "mullet" haircut.

8. The controlling mechanisms of bookers, censors, and markets can often lead to little innovation and limited exposure in the most lucrative venues and media on the part of new comedians and those from traditionally marginalized groups. Chris Rock makes this point in passing, and speaks to its probable causes, when discussing the "whiteness" of sketches during his time on *Saturday Night Live*: "That's how it was in comedy clubs too. One black comic goes on at nine o'clock, they will not be putting me on at nine-fifteen. Same goes with women. It was just men in power overreacting, overthinking things" (qtd. in Shales and Miller 2002, 385).

9. A reviewer of a James's stand-up performances of just a few months prior thought that his stand-up "wasn't so much enjoyed as it was endured," going on to justify this charge by explaining how "the material changed but James' delivery remained the same. He set-up with a 'And what about?' observation. Threw out his punchline in a staccato voice that drew up in inflection. Then James tagged the joke (added smaller jokes to the main gag) by acting out the punchline. . . . James flitted from topic to topic with no through-line: from federalism to television commercials to Los Angeles. It was the standup equivalent of spraying a deck of cards into the air." (Clark 1996a)

Chapter 4

1. When a comedian has been successful in other fields and has thus been absent from the stand-up circuit for a stretch of time, there is a sense that he or she must return to the stage if he or she still wants to claim that identity. Martin Lawrence's *Runteldat* (2002*) and Robin Williams's *Live on Broadway* (2002*) both emerged from tours that saw them performing stand-up comedy for the first time in several years.

2. Barry Lee Pearson notes how the "artist tells his story to someone else in the context of an interview, or less often as part of an onstage act, and his tale reflects the presence of an audience" (1984, 29). Rosenberg notes how "non-musical aspects of the musician's career become increasingly significant" and how skills involve "the projection of personal charisma, the facility to handle relationships with 'fans' on and off-stage, and the manipulation of performance situations" (1986, 155, 157).

3. While being on television or radio does not assure that everyone who could have heard or seen a comedian's performance did so, it is not disingenuous to suggest that a person who is in the audience of a stand-up comedy performance also seeks out broadcasts of stand-up comedy.

4. The spelling of the show alternated variously between "Shakey" and "Shaky."

5. See also, inter alia, Mietkiewicz 1995; Hepfner 1999; Dunn 2003; Rankin 2004, 1.

6. The other central narrative for James, both on stage and off, is his constant touring and travels through Canada: it forms much of the discussion of the next chapter.

7. When George Carlin performed in St. John's in 2004, his first and only time in Newfoundland, he said in an aside that all his material used American references, but that it didn't particularly matter as "we're all one culture, really": the assertion passed without opprobrium, largely (most likely) out of a sense of excitement of such a performer coming to town, but it is certainly not how Newfoundlanders understand themselves, even compared to the rest of the Atlantic provinces and certainly to the rest of Canada.

8. "Living next to you is in some ways like sleeping with an elephant. No matter how friendly and even-tempered is the beast, if I can call it that, one is affected by every twitch and grunt" (Pierre Trudeau, from an address to the Press Club in Washington, D.C., March 25, 1969).

9. A second, more implicit way the Maritime persona is developed is through the opening music: at the beginning of the shows on the Nova Scotia tour, following an announcement by his tour producer Terry McRae, a short, exuberant pop-Celtic instrumental piece is played over the PA system, at a volume considerably higher than the music playing as the audience is being seated. It is identifiably proto-Celtic through the use of bodhran, Uillean pipes, and tin whistle, and it accompanies the dimming of the house lights, the raising of the stage lights, and the introduction, again by McRae, of "Ladies and Gentlemen, Ron James." It is the same music that opens *The Road Between My Ears* special (2003*).

10. "And I think that's a good place for a comedian to be—you never want to be a card-carrying member of the country club; you always want to be out on the porch, looking in through the picture window and making fun of them" (James, qtd. in Oswald 2004, F2). "I think the last place a comedian wants to find himself is a card-carrying member of the country club. It's always important to be standing outside the circle of power. You definitely want to be on the porch looking into the picture window" (James, qtd. in Rankin 2005). "In terms of Canada, [James] says he thinks Maritimers are welcome right across the map. 'Because we come from a have-not region, we haven't exactly been card-carrying members to the country club of Central Canada. I think we've really built the west'" (in Furlong 2006).

11. "I got off the plane there to take the shuttle to the hotel, and the driver looks at me and goes, 'Where you going to, my darling, my honey? My little partridgeberry? Where you going to, my love?' And I thought to myself, 'Jeez, if it wasn't for unemployment in Atlantic Canada, the West would have to hire real Mexican labour.' 'Cause we're hewers of wood and drawers of water out there" (James, qtd. in Cooke 2005).

12. In performance, this is said with a strong North Shore accent and is often addressed to "Martha" as he walks in purposeful indignation across the stage.

Chapter 5

1. "To be able to see these places and experience new places, that is a real plus to me. I talk a lot about new places and my experiences travelling it. I always come away from a new place with 20 minutes of new material" (James, qtd. in Callahan 2002). "This is what's really heightened my awareness of the country, is pulling into a Corner Brook or a Fort McMurray on a Wednesday night and walking around. Anywhere you go, you walk around and you walk on stage with at least 10 minutes of material about them. It's interesting that I'm able to wrap my head around some idiosyncrasy or personality characteristic of a place and put it up on stage. I think no matter where people live they like to be immortalized, get some kind of recognition that they're not forgotten in the big picture" (James, qtd. in Lewis 2002). "I got a haircut in Charlottetown and everybody was chinwagging in the shop and I walked on stage that night with 20 minutes of new material" (James, qtd. in Foley 2004).

2. This refers to a routine in which he describes sitting behind an old Anglican lady who breaks wind in a particularly malodorous way: the comparison is the gas in the trenches of World War I. Because of this routine, he needs the distortive effects of a microphone, which has precluded him from switching to hands-free (see the discussion in chapter 2). In the Halifax shows, he locates these Sunday mornings as transpiring at St. George's Round Church, a local landmark, which evinces recognition from the audience.

3. This is a routine in which how he describes how Canadians, when riding in a boat, no matter how otherwise sophisticated, will wave enthusiastically at the passengers of any boat they pass, who in turn do likewise. It is punctuated by particularly frenetic waving.

4. James contrasts the sympathy his wife got during her pregnancies—friends and relatives rubbing her belly—with his own experience after a vasectomy, comprising a bag of frozen peas and the use of the remote control ("I had to get *neutered* to get that thing in my hand").

5. Reconstructed from fieldnotes. James did not give me permission to record his performances. Also there's this: "He knew he hit humour's big time when, while on a recent tour of Northern Ontario, he was 'in this town called Atikokan, which is up on the Voyager Highway, right across from Quetico Park, you know? Way, way, way up there. At the end of the show, this man and his wife came up to me and gave me a big, brown paper bag. It was really heavy. They handed me the bag and, like, my arms went down and I

said, "What the hell is this?" I opened it up and it was a seven-pound sirloin moose roast! I came home and people said: "Boy, you know you've made it in Canadian show business when you're getting paid in Moose meat!"" (James, qtd. in Spevack 2000).

6. This credibility is similar to the "signifiers of authenticity" Peter Narváez has written about in the blues tradition (2005), and Barry Lee Pearson's work on the bluesman's story as a strategy for the reception of his repertoire (1984) would further add to this discussion. Martin Lovelace (1983), in his study of the life history as a source for folklife data, and John Cowley (1993), in his study of the bluesman as ethnographer, each suggested that, although these texts were not created with the same questions in mind as those of the ethnographer per se, they can be legitimately used as ethnographic source material.

7. Novalis's aphorism on the essence of Romantic poetry, "The art of estranging in a pleasant manner, making an object unfamiliar and yet familiar and attractive, that is romantic poetics" (1962, 502, Fragment 3053), has merged with Chesterton's on the role of the imagination ("not to make strange things settled, so much as to make settled things strange" [1907, 84]), and then been adapted to the more proverbial "making the strange familiar and the familiar strange" and adopted by artists, semioticians, and ethnographers alike as a definitional dictum. In his essay "On Ethnographic Surrealism," anthropologist James Clifford makes the point thus: "The ethnographic label suggests a characteristic attitude of participant observation among the artefacts of a defamiliarised cultural reality. The surrealists were intensely interested in exotic worlds, among which they included a certain Paris. Their attitude, while comparable to that of the fieldworker who strives to render the unfamiliar comprehensible, tended to work in the reverse sense, making the familiar strange. The contrast is in fact generated by a continuous play of the familiar and the strange, of which ethnography and surrealism are two elements" (1989, 121).

8. A three-disc "Collector's Edition" of the special was released in January of 2009, featuring the entirety of all three concerts. In the New York show, filmed at the world famous Apollo Theater, he emphasizes how he wants to do a good show "'cause it's the Apollo *Theatre* / and I know if it *ain't* good you all'll let me *know*." He transitions to a reference to Britney Spears on the MTV Video Music Awards, which had aired three nights previously.

9. For those even passingly familiar with the Cosby oeuvre, it may be of interest to note that "Buck Buck" later includes the first appearance of his Fat Albert character, a serious Buck Buck contender.

10. Guha Shankar, of the American Folklife Center at the Library of Congress, used this expression ("deep hanging out") as the best description of ethnography he knew during a conversation at the American Folklore Society meeting in Milwaukee, WI, in October of 2006. I continue to use it in my classes as it is the most effective definition to cross my path.

11. See Amy Shuman's discussion of "entitlement" (2005, 9–12).

12. Urry (1990) allows for a distinction between "traveller" and "tourist," mainly through the emic perception of the latter being subject to mass production: however,

when his focus is not on the concept of tourism as a consumable, that distinction is largely a matter of emphasis.

13. "Life on the Road" is one of the settings Keith Moore suggests in his "Fantasy Theme Analysis" of Denver stand-up comedians (1997, 128); Eric Shouse frames his study of comedian's backstage stories with the concept of the comedian as "Road Warrior" (2004).

14. And it appears in James's press: "The highly animated comic, who last played P.E.I. two years ago, said he's developed a lot of new material since then, much of it based on the adventures he's had on his travels across Canada. A keen observer of humanity, he said he tries to keep a poet's ear as he travels from place to place" (Gallant 2003); "Like the touring vaudeville comedians of the 19th century, 46-year-old James travels the country performing at its far reaches and it is in the small towns and remote regions that he finds much of his comedic inspiration and exasperation" (Clark 2004).

Chapter 6

1. The Federal Communications Commission (FCC) follows Title 18 § 1464 of the United States Code, "Broadcasting Obscene Language": "Whoever utters any obscene, indecent, or profane language by means of radio communication shall be fined under this title or imprisoned not more than two years, or both." See FCC 2007.

2. In Canada and Europe, where state broadcasters established a presence prior to private broadcasters, the influence of corporate interest has been somewhat less and, relatedly, a standard for the medium emerged prior to the influence of corporate interest.

3. "A fifth segment [of off-screen space, following up, down, right, and left] cannot be defined with the same seeming geometric precision, yet no one will deny that there is an off-screen space 'behind the camera' that is quite distinct from the four segments of space bordering the frame lines although the characters in the film generally reach this space by passing just to the right or the left of the camera" (Burch 1973, 17).

4. Cf. "While a folk preacher may not necessarily be longwinded in a natural church context, the presence of a strict control over the amount of time allowed to him during a broadcast must have an inhibiting effect" (Clements 1974, 324).

5. On occasion, cast members who came from stand-up would use the "Weekend Update" section to perform reworked routines as "editorials" or "commentaries": Chris Rock, Adam Sandler, David Spade, Norm MacDonald, and Colin Quinn, to name a few, all made significant names for themselves through these segments.

6. Voiceover: "At this point in his monologue, Martin begins a commentary on what he considers the decline in standards of feminine hygiene in this country. Although we at Saturday Night Live take no stand on this issue one way or the other, network policy prevents us from re-broadcasting this portion of his remarks. In summary, Martin feels, or felt at the time, that the failure of many young women to bathe thoroughly is a serious problem that demands our attention. He explores this problem, citing numerous examples from his personal experience, and ends by proposing several imaginative

solutions. It was a frank and lively presentation, and nearly cost us all our jobs. We now return to the conclusion of Martin's monologue" (*Saturday Night Live Transcripts* 1993).

7. More famously, in October of 1993, Hicks's entire routine was cut by Letterman's producers on the new *Late Show* (see True 2002, 209–27).

8. The Canadian equivalent to the FCC, the Canadian Radio-Television and Telecommunications Commission, does regulate cable television.

9. As of this writing, the latest live broadcasting technology—streaming audio and video—has yet to be used for stand-up performances in any systematic way.

10. Jay Leno recounts an earlier effort at televised stand-up, where the performers were shot without an audience in the morning and then filmed in the afternoon as members of the audience and a laugh-track was added in post-production. Incredibly bad continuity meant that Leno was in the audience for his own performance (1996, 158–60).

Chapter 7

1. A performance of "Seven Words" in Milwaukee in July of 1972—two months after its recording for *Class Clown* but prior to that album's September release—led to obscenity charges, which were dismissed when it went to trial that December, at which the recorded routine was played as evidence (Stingl 2007). In October of 1973, "Filthy Words"—a continuation of "Seven Words" that appears on *Occupation: Foole* (Carlin 1973*)—was broadcast on WBAI radio in New York, which led to the Supreme Court Case *FCC v. Pacifica Foundation et al.* In a five-to-four ruling, the Court held that there is a heretofore undefined difference between "obscene" and "indecent" language; that the routine was the latter; and that, whereas "obscene" material is not permitted on the public airwaves, "indecent" material is permitted, building on the FCC's original claim that it "never intended to place an absolute prohibition on the broadcast of this type of language, but rather sought to channel it to times of day when children most likely would not be exposed" (*FCC v. Pacifica Foundation et al.* 1978). There was never a suggestion that the material shouldn't appear on record, however.

2. In February of 1990, Carlin purchased the Little David label (save for the name). He now owned the masters to all his albums since *FM & AM*. This allowed for the first spate of CD reissues through Eardrum/Atlantic: *Classic Gold* (Carlin 1993*) comprises *FM & AM*, *Class Clown*, and *Occupation: Foole*. Since then he oversaw the reissue of all of his Little David albums on CD (starting in 1999) and his HBO specials on DVD (starting in 2000). In 2001 he launched Laugh.com, an online comedy store and label that also produced interviews with comedians on the art of comedy, including *Carlin on Comedy* (2002*).

3. Woody Allen's comic essay "A Twenties Memory" (1972) is similar to his "Lost Generation" routine from *Woody Allen Vol. 2* (1965*), while Steve Martin's "Cruel Shoes" (1979) is explicitly contiguous with his routine of the same name on *Comedy Is Not Pretty* (1979*). These, however, are the exceptions.

4. I have rearranged the sections from the book to correspond with the order of the performance.

REFERENCES

References marked with an asterisk (*) in the text citations refer to audio or video recordings: see the "Discography and Videography" section.

Abrahams, Roger D. 1975. "Negotiating Respect: Patterns of Presentation among Black Women." *Journal of American Folklore* 8 (347): 58–80.

Adorno, Theodor. 1991. *The Culture Industry: Selected Essays on Mass Culture*. London: Routledge.

Allen, Tim. 1994. *Don't Stand Too Close to a Naked Man*. New York: Hyperion.

Anders, Gunther. 1957. "The Phantom World of TV." Translated by Norbert Guterman. In *Mass Culture: The Popular Arts in America*, edited by Bernard Rosenberg and David Manning White, 358–67. Glencoe, IL: The Free Press.

Anderson, Benedict. 1991. *Imagined Communities: Reflections on the Origins and Spread of Nationalism*. Rev. ed. London: Verso.

Angelo, Megan. 2011. "Writers' New Form: Tweet-Up Comedy." *New York Times*, November 6.

Apte, Mahadev L. 1992. "Humor." In Bauman 1992b, 67–75.

Augestad, Kate. 2004. "Music Technology and Vocal Performance." Paper presented at New Media Conference: New Media as Culture Techniques and as Fora for Communicative Action, Bergen, Norway. May 28. Accessed February 4, 2008. http://www.kulturteknikker.hivolda.no/default.asp?kat=655&id=2440&sp=1.

Auslander, Philip. 1998. "Seeing Is Believing: Live Performance and the Discourse of Authenticity in Rock Culture." *Literature and Psychology* 44 (4): 1–26.

———. 1999. *Liveness: Performance in a Mediatized Culture*. New York: Routledge.

Austin, Bruce A. 1982. "The Motion Picture Audience: A Neglected Aspect of Film Research." Paper presented at the meeting of the Ohio University Film Conference, Athens, OH.

Badone, Ellen. 2004. "Crossing Boundaries: Exploring the Borderlands of Ethnography, Tourism, and Pilgrimage." In *Intersecting Journeys: The Anthropology of Pilgrimage and Tourism*, edited by Badone Roseman and Sharon R. Roseman, 180–89. Urbana: University of Illinois Press.

Baker, Houston A. 1984. *Blues, Ideology, and Afro-American Literature: A Vernacular Theory*. Chicago: University of Chicago Press.

Barr, Roseanne. 1989. *Roseanne: My Life as a Woman*. New York: Harper and Row.

Bascom, William. 1965. "The Forms of Folklore: Prose Narratives." *Journal of American Folklore* 78: 3–19.

Baudrillard, Jean. 1994. *Simulacra and Simulation*. Translated by Sheila Faria Glaser. Ann Arbor: University of Michigan Press.

Bauman, Richard. 1971. "Differential Identity and the Social Base of Folklore." *Journal of American Folklore* 84 (331): 31–41.

———. 1975. "Verbal Art as Performance." *American Anthropologist* New Series 77 (2): 290–311.

———. 1992a. "Performance." In Bauman 1992b, 41–49.

———, ed. 1992b. *Folklore, Cultural Performances, and Popular Entertainments: A Communications-Centered Approach.* New York: Oxford University Press.

Beavers, Herman. 1997. "'The Cool Pose': Intersectionality, Masculinity, and Quiescence in the Comedy and Films of Richard Pryor and Eddie Murphy." In *Race and the Subject of Masculinities*, edited by Harry Stecopoulos and Michael Uebel, 253–85. Durham: Duke University Press.

Bell, Michael J. 1983. *The World from Brown's Lounge: An Ethnography of Black Middle-Class Play.* Urbana: University of Illinois Press.

Belzer, Richard, Larry Charles, and Rick Newman. 1988. *How to Be a Stand-Up Comic.* New York: Citadel.

Ben-Amos, Dan. 1971. "Toward a Definition of Folklore in Context." *Journal of American Folklore* 84 (331): 3–15.

———. 1976. "Analytical Categories and Ethnic Genres." In *Folklore Genres*, edited by Dan Ben-Amos, 215–42. Austin: University of Texas Press.

Berger, Phil. 2000. *The Last Laugh: The World of Stand-Up Comics.* Updated ed. New York: Cooper Square.

Bergson, Henri. 1900. *Le Rire: Essai sur la signification du comique.* Paris: Alcan.

Bethke, Robert D. 1976. "Storytelling at an Adirondack Inn." *Western Folklore* 35 (2): 123–39.

Bird, S. Elizabeth. 1992. *For Enquiring Minds: A Cultural Study of Supermarket Tabloids.* Knoxville: University of Tennessee Press.

Borns, Betsy. 1987. *Comic Lives: Inside the World of American Stand-Up Comedy.* New York: Simon and Schuster.

Bouw, Brenda. 2001. "Funny Money: Comic Actor Ron James Gave Up His Hollywood Dream for the Canadian Acting Scene, Where Getting out of Debt Takes Perseverance and Talent." *Financial Post*, December 29.

Brady, Erika. 1999. *A Spiral Way: How the Phonograph Changed Ethnography.* Jackson: University Press of Mississippi.

Brand, Russell. 2007. *My Booky Wook.* London: Hodder & Stoughton.

Brodie, Ian. 2005. "Stand-Up Comedy and the Negotiation of Cultural Risk." Paper presented at the annual meeting of the American Folklore Society, Atlanta, GA.

———. 2006a. "History, Mimicry, Poetry, Poo: Ron James on Tour." Paper presented at the annual meeting of the Folklore Studies Association of Canada/Association canadienne de folklore et d'ethnologie, Toronto, ON.

———. 2006b. "'If It Wasn't for Unemployment in Atlantic Canada the West Would Have to Hire Real Mexican Labour': Regional Antagonisms in the Comedy of Ron James." Paper presented at the annual meeting of the American Folklore Society, Milwaukee, WI.

———. 2007a. "Stand-Up Comedy and/as Legend-Telling." Paper presented at the

Perspectives on Contemporary Legend Conference, the annual meeting of the International Society for Contemporary Legend Research, Logan, UT.

———. 2007b. "It's Funny because It's True: Stand-Up Comedy as Vernacular Ethnography." Paper presented at the joint annual meeting of the American Folklore Society and the Folklore Studies Association of Canada/Association canadienne de folklore et d'ethnologie, Quebec.

———. 2008a. "Live to Tape: Stand-Up Recordings." Paper presented at the annual meeting of the Folklore Studies Association of Canada/Association canadienne de folklore et d'ethnologie, Sydney, NS.

———. 2008b. "Stand-Up Comedy as a Genre of Intimacy." *Ethnologies* 30 (2): 153–80.

———. 2009. "Three Modes of the 'Outsider': Approaches to Stand-Up Comedy and Otherness." Paper presented at the annual meeting of the Folklore Studies Association of Canada/Association canadienne de folklore et d'ethnologie, Ottawa, ON.

Bruce, Lenny. 1967. *The Essential Lenny Bruce*. Compiled and edited by John Cohen. New York: Bell.

Brusseau, James. 2000. "Violence and Baudrillardian Repetition in Bret Easton Ellis's *American Psycho*." In *Phenomenological Approaches to Popular Culture*, edited by Michael T. Carroll and Eddie Tafoya, 35–47. Bowling Green, OH: Bowling Green State University Popular Press.

Bryant, Jerry H. 2003. *"Born in a Mighty Bad Land": The Violent Man in African-American Folklore and Fiction*. Bloomington: Indiana University Press.

Burch, Noël. 1973. *Theory of Film Practice*. Translated by Helen Lane. New York: Praeger.

Burns, Elizabeth. 1972. *Theatricality*. London: Longman.

Butler, Brett. 1996. *Knee Deep in Paradise*. New York: Hyperion.

Butler, Gary R. 1990. *Saying Isn't Believing: Conversation, Narrative, and the Discourse of Belief in a French Newfoundland Community*. St. John's, NL: ISER.

Byrne, Pat. 1987. "The Three Sisters: An Ethnography of Three 'Carlton Showband' Fans." *Culture & Tradition* 11: 58–68.

Caillois, Roger. 1961. *Man, Play, and Games*. Translated by Meyer Barash. Urbana: University of Illinois Press.

Callahan, Melanie. 2002. "Ron James Can't Wait to Bring Comedy Show to Province." *Corner Brook (NL) Western Star*, September 12.

Canadian Satellite Radio. 2005–2008. *XM Satellite Radio Canada*. Accessed August 6, 2008. http://www.xmradio.ca/.

Cantwell, Robert. 1993. "When We Were Good: Class and Culture in the Folk Revival." In Rosenberg 1993, 35–60.

Carlin, George. 1982. Interview by Sam Merrill. *Playboy*, January. Accessed July 31, 2008. http://www.playboy.com/magazine/interview_archive/george-carlin-1982/george -carlin.html.

———. 2007. "6 Questions: George Carlin." *Billboard.com*. Accessed July 29, 2008. http://www.billboard.com/bbcom/search/google/article_display.jsp?vnu_content _id=1003819742.

———. 2008. "HBO.com Exclusive George Carlin Interview." *HBO.com*. Accessed July 25, 2008. http://www.hbo.com/events/george-carlin/interview.html.

Carson, Johnny. 1979. "Johnny Carson: The Rolling Stone Interview." By Timothy White. *Rolling Stone*, March 22. Accessed September 26, 2008. http://www.rollingstone.com/artists/johnnycarson/articles/story/6862856/johnny_carson.

Carter, Judy. 1989. *Stand-Up Comedy: The Book*. New York: Dell.

———. 2001. *The Comedy Bible*. New York: Simon and Schuster.

Cavett, Dick. 2008. "Mamas, Don't Let Your Babies Grow Up to Be . . ." *Talk Show: A New York Times Blog*, August 15. Accessed October 8, 2008. http://cavett.blogs.nytimes.com/2008/08/15/mamas-dont-let-your-babies-grow-up-to-be/.

Chesterton, G. K. 1907. "In Defence of China Shepherdesses." In his *The Defendant*, 81–89. London: Dent.

Chiaro, Delia. 1992. *The Language of Jokes: Analysing Verbal Play*. London: Routledge.

Cho, Henry. 2006. *Henry Cho: Actor, Comedian, Rancher*. Accessed November 9, 2008. http://www.choindustries.com/.

CK, Louis. 2011a. "A Statement from Louis CK." Blog post, December 13. louisck.net.

———. 2011b. "Another statement from Louis CK." Blog post, December 21. louisck.net.

Clark, Andrew. 1996a. "Newfoundland's Accidental Standup Shaun Majumder Falls Backwards into Laugh Circuit." *Toronto Star*, March 7.

———. 1996b. "Laughter Gets Lifted from the Delete Bin: CD Series Bodes Well for Comics." *Toronto Star*, May 23.

———. 2004. "Ron James Turns Crackling Wit on Canadian Foibles." *Toronto Star*, June 18.

Clements, William M. 1974. "The Rhetoric of the Radio Ministry." *Journal of American Folklore* 37 (346): 318–27.

Clifford, James. 1989. "On Ethnographic Surrealism." In his *The Predicament of Culture: Twentieth-Century Ethnography, Literature, and Art*, 117–51. Cambridge, MA: Harvard University Press.

Collins, Ronald K. L., and David M. Skover. 2002. *The Trials of Lenny Bruce*. Naperville, IL: Sourcebooks.

Cooke, Stephen. 2005. "Comedic Quest." *Halifax (NS) Chronicle-Herald*, November 5.

Corner Brook (NL) Western Star. 2002. "Comedian James Plans Four Stops in Province." August 29.

———. 2005. "Gone with Ron: James Bringing Comedic Rant to Corner Brook Nov. 4." October 27.

Corrigan, Kelly. 2001. "Ron James." *View Magazine* (Hamilton), May 24. Accessed November 1, 2008. http://www.viewmag.com/viewstory.php?storyid=25.

Cosby, Bill. 1986. *Fatherhood*. Introduction and afterword by Alvin F. Poussaint. New York: Dolphin Doubleday.

Cosgrove, Stuart. 1984. "The Zoot-Suit and Style Warfare." *History Workshop* 18: 77–91.

Cowley, John. 1993. "Shack Bullies and Levee Contractors: Bluesmen as Ethnographers." In *Songs about Work*, edited by Archie Green, 134–62. Bloomington: Folklore Institute, Indiana University.

Crick, Malcolm. 1985. "'Tracing' the Anthropological Self: Quizzical Reflections on Fieldwork, Tourism, and the Ludic." *Social Analysis* 17: 71–92.

Dangerfield, Rodney. 2005. *It's Not Easy Bein' Me*. New York: Harper Entertainment.

Davies, Christie. 1990. *Ethnic Humor around the World: A Comparative Analysis*. Bloomington: University of Indiana Press.

DeGeneres, Ellen. 1995. *My Point . . . And I Do Have One*. New York: Bantam.

Del Negro, Giovanna P. 2005. "Torch Singer, Dominatrix Goddess: Music and Hybrid Identity in the Performance of Judy Tenuta." Paper presented at the annual meeting of the American Folklore Society, Atlanta, GA.

———. 2006. "'If I Embarrass You Tell Your Friends,' or 'This Next Story Is a Little Risqué': Recovering the Jewish Women Comic Giants of the 1950s and Early 1960s." Paper presented at the annual meeting of the American Folklore Society, Milwaukee, WI.

———. 2010. "The Bad Girls of Jewish Comedy: Gender, Class, Assimilation, and Whiteness in Postwar America." In *A Jewish Feminist Mystique? Jewish Women in Postwar America*, edited by Hasia Diner, Shira Kohn, and Rachel Kranson, 144–59. Piscataway, NJ: Rutgers University Press.

Double, Oliver. 1997. *Stand-Up: On Being a Comedian*. London: Methuen.

Doyle, John. 2003. "Enough of the Headscarf-and-Handbag Humour, B'y." *Globe and Mail* (Toronto, ON), October 1.

———. 2004. "Superior? Stop Kidding Yourself, Canada." *Globe and Mail* (Toronto, ON), January 28.

———. 2005. "Comic Riffs and a Comic Opera." *Globe and Mail* (Toronto, ON), December 9.

Dresser, Norine. 1994. "The Case of the Missing Gerbil." *Western Folklore* 53 (3): 229–42.

Dundes, Alan. 1964. "Texture, Text, and Context." *Southern Folklore Quarterly* 28 (4): 251–65.

———. 1965. "What Is Folklore?" Introduction to *The Study of Folklore*, edited by Alan Dundes, 1–3. Englewood Cliffs, NJ: Prentice-Hall.

———. 1971. "Folk Ideas as Units of Worldview." *Journal of American Folklore* 84 (331): 93–103.

Dunn, Sharon. 2003. "'I Don't Get Rich, I Get Recognized': Yes, It's Ron James, That Guy from the Show about Canoes." *National Post* (Toronto, ON), June 2.

Eco, Umberto. 1986. "The Comic and the Rule." In his *Travels in Hyperreality*, translated by William Weaver, 269–77. New York: Harvest-Harcourt Brace.

Ellis, Bill. 1989. "When Is a Legend? An Essay in Legend Taxonomy." In *The Questing Beast: Perspectives on Contemporary Legend IV*, edited by Gillian Bennett and Paul Smith, 31–53. Sheffield, UK: Sheffield Academic Press.

———. 2001. *Aliens, Ghosts, and Cults: Legends We Live*. Jackson: University Press of Mississippi.

———. 2003. "Making a Big Apple Crumble: The Role of Humor in Constructing a Global Response to Disaster." In Narváez 2003, 35–79.

Everett, Holly. 2003. "'The Association I Have with This Guitar Is My Life': The Guitar as Artifact and Symbol." *Popular Music and Society* 26 (3): 331–50.

FCC (Federal Communications Commission). 2007. "Obscenity, Indecency & Profanity—Frequently Asked Questions." April 27. *FCC Home Page*. Accessed November 11, 2007. http://www.fcc.gov/eb/oip/FAQ.html.

FCC v. Pacifica Foundation et al. 1978. 438 U.S. 726.

Fine, Gary Alan. 1992. *Manufacturing Tales: Sex and Money in Contemporary Legends*. Knoxville: University of Tennessee Press.

Fisher, Rhoda L., and Seymour Fisher. 1984. "The Comic's Quest for Goodness." *Western Folklore* 43: 71–79.

Fiske, John. 1989. *Understanding Popular Culture*. London: Routledge.

Foley, Doug. 2004. "Comedian Honed Craft on the Road." *Hamilton Spectator* (Hamilton, ON), March 17.

Fowke, Edith. 1988. *Red Rover, Red Rover: Children's Games Played in Canada*. Toronto: Doubleday.

Franklin, Joe. 1979. *Joe Franklin's Encyclopedia of Comedians*. New York: Bell.

Freedman, Jim. 1983. "Will the Sheik Use His Blinding Fireball? The Ideology of Professional Wrestling." In *The Celebration of Society: Perspectives on Contemporary Cultural Performance*, edited by Frank E. Manning, 67–79. Bowling Green, OH: Bowling Green State University Popular Press.

French, Daniel B. 1998. "Through the Eyes of the Comic Mask: An Ethnographic Exploration of the Identity of a Stand-Up Comedian." PhD diss., University of South Florida.

Freud, Sigmund. 1976. *Jokes and Their Relation to the Unconscious*. Translated by James Strachey. Penguin Freud Library 6. London: Penguin.

Frings, Manfred. 2003. *Life Time: Max Scheler's Philosophy of Time: A First Inquiry and Presentation*. Dordrecht and Boston: Kluwer Academic Publishers.

Frith, Simon. 1996. *Performing Rites: On the Value of Popular Music*. Cambridge, MA: Harvard University Press.

Fulton, DoVeanna S. 2004. "Comic Views and Metaphysical Dilemmas: Shattering Cultural Images through Self-Definition and Representation by Black Comediennes." *Journal of American Folklore* 117 (463): 81–96.

Furlong, Melanie. 2006. "Tourists Do Say the Darndest Things; Visitors Still Looking for Supposedly Ubiquitous Fishermen of Nova Scotia." *Halifax (NS) Chronicle-Herald*. January 21.

Gallant, Doug. 2003. "Ron James Brings Comedy to Confederation Centre Stage." *Charlottetown (PE) Guardian*, November 7.

Geertz, Clifford. 1971. "Deep Play: Notes on the Balinese Cockfight." *Myth, Symbol, and Culture*, edited by Clifford Geertz, 1–37. New York: W. W. Norton.

Gelo, Daniel J. 1999. "Powwow Patter: Indian Emcee Discourse on Power and Identity." *Journal of American Folklore* 112 (443): 40–57.

George, Nelson. 1998. *Hip Hop America*. New York: Viking.

Georges, Robert A. 1969. "Toward an Understanding of Storytelling Events." *Journal of American Folklore* 82 (326): 313–28.

Goffman, Erving. 1959. *The Presentation of Self in Everyday Life*. Garden City: Anchor Books.

Goldman, Albert. 1974. *Ladies and Gentlemen—Lenny Bruce!* With Lawrence Schiller. New York: Penguin.

Goldstein, Kenneth S. 1976. "Monologue Performance in Great Britain." *Southern Folklore Quarterly* 40 (1–2): 7–29.

———. 1982. "The Impact of Recording Technology on the British Folksong Revival." In *Folk Music and Modern Sound*, edited by William Ferris and Mary L. Hart, 3–13. Jackson: University Press of Mississippi.

Goodsell, Charles. 1988. "The Architecture of Parliaments: Legislative Houses and Political Culture." *British Journal of Political Science* 18 (3): 287–302.

Gordon, Max. 1980. *Live at the Village Vanguard*. New York: St. Martin's.

Gramsci, Antonio. 1971. *Selections from the Prison Notebooks*. Edited and translated by Quintin Hoare and Geoffrey Nowell-Smith. London: Lawrence & Wishart.

Green, Adam. 2004. "Standup for the Lord." *New Yorker*, August 9 and 16, 46–54.

Gregory, Dick. 1964. *Nigger: An Autobiography*. With Robert Lipsyte. New York: Dutton.

Halifax (NS) Daily News. 1999. "Speed Read." June 6.

———. 2002. "Speed Read." August 6.

Harrop, John. 1992. *Acting*. London: Routledge.

Hayward, Karla. 2005. "Get Laughs or Die." *St. John's (NL) Telegram*, October 28.

Hebdige, Dick. 1979. *Subculture: The Meaning of Style*. London: Methuen.

Hellmann, John M., Jr. 1973. "'I'm a Monkey': The Influence of the American Blues Argot on the Rolling Stones." *Journal of American Folklore* 86 (342): 367–73.

Henken, Elissa R. 2006. "Genre Selection: Legend or Joke." Paper presented at the annual meeting of the American Folklore Society, Milwaukee, WI.

Hepfner, Lisa. 1999. "Maritime Roots Provide Ocean of Inspiration." *Hamilton (ON) Spectator*, November 12.

Hicks, Bill. 2004. *Love All the People: Letters, Lyrics, Routines*. London: Constable & Robertson.

Hills, Matt. 2002. *Fan Cultures*. London: Routledge.

Holt, Jim. 2008. *Stop Me If You've Heard This: A History and Philosophy of Jokes*. New York: W. W. Norton.

Horowitz, Josh. 2007. "Pee-Wee's Big Return? Paul Reubens Discusses Plans for Two Pee-Wee Films." *MTV Movie News*, December 11. Accessed November 1, 2008. http://www.mtv.com/movies/news/articles/1576172/20071210/story.jhtml.

Hutchinson, Robert S., ed. 1963. *Joe Miller's Jests: or, the Wit's Vade-mecum*. New York: Dover Publications.

Hymes, Dell. 1975. "Breakthrough into Performance." In *Folklore: Performance and Communication*, edited by Dan Ben-Amos and Kenneth S. Goldstein, 11–74. The Hague: Mouton.

James, Ron. 2005a. Interview with author. November 16.

———. 2005b. "Ron James: How Much Do I Love Canada?" Interview by Sarah Hampson. *Toronto Globe and Mail*, December 3.

Jansen, William Hugh. 1959. "The Esoteric-Exoteric Factor in Folklore." *Fabula: Journal of Folklore Studies* 2: 205–11.

Jet. 1996. "Martin Lawrence Picked up by Police for Strange Behavior; Suffered Exhaustion, Dehydration: Doctor." May 27.

———. 1999. "Martin Lawrence Recovers from Coma Caused by Jogging in Near 100-Degree Heat." September 13.

Kaufman, Will. 1997. *The Comedian as Confidence Man: Studies in Irony Fatigue.* Detroit: Wayne State University Press.

Kibler, M. Alison. 1999. "Gender Conflict and Coercion on A&E's *An Evening at the Improv.*" *Journal of Popular Culture* 32 (4): 45–57.

Kiesler, Sara, and Jonathon M. Cummings. 2002. "What Do We Know about Proximity and Distance in Work Groups? A Legacy of Research." In *Distributed Work*, edited by Pamela Hinds and Sara Kiesler, 57–82. Boston: MIT Press.

Kirchhoff, H. J. 1994. Review of *Up and Down in Shaky Town*, by Ron James, and *Skinny Guy with a Gut*, by Dave MacKenzie. *Globe and Mail* (Toronto, ON), April 30.

Kirshenblatt-Gimblett, Barbara. 1989. "Objects of Memory: Material Culture as Life Review." In *Folk Groups and Folklore Genres: A Reader*, edited by Elliott Oring, 329–38. Logan: Utah State University Press.

Klein, Barbro. 2006. "An Afternoon's Conversation at Elsa's." In *Narrating, Doing, Experiencing: Nordic Folkloristic Perspectives*, edited by Annikki Kaivola-Bregenhøj, Barbro Klein, and Ulf Palmenfelt, 79–100. Studia Fennica Folkloristica 16. Helsinki: Finnish Literature Society.

Klein, Robert. 1977. "Mind over Matter: An Interview with Robert Klein." By Diane U. Eisenberg. In Mintz 1977, 3–10.

Knelman, Martin. 1999. *The Joker Is Wild: The Triumphs and Tribulations of Jim Carrey.* Toronto: Penguin.

Koven, Mikel J. 2003. "Traditional Narrative, Popular Aesthetics, *Weekend at Bernie's*, and Vernacular Cinema." In Narváez 2003, 294–310.

Koziski, Stephanie. 1984. "The Standup Comedian as Anthropologist: Intentional Culture Critic." *Journal of Popular Culture* 18 (2): 57–76.

Kugelmass, Jack. 2003. "Wishes Come True: Designing the Greenwich Village Halloween Parade." In Narváez 2003, 171–97.

Ladenheim, Melissa. 1987. "'I Was Country When Country Wasn't Cool': An Ethnography of a Country Music Fan." *Culture & Tradition* 11: 69–85.

Lahr, John. 2000. "The Izzard King." In his *Show and Tell: New Yorker Profiles*, 171–82. New York: Overlook Press.

Lax, Eric. 1992. *Woody Allen: A Biography.* New York: Vintage.

Lee, Rachel C. 2004. "'Where's My Parade?': Margaret Cho and the Asian American Body in Space." *TDR: The Drama Review* 48 (2): 108–32.

Leno, Jay. 1996. *Leading with My Chin.* With Bill Zehme. New York: Harper Collins.

Lewis, Nick. 2002. "Ron James Is Happy Making Canadians Laugh." *Calgary (AB) Herald*, November 3.

Limon, John K. 2000. *Stand-Up Comedy in Theory, or, Abjection in America*. London: Duke University Press.

———. 2001. "Spritzing, Skirting: Standup Talk Strategies." In *Talk Talk Talk: The Cultural Life of Everyday Conversation*, edited by S. I. Salamensky, 105–18. New York: Routledge.

Lisk, Dean. 2005. "Gone with Ron in Town." *Halifax (NS) Daily News*, November 11.

Lo, Kwai-Cheung. 1998. "Look Who's Talking: The Politics of Orality in Transitional Hong Kong Mass Culture." *Modern Chinese Literary and Cultural Studies in the Age of Theory: Reimagining a Field*. Special issue of *boundary 2* 25 (3): 151–68.

Lockheart, Paula. 2003. "A History of Early Microphone Singing, 1925–1939: American Mainstream Popular Singing at the Advent of Electronic Microphone Amplification." *Popular Music and Society* 26 (3): 367–85.

Lombana, Andres. 2007. "The Bastard Son of Comedy." *Confessions of an Aca/Fan: The Official Weblog of Henry Jenkins*. April 5. Accessed October 30, 2008. http://www .henryjenkins.org/2007/04/the_bastard_son_of_comedy.html.

Lonergan, Bernard. 1957. *Insight*. London: Darton Longman and Todd.

Lopez, George. 2004. *Why You Crying? My Long, Hard Look at Life, Love, and Laughter*. With Armen Keteyian. New York: Touchstone.

Lord, Albert B. 1960. *The Singer of Tales*. Cambridge: Harvard University Press.

Lovelace, Martin. 1983. "The Presentation of Folklife in the Biographies and Autobiographies of English Rural Workers." PhD diss., Memorial University of Newfoundland.

Lull, James. 1990. *Inside Family Viewing: Ethnographic Research on Television's Audiences*. London: Routledge.

Mac, Bernie. 2003. *Maybe You Never Cry Again*. With Pablo F. Fenjves. New York: ReganBooks HarperCollins.

MacDonald, Gayle. 2002. "True North Strong and Plaid." *Globe and Mail*. April 13.

Macdonald, Ron Foley. 1999. "James's Shakeytown Is All Ups, No Downs." *Halifax (NS) Daily News*, June 18.

Martin, Steve. 1979. *Cruel Shoes*. New York: Putnam.

———. 2007. *Born Standing Up: A Comic's Life*. New York: Scribner.

McCarl, Robert. 1986. "Occupational Folklore." In *Folk Groups and Folklore Genres: An Introduction*, edited by Elliott Oring, 71–89. Logan: Utah State University Press.

McCracken, Allison. 1999. "'God's Gift to Us Girls': Crooning, Gender, and the Re-creation of American Popular Song, 1928–1933." *American Music* 17 (4): 365–95.

McIlvenny, Paul, Sari Mettovaara, and Ritva Tapio. 1993. "'I Really Wanna Make You Laugh': Stand-Up Comedy and Audience Response." In *Folia, Fennistica & Linguistica: Proceedings of the Annual Finnish Linguistics Symposium, May 1992*, edited by Matti K. Suojanen and Auli Kulkki-Nieminen, 225–47. Tampere University Finnish and General Linguistics Department Publications 16. Tampere, Finland: Tampere University.

McKay, John. 2000. "Canadian History Served Up in *Blackfly*." *Corner Brook (NL) Western Star*, December 30.

McLaughlin, Thomas. 1997. "Theory outside the Academy." Introduction to his *Street Smarts and Critical Theory*, 3–30. Madison: University of Wisconsin Press.

McLuhan, Marshall. 1964. *Understanding Media: The Extensions of Man*. 2nd ed. New York: McGraw Hill.

McRobbie, Angela. 1998. *British Fashion Design: Rag Trade or Image Industry?* London: Routledge.

Mietkiewicz, Henry. 1995. "How California Brings Out the Canadian in Ron James." *Toronto Star*, April 6.

Mills, Theodore M. 1967. *The Sociology of Small Groups*. Prentice-Hall Foundations of Modern Sociology. Englewood Cliffs, NJ: Prentice-Hall.

Mintz, Lawrence E., ed. 1977. *Standup Comedy*. Special issue of *American Humor* 4 (2): 1–46.

———. 1998. "Stand-Up Comedy as Social and Cultural Mediation." In *What's So Funny? Humor in American Culture*, edited by Nancy A. Walker, 193–204. Wilmington, DE: Scholarly Resources.

Misje, Anne-Karin. 2002. "Stand-Up Comedy as Negotiation and Subversion." In *Popular Imagination: Essays on Fantasy and Cultural Practice*, edited by Sven-Erik Klinkmann, 87–112. NNF Publications 12. Turku, Finland: Nordic Network of Folklore.

Mitges, Lynn. 2006. "Making the Most of a Blood Sport." *Vancouver (BC) Province*, April 26.

Mock, Roberta. 1999. "Female Jewish Comedians: Grotesque Mimesis and Transgressing Stereotypes." *New Theatre Quarterly* 15 (2): 99–108.

Moore, Jacquie. 2005. "A Funny Thing Happened on the Way to the Centennial: Manic Maritimer Ron James Returns to Riff on Pogey Culture, Elk Snot, and King Ralph." *Calgary (AB) Herald*, September 16.

Moore, Keith P. J. 1997. "A Fantasy Theme Analysis of the Community of Professional Comedians in Denver, Colorado." PhD diss., University of Denver.

Mukerji, Chandra. 1978. "Bullshitting: Road Lore among Hitchhikers." *Social Problems* 25 (3): 241–52.

Mullen, Patrick B. 1970. "A Negro Street Performer: Tradition and Innovation." *Western Folklore* 29 (2): 91–103.

Nachman, Gerald. 2003. *Seriously Funny: The Rebel Comedians of the 1950s and 1960s*. New York: Pantheon.

Nahm, H. Y. 2008. "Comedy's Southern Squire." *Goldsea American Asian Daily*. Accessed November 9, 2008. http://goldsea.com/Personalities2/Chohenry/chohenry.html.

Narváez, Peter. 1986. "Joseph R. Smallwood, 'The Barrelman': The Broadcaster as Folklorist." In Narváez and Laba 1986a, 47–64.

———. 1992. "Folk Talk and Hard Facts: The Role of Ted Russell's 'Uncle Mose' on CBC's 'Fishermen's Broadcast.'" In *Studies in Newfoundland Folklore: Community and Process*, edited by Gerald Thomas and J.D.A. Widdowson, 191–212. St. John's, NL: Breakwater.

———. 1993. "*Living Blues* Journal: The Paradoxical Aesthetics of the Blues Revival." In Rosenberg 1993, 241–57.

———, ed. 2003. *Of Corpse: Death and Humor in Folklore and Popular Culture*. Logan: Utah State University Press.

———. 2005. "Marginal to Vernacular Blues: Australian and Canadian Blues Scenes." Paper presented at Post-Colonial Distances: The Study of Popular Music in Canada and Australia, the annual meeting of the International Association for the Study of Popular Music Canada, St. John's, NL.

Narváez, Peter, and Martin Laba, eds. 1986a. *Media Sense: The Folklore Popular Culture Continuum.* Bowling Green, OH: Bowling Green State University Popular Press.

———. 1986b. "The Folklore-Popular Culture Continuum." In Narváez and Laba 1986a, 1–8.

Nathanson, Ian. 2001. "James' Laugh-a-Minute Performance Perfect." *Ottawa (ON) Sun*, February 3.

Newhart, Bob. 2006. *I Shouldn't Even Be Doing This! And Other Things that Strike Me as Funny.* New York: Hyperion.

Novalis [Georg Philipp Friedrich von Hardenberg]. 1962. *Werke und Briefe.* Edited by Alfred Kelletat. Munich: Winkler.

O'Donnell, Rosie. 2002. *Find Me.* New York: Warner Books.

O'Meally, Robert. 1991. *Lady Day: The Many Faces of Billie Holiday.* New York: Arcade.

Oppenheimer, Jerry. 2002. *Seinfeld.* New York: HarperCollins.

Oring, Elliott. 1992. *Jokes and Their Relations.* Lexington: University Press of Kentucky.

Oswald, Brad. 2004. "Jokin' with James." *Winnipeg (MB) Free Press*, November 20.

Oswalt, Patton. 2011. Interview with Genevieve Koski. *The A.V. Club*, August 31. http://www.avclub.com/article/patton-oswalt-61121.

Parker, Zoe. 2002. "Standing Up for the Nation: An Investigation of Stand-Up Comedy in South Africa Post-1994 with Specific Reference to Women's Power and the Body." *South African Theatre Journal* 16: 8–29.

Paton, George E. C. 1988. "The Comedian as a Portrayer of Social Morality." In *Humour in Society: Resistance and Control*, edited by Chris Powell and George E. C. Paton, 206–33. London: Palgrave MacMillan.

Pearson, Barry Lee. 1984. *"Sounds So Good to Me": The Bluesman's Story.* Philadelphia: University of Pennsylvania Press.

Pedersen, Stephen. 2001a. "James Serious about Stand-up; Comedian Brings New Show to N.S." *Halifax (NS) Chronicle-Herald*, November 6.

———. 2001b. "Fast-Quipping James Gives Funnybone a Real Workout." *Halifax (NS) Chronicle-Herald*, November 15.

Ping-kwan, Leung. 2000. "Urban Cinema and the Cultural Identity of Hong Kong." In *The Cinema of Hong Kong: History, Arts, Identity*, edited by Poshek Fu and David Desser, 227–51. Cambridge: Cambridge University Press.

Playboy. 1961. "Playboy Panel: Hip Comics and the New Humor." March.

Porter, Jennifer E. 1999. "To Boldly Go: *Star Trek* Convention Attendance as Pilgrimage." In *Star Trek and Sacred Ground: Explorations in Star Trek, Religion, and American Culture*, edited by Jennifer Porter and Darcee L. McLaren, 245–70. Albany: SUNY Press.

Posen, I. Sheldon. 1993. "On Folk Festivals and Kitchens: Questions of Authenticity in the Folksong Revival." In Rosenberg 1993, 127–36.

Posner, Michael. 2001. "*Blackfly* Set to Buzz." *Globe and Mail* (Toronto, ON), January 1.

Price, Darby Li Po. 1998. "Laughing without Reservation: Indian Standup Comedians." *American Indian Culture and Research Journal* 22 (4): 255–71.

Pryor, Richard. 1995. *Pryor Convictions and Other Life Sentences*. With Todd Gold. New York: Pantheon.

———. 2004. Foreword to *Made You Laugh! The Funniest Moments in Radio, Television, Stand-Up, and Movie Comedy*, by Joe Garner, ix–x. Kansas City: Andrews McMeel.

Pulliam, Gregory J. 1991. "Stock Lines, Boat-Acts, and Dickjokes: A Brief Annotated Glossary of Standup Comedy Jargon." *American Speech* 66: 164–70.

Radner, Joan Newlon, and Susan S. Lanser. 1993. "Strategies of Coding in Women's Cultures." In *Feminist Messages: Coding in Women's Folk Culture*, edited by Joan Radner, 1–29. Urbana: University of Illinois Press.

Rahman, Jacquelyn. 2004. "It's a Serious Business: The Linguistic Construction of Middle-Class White Characters by African American Narrative Comedians." PhD diss., Stanford University.

Rankin, Bill. 2004. "Funnyman Ron James Has Wind in His Sails." *Halifax (NS) Daily News*, December 7.

———. 2005. Poking Fun at the Giant Perogy and Other Prairie Foibles. *Edmonton (AB) Journal*, December 8.

Rasmussen, Susan J. 1997. "Between Ritual, Theatre, and Play: Blacksmith Praise at Tuareg Marriage." *Journal of American Folklore* 110 (435): 3–27.

Ressner, Jeffrey. 1998. "As for the Old Master . . ." *Time*, August 10. Accessed July 25, 2007. http://www.time.com/time/magazine/article/0,9171,988894,00.html.

Rickles, Don. 2007. *Rickles' Book*. New York: Simon and Schuster.

Riesman, David. 1970. "The Oral Tradition, the Written Word and the Screen Image." In *Film and the Liberal Arts*, edited by T. J. Ross, 251–59. Toronto: Holt, Rinehart, and Winston.

Rivers, Joan. 1986. *Enter Talking*. With Richard Merryman. New York: Delacorte.

Robidoux, Michael A. 2001. *Men at Play: A Working Understanding of Professional Hockey*. Montreal: McGill-Queen's University Press.

Rock, Chris. 1997. *Rock This!* New York: Diane.

———. 2007. Interview by Brian Haitt. *Rolling Stone*, November 15, 154–56.

Rock, Chris, and Don Rickles. 2008. "Mind If I Joke?" Interview by Devin Friedman. *GQ*, August, 128–32.

ronjames.ca. 2004. "Ron's Official Bio." Accessed June 6, 2006.

Rosenberg, Neil V. 1972. Review of *Nobody: The Story of Bert Williams*, by Ann Charters; *Recording the Blues*, by Robert M. W. Dixon and John Godrich; and *Blacks, Whites, and the Blues*, by Tony Russell. *Western Folklore* 30 (2): 147–49.

———. 1985. *Bluegrass: A History*. Urbana: University of Illinois Press.

———. 1986. "Big Fish, Small Pond: Country Musicians and Their Markets." In Narváez and Laba 1986a, 149–66.

———, ed. 1993. *Transforming Tradition: Folk Music Revivals Examined*. Urbana: University of Illinois Press.

Rosenkranz, Karl. 1977. *Georg Wilhelm Friedrich Hegels Leben*. Darmstadt: Wissenschaftliche Buchgesellschaft.

Roth, LuAnne K. 2003. "Dancing Skeletons: The Subversion of Death among Deadheads." In Narváez 2003, 263–93.

Roubo, Kelly. 2003. Interview with author. March 21.

Rubinoff, Joel. 2001. "Ron James Stands on Guard for Comedy." *Guelph (ON) Mercury*, November 15.

Russell, I. Willis, and Mary Gray Porter. 1973. "Among the New Words." *American Speech* 48 (1–2): 131–43.

Rutter, Jason. 2000. "The Stand-Up Introduction Sequence: Comparing Comedy Compères." *Journal of Pragmatics* 32: 463–83.

Sankey, Jay. 1998. *Zen and the Art of Stand-Up Comedy*. New York: Taylor and Francis.

Saturday Night Live Transcripts. 1993. Martin Lawrence monologue. Accessed June 17, 2008. http://snltranscripts.jt.org/93/93nmono.phtml.

Schechter, Harold. 1988. *The Bosom Serpent: Folklore and Popular Art*. Iowa City: University of Iowa Press.

Schulman, Norma. 1994. "The House That Black Built: Television Stand-Up Comedy as Minor Discourse." *Journal of Popular Film and Television* 22 (3): 108–15.

Schwensen, David. 2005. *Comedy FAQs and Answers: How the Stand-Up Biz Really Works*. New York: Watson-Guptill.

Seizer, Susan. 2011. "On the Uses of Obscenity in Live Stand-Up Comedy." *Anthropological Quarterly* 84 (1): 209–34.

Shales, Tom, and James Andrew Miller. 2002. *Live from New York: An Uncensored History of Saturday Night Live*. Boston: Little, Brown.

Shouse, Eric. 2004. "Outlaw Heroes and Road Warriors: Standup Comedy and the Quest for Fame." PhD diss., University of South Florida.

Shuker, Roy. 2001. *Understanding Popular Music*. London: Routledge.

Shuman, Amy. 2005. *Other People's Stories: Entitlement Claims and the Critique of Empathy*. Urbana: University of Illinois Press.

Singer, Milton B. 1972. *When a Great Tradition Modernizes: An Anthropological Approach to Indian Civilization*. New York: Praeger.

Sirius Canada. 2008. *Sirius Satellite Radio Canada*. Accessed August 6, 2008. http://www.siriuscanada.ca/.

Smith, L. Mayne. 1965. "An Introduction to Bluegrass." *Journal of American Folklore* 78 (309): 245–56.

Smith, Ronald L. 1997. *Cosby: The Life of a Comedy Legend*. Rev. ed. New York: Prometheus Books.

———. 1998. *Comedy Stars at 78 RPM: Biographies and Discographies of 89 American and British Recording Artists, 1896–1946*. Jefferson, NC: McFarland and Company.

Smulders, Marilyn. 2003. "Ron James Tackles Middle Age, 9/11." *Halifax (NS) Daily News*, October 2.

Spence, Louise. 1995. "'They Killed off Marlena, but She's on Another Show Now': Fantasy, Reality, and Pleasure in Watching Daytime Soap Operas." In *To Be Continued . . . : Soap Operas around the World*, edited by Robert C. Allen, 182–98. London: Routledge.

Speroni, Charles, comp. and trans. 1964. *Wit and Wisdom of the Italian Renaissance*. Berkeley: University of California Press.

Spevack, Leatrice. 2000. "Ron James Is in It Just for Laughs." *Toronto Star*, March 12.

Stanley, Alessandra. 2008. "Who Says Women Aren't Funny?" *Vanity Fair*, April, 182–91, 251.

Stebbins, Robert A. 1990. *The Laugh-Makers: Stand-Up Comedy as Art, Business, and Life-Style*. Montreal: McGill-Queen's University Press.

Stephenson, Pamela. 2001. *Billy*. London: HarperCollins.

Stingl, Jim. 2007. "Carlin's Naughty Words Still Ring in Officer's Ears." *JS Online (Milwaukee Journal-Sentinel)*, June 30. Accessed July 28, 2008. http://www.jsonline.com/story/index.aspx?id=626471.

Stone, Kay. 1997. "Social Identity in Organized Storytelling." *Western Folklore* 56 (3–4): 233–41.

Storey, John. 1998. *An Introduction to Cultural Theory and Popular Culture*. 2nd ed. Athens: University of Georgia Press.

Sutton-Smith, Brian. 1972. *The Folkgames of Children*. Publications of the American Folklore Society Bibliographical and Special Series 24. Austin: University of Texas Press.

———. 2001. *The Ambiguity of Play*. Cambridge, MA: Harvard University Press.

Szwed, John. 2002. *So What: The Life of Miles Davis*. New York: Simon & Schuster.

Taft, Michael. 2006. *The Blues Lyric Formula*. London: Routledge.

Thomas, Jeannie B. 1997. "Dumb Blondes, Dan Quayle, and Hillary Clinton: Gender, Sexuality, and Stupidity in Jokes." *Journal of American Folklore* 110 (437): 277–313.

Time. 1959. "The Sickniks." July 13.

———. 1960a. "The Giant Killer." February 29.

———. 1960b. "The Third Campaign." August 15.

Toelken, Barre. 1979. *The Dynamics of Folklore*. Boston: Houghton Mifflin.

Tokofsky, Peter I. 1997. "Communal Creation Revisited: Authorship and Creativity in the Elzacher *Fasnet*." *Western Folklore* 56 (3–4): 215–32.

True, Cynthia. 2002. *American Scream: The Bill Hicks Story*. London: Pan Macmillan.

Turner, Victor. 1974. *Dramas, Fields, and Metaphors: Symbolic Action in Human Society*. Ithaca, NY: Cornell University Press.

Tye, Diane. 1987. "An Ethnography of a Beatles Fan." *Culture & Tradition* 11: 41–57.

———. 1988. "Local Characters and the Community: A Case Study of Tradition and Individual Nonconformity in the Maritimes." PhD diss., Memorial University of Newfoundland.

———. 1989. "Local Character Anecdotes: A Nova Scotia Case Study." *Western Folklore* 48 (3): 181–99.

United Press. 1987. "One Killed, One Stabbed at Opening of Murphy Film." December 20.

Urry, John. 1990. "The 'Consumption' of Tourism." *Sociology* 24 (1): 23–35.

Van Fuqua, Joy. 2003. "'What Are Those Little Girls Made Of?': *The Powerpuff Girls* and Consumer Culture." In *Prime Time Animation*. edited by Carol A. Stabile and Mark Harrison, 205–19. London: Routledge.

von Sydow, C. W. 1948. *Selected Papers on Folklore*. Copenhagen: Rosenkilde and Bagger.

Ward, Bruce. 2005. "Career of Canuck Comic Ron James Soars." CanWest News (newswire), January 27.

Warren, Roz, ed. 1995. *Revolutionary Laughter: The World of Women Comics*. Women's Glib Contemporary Women's Humor 8. Freedom, CA: The Crossing Press.

Werbin, Stu. 1972. "How George Carlin Showed His Hair." *Rolling Stone*, August 17. Accessed September 26, 2008. http://www.rollingstone.com/news/story/21454948/how_george_carlin_showed_his_hair (in excerpt).

White, Shane, and Graham J. White. 1998. *Stylin': African American Expressive Culture from Its Beginnings to the Zoot Suit*. Ithaca, NY: Cornell University Press.

Williams, Raymond. 1976. *Keywords: A Vocabulary of Culture and Society*. New York: Oxford University Press.

XM Satellite Radio. 2001–2008. *XM Satellite Radio—America's #1 Satellite Radio Service*. Accessed August 6, 2008. http://www.xmradio.com/.

Zall, P. M., ed. 1963. *A Hundred Merry Tales and Other English Jestbooks of the Fifteenth and Sixteenth Centuries*. Lincoln: University of Nebraska Press.

DISCOGRAPHY AND VIDEOGRAPHY

Allen, Woody. 1964. *Woody Allen*. LP. Colpix.

———. 1965. *Woody Allen Vol. 2*. LP. Colpix.

Ansari, Aziz. 2012. *Dangerously Delicious*. Digital video download. www.asizansari.com.

Aukerman, Scott. 2009–2011. *Comedy Death Ray Radio*. Podcast. earwolf.com.

Aukerman, Scott, and Eugene Mirman. 2010. Appearance on Aukerman 2009–2011, November 10.

Barker, Irwin. 2008. Performance in "Hardly Working" episode of *Winnipeg Comedy Festival*. Network television broadcast. January 15. CBC.

Bell, W. Kamau. 2013. Appearance on *Nerdist*. Podcast. May 8. nerdist.com.

Berman, Shelley. 1959. *Inside Shelley Berman*. LP. Verve.

Best of the Improv, Vol. 1. 2001. DVD. Loch Vision.

Billing, Ninder, and David Upshal, dirs. 2002. *Heroes of Black Comedy*. Television program. Comedy Central.

Blieden, Michael, dir. 2005. *The Comedians of Comedy*. Motion picture. Netflix.

Bruce, Lenny. 1992. *The Lenny Bruce Performance Film*. Directed by John Magnusson. VHS and CD. Rhino Home Video.

Carlin, George. 1967. *Take-Offs and Put-Ons*. LP. RCA.

———. 1972a. *FM & AM*. LP. Little David.

———. 1972b. *Class Clown*. LP. Little David.

———. 1973. *Occupation: Foole*. LP. Little David.

———. 1974. *Toledo Window Box*. LP. Little David.

———. 1975. *An Evening with Wally Londo Featuring Bill Slaszo*. LP. Little David.

———. 1977a. *On Location: George Carlin at USC*. Cable television recording. March 5. HBO.

———. 1977b. *On the Road*. LP. Little David.

———. 1977c. *Indecent Exposure: Some of the Best of George Carlin*. LP. Little David.

———. 1978. *On Location: George Carlin at Phoenix*. Cable television recording. July 23. HBO.

———. 1981. *A Place for My Stuff*. LP. Atlantic.

———. 1982. *Carlin at Carnegie*. Cable television recording. HBO.

———. 1984a. *Carlin on Campus*. Cable television recording. HBO.

———. 1984b. *Carlin on Campus*. LP. Eardrum.

———. 1984c. *The George Carlin Collection*. LP. Little David.

———. 1986a. *Playin' with Your Head*. Cable television recording. May 2. HBO.

———. 1986b. *Playin' with Your Head*. LP. Eardrum.

———. 1988. *What Am I Doing in New Jersey?* Cable television recording. HBO.

———. 1990a. *Doin' It Again*. Cable television recording. HBO.

———. 1990b. *Parental Advisory—Explicit Lyrics*. LP. Eardrum.

———. 1992a. *Jammin' in New York*. Cable television recording. HBO.

———. 1992b. *Jammin' in New York*. LP. Eardrum.

———. 1993. *Classic Gold* . Reisssue of 1972a*, 1972b*, and 1973*. Liner notes by Tony Hendra. CD. Atlantic.

———. 1996a. *Back in Town*. Cable television recording. HBO.

———. 1996b. *Back in Town*. CD. Eardrum.

———. 1997. *George Carlin: 40 Years of Comedy*. February 27. Cable television recording. HBO.

———. 2002. *George Carlin on Comedy*. CD. Laugh.com.

———. 2005. *Life Is Worth Losing*. Cable television live broadcast. November 5. HBO.

———. 2008a. *It's Bad for Ya*. Cable television live broadcast. March 1. HBO. (Also 2008. DVD. MPI Home Video.)

———. 2008b. *It's Bad for Ya*. CD. Atlantic.

Carvey, Dana. 2008. *Squatting Monkeys Tell No Lies*. Cable television recording. June 14. HBO.

Cary, Donick, writer. 1998. "The Last Temptation of Krust." Episode 5F10 of *The Simpsons*. Television recording. February 22. FOX.

Cho, Margaret. 1994. Episode of *HBO Comedy Half-Hour*. Cable television recording. HBO.

———. 2000. *I'm the One That I Want*. Motion picture. Directed by Lionel Coleman. Cho Taussig Productions.

———. 2002. *Notorious C.H.O.* Motion picture. Directed by Lorene Machado. Cho Taussig Productions.

———. 2005. *Margaret Cho: Assassin*. Motion picture. Directed by Kerry Asmussen and Konda Mason. Cho Taussig Productions.

CK, Louis. 2010. *Hilarious*. Motion Picture. Directed by Louis CK. Epix.

———. 2011. *Live at the Beacon Theater*. Digital video download. louisck.net.

Clay, Andrew "Dice." 1990. *The Day the Laughter Died*. CD. American Recordings.

———. 1991. *Dice Rules*. Motion picture. Directed by Jay Dubin. Twentieth Century Fox.

———. 1994. *Dice Live at Madison Square Garden*. CD. American Recordings.

Clift, Robert A., and Hillary Demmon, dirs. 2012. *Road Comics: Big Work on Small Stages*. Documentary film. Ruby Lane Pictures.

Cosby, Bill. 1963. *Bill Cosby Is a Very Funny Fellow . . . Right!* LP. Warner.

———. 1964. *I Started Out as a Child*. Liner notes by Allan Sherman. LP. Warner.

———. 1965. *Why Is There Air?* Liner notes by Stan Cornyn. LP. Warner.

———. 1967. *Revenge*. LP. Warner.

———. 1968a. *To Russell, My Brother, Whom I Slept With*. LP. Warner.

———. 1968b. *200 M.P.H.* LP. Warner.

———. 1969. *It's True! It's True!* LP. Warner.

———. 1972. "The Golfer." *Just for Laughs!* Vol. 2. Various artists. LP. Scepter.

———. 1982. *Himself*. LP. Motown.

———. 1983. *Bill Cosby: Himself*. Motion picture. Directed by Bill Cosby. Twentieth Century Fox.

———. 1992. *At His Best*. CD. MCA.

Cross, David. 1996. Episode of *HBO Comedy Half-Hour*. Cable television recording. HBO.

———. 1999. *The Pride Is Back*. Cable television recording. September 18. HBO.

Dangerfield, Rodney, host. 1988. *Nothin' Goes Right*. Cable television recording. August 10. HBO.

Daniels, Greg, writer. 1994. "Homer Badman." Episode 2F06 of *The Simpsons*. Television recording. November 27. FOX.

David, Larry. 1999. *Curb Your Enthusiasm*. Cable television recording. October 17. HBO.

DeGeneres, Ellen. 1996. *Taste This*. CD. Atlantic.

———. 2003. *Here and Now*. Cable television recording. HBO. (Also 2004. DVD. HBO Home Video.)

Delaney, Rob. 2012. *Live at the Bowery Ballroom*. Streaming content. Netflix.

Elliott, Lorne. 2000. *More Lorne Elliott (Than You Probably Need in Your Life)*. CD. Independent release.

English, John, dir. 1944. *San Fernando Valley*. Motion picture. Republic Pictures.

Evans, Lee. 2002. *Wired and Wonderful—Live at Wembley*. DVD. Off the Wall Productions.

Foxx, Redd. 1997. *The Best of*. CD. Capitol.

Frink, Don, and John Payne, writers. 2002. "The Bart Wants What It Wants." Episode DABF06 of *The Simpsons*. Television recording. February 17. FOX.

Gaffigan, Jim. 2012. *Mr. Universe*. Digital video download. www.jimgaffigan.com.

Glass, Todd. 2010. Appearance on Aukerman 2009–2011, January 22.

Gregory, Dick. 1961. *Dick Gregory in Living Black and White*. LP. Colpix.

Griffin, Eddie. 1997. *Eddie Griffin: Voodoo Child*. Cable television recording. HBO. (Also 2005. DVD. Image Entertainment.)

———. 2003. *DysFunktional Family*. Motion picture. Directed by George Gallo. Eddie Live LLC/Miramax.

Harvey, Steve. 1997. *One Man*. Cable television recording. HBO. (Also 2001. DVD. UrbanWorks Entertainment.)

Hedberg, Mitch. 1998. Performance on *Premium Blend*. Television recording. Comedy Central. Released on DVD of Hedberg 2003*.

———. 1999. Episode of *Comedy Central Presents*. Television recording. January 5. Comedy Central. Released on DVD of Hedberg 2003* with aired and unedited versions.

———. 2002. *Strategic Grill Locations*. CD. Comedy Central Records.

———. 2003. *Mitch All Together*. CD & DVD. Comedy Central Records.

———. 2004. Performance on "2004 Gala" episode of *Just for Laughs*. Television recording. CBC. Accessed July 5, 2009. http://www.youtube.com/watch?v=J-zFQ9fOTSU.

Hendricks, Bruce, dir. 2008. *Hannah Montana/Miley Cyrus: Best of Both Worlds Concert Tour*. Motion picture. Walt Disney.

Hicks, Bill. 2002. *Love Laughter and Truth*. Liner notes by Jeff Rougvie. CD. Rykodisc.

Hughley, D. L. 1999. *Goin' Home.* Cable television recording. HBO.

———. 2007. *Unapologetic.* Cable television recording. September 22. HBO.

Ice T. 2002. Interview in "The Original Kings of Comedy," episode 2 of Billing and Upshal 2002.

James, Ron. 1996. Performance on "Shaun Majumder and Ron James" episode of *Comedy at Club 54.* Produced and hosted by Ben Guyatt. Television recording. CHCH Television.

———. 1997. *Up and Down in Shakey Town: One Canadian's Journey through the California Dream.* Broadcast television recording. The Comedy Network.

———. 2003. *The Road Between My Ears.* Broadcast television recording. October 3. CBC. (Also 2003. *The Road Between My Ears: 100 Minute Performer's Cut.* DVD. Morningstar Entertainment/CBC Home Video.)

———. 2004. Performance on "Sleeping with the Elephant" episode of *Winnipeg Comedy Festival.* Network television broadcast. January 28. CBC.

———. 2005. *Quest for the West.* Broadcast television recording. December 9. CBC. (Also 2005. DVD. Morningstar Entertainment/CBC Home Video.)

———. 2006. *West Coast Wild.* Broadcast television recording. December 31. CBC. (Also 2006. DVD. Morningstar Entertainment/CBC Home Video.

———. 2007. *Back Home.* Broadcast television recording. December 31. CBC. (Also 2007. DVD. Morningstar Entertainment/CBC Home Video.)

———. 2008. *Manitoba Bound.* Broadcast television recording. December 31. CBC.

———. 2009. *The Ron James Show.* Television series. CBC.

Kasher, Moshe. 2012. *Live in Oakland.* Streaming content. Netflix.

Kaufman, Andy. 1979. *Andy's Funhouse.* Network variety special. August 28. ABC.

King, Alan. 1969. *The Alan King Show.* Network variety special. January 18. ABC.

Klein, Robert. 1975. *An Evening with Robert Klein.* Cable television live broadcast. HBO. Released on Klein 2007*.

———. 2005. *The Amorous Busboy of Decatur Avenue.* Cable television recording. December 3. HBO. Released on Klein 2007*.

———. 2007. *The HBO Specials 1975–2005.* 4 DVD set. SRO Entertainment.

Laughing Out Loud: America's Funniest Comedians. 2003. DVD. Madacy Entertainment Group.

Lawrence, Martin. 1994. *You So Crazy.* Cable television recording. April 27. HBO.

———. 2002. *Martin Lawrence Live: Runteldat.* Motion picture. Directed by David Raynr. Runteldat Entertainment/Paramount. (Also 2002. DVD. Paramount Home Video.)

Lee, Spike, dir. 2000. *The Original Kings of Comedy.* Motion picture. MTV Films/Paramount. (Also 2000. DVD. Paramount Home Video.)

Leguizamo, John. 1998. *Freak.* Cable television recording. October 10. HBO.

MacDonald, Mike. 1991. *On Target.* Network television recording. March 22. CBC.

———. 1992. *My House. My Rules.* Network television recording. March 20. CBC.

———. 1993. *Happy as I Can Be.* Network television recording. November 14. CBC.

Markham, Pigmeat. 1968[?]. *Tune Me In.* LP. Chess.

Maron, Marc. 2013. *Thinky Pain*. Streaming content. Netflix.

Martin, Demetri. 2006. *These Are Joke*s. CD. Comedy Central Records.

Martin, Steve. 1979. *Comedy Is Not Pretty*. LP. Warner Brothers.

McIntyre, Michael. 2007. Performance on *Live at the Apollo*. Television recording. November 26. BBC. Available online in three parts: pt. 1, http://www.youtube.com/watch?v=Es2l4yUBY6M; pt. 2, http://www.youtube.com/watch?v=CLPyPJTwEC4; pt. 3, http://www.youtube.com/watch?v=_YsJ186p17U. Accessed November 10, 2008.

Miller, Dennis. 1994. *Live from Washington D.C.: They Shoot HBO Specials, Don't They?* Cable television recording. April 20. HBO.

Moore, Rudy Ray. 1978. *Rude*. Motion picture. Directed by Cliff Roquemore. Independent release. (Also 1988. VHS. Xenon Home Video.)

Murphy, Eddie. 1982. *Eddie Murphy*. LP. Columbia.

———. 1983a. *Delirious*. Cable television recording. HBO.

———. 1983b. *Comedian*. LP. Columbia.

———. 1987. *Raw*. Motion picture. Directed by Robert Townsend. Paramount. (Also 2004. DVD. Paramount Home Video.)

———. 1997. *Greatest Comedy Bits*. CD. Columbia.

Newhart, Bob. 1960. *The Button-Down Mind of Bob Newhart*. LP. Warner.

———. 2006. *Button-Down Concert*. DVD. Twentieth Century Fox Home Entertainment.

Notaro, Tig. 2012. *Live*. Online release. louisck.net.

Ortega, Kenny, dir. 2009. *This Is It*. Motion picture. Columbia Pictures.

Pardo, Jimmy. 2006–. *Never Not Funny*. Podcast. pardcast.com.

Provenza, Paul, dir. 2005. *The Aristocrats*. Motion picture. Thinkfilm. (Also 2005. DVD. Thinkfilm.)

Pryor, Richard. 1971. *Live and Smokin'*. Motion picture. Directed and produced by Michael Blum. Independent release. (Also 2001. DVD. MPI Media.)

———. 1974. *That Nigger's Crazy*. LP. Partee/Stax.

———. 1975. *. . . Is It Something I Said?* LP. Warner Brothers.

———. 1976. *Bicentennial Nigger*. LP. Warner Brothers.

———. 1977a. *The Richard Pryor Special?* Network variety special. May 5. NBC.

———. 1977b. *The Richard Pryor Show*. Network variety series. September 13, 20, 27; October 20. NBC.

———. 1979a. *Richard Pryor: Live in Concert*. Motion picture. Directed by Jeff Margolis. Special Event Entertainment.

———. 1979b. *Wanted/Richard Pryor—Live in Concert*. LP. Warner Brothers.

———. 1982a. *Richard Pryor Live on the Sunset Strip*. Motion picture. Directed by Joe Layton. Columbia Pictures.

———. 1982b. *Live on the Sunset Strip*. LP. Warner Brothers.

———. 1983a. *Richard Pryor . . . Here and Now*. Motion picture. Directed by Richard Pryor. Columbia Pictures.

———. 1983b. *Here and Now*. LP. Warner Brothers.

Quinn, Colin. 2002. Interview in "Chris Rock," episode 1 of Billing and Upshal 2002.

Rascals. 2003. *Rascals Presents Comedy Knockouts*. DVD compilation. Razor & Tie.

Regan, Brian. 1997. *Live*. CD. Uproar.

Rock, Chris. 1994. "Big Ass Jokes." Episode of *HBO Comedy Half Hour*. Cable television recording. HBO. Released on DVD of Rock 2004*.

———. 1996. *Bring the Pain*. Cable television recording. HBO. (Also 2002. DVD. HBO Home Video.)

———. 1997. *Roll with the New*. CD. Dreamworks.

———. 1999a. *Bigger & Blacker*. Cable television recording. HBO. (Also 2000. DVD. HBO Home Video.)

———. 1999b. *Bigger & Blacker*. CD. Dreamworks.

———. 2004. *Never Scared*. Cable television recording. HBO. (Also 2004. DVD. HBO Home Video.)

———. 2008. *Kill the Messenger*. Cable television recording. HBO. (Also 2009. DVD, 3 disc Collector's Edition. HBO Home Video.)

Rodriguez, Paul. 1991. *Behind Bars and Live in San Quentin*. Cable television live broadcast. August 4. HBO. (Also 2007. DVD. UrbanWorks Entertainment.)

Rollins, Henry. 1992a. *Talking from the Box*. Video. 2.13.61.

———. 1992b. *Live at McCabe's*. CD. Quarterstick Records.

Sandler, Adam. 1993. *They're All Gonna Laugh at You!* CD. Warner Brothers.

Seinfeld, Jerry, performer. 1990. "The Stakeout." *Seinfeld*. Television recording. NBC.

———. 1998a. *I'm Telling You for the Last Time*. Cable television live broadcast. August 9. HBO. (Also 1999. DVD. HBO Home Video.)

———. 1998b. *I'm Telling You for the Last Time*. CD. Uptown/Universal.

———. 2002. *Comedian*. Motion picture. Directed by Christian Charles. Miramax.

Shandling, Garry, host. 1995. *1995 Young Comedians Special*. Cable television recording. HBO.

Sigurdson, Erica. 2004. Performance in "Prairie Crop" episode of *Winnipeg Comedy Festival*. Network television broadcast. June 5. CBC.

Silverman, Sarah. 2005. *Jesus Is Magic*. Motion picture. Directed by Liam Lynch. Roadside Attractions.

Small, Leslie, dir. 2002. *Cedric the Entertainer's Starting Line Up*. DVD. UrbanWorks Entertainment.

Tompkins, Paul F. 2009. *Freak Wharf*. CD. A Special Thing.

Wayans, Damon. 1990. *The Last Stand?* Cable television recording. HBO.

Williams, Robin. 2002. Live on Broadway. Cable television live broadcast. July 14. HBO. (Also 2002. DVD. Sony.)

Wilson, Flip. 1972. Geraldine: Don't Fight the Feeling. LP. Little David.

INDEX

CPSIA information can be obtained at www.ICGtesting.com
Printed in the USA
BVOW08s0440080116

431792BV00002B/5/P